T0248416

THE SPECIAL RELATIONSHIP

THE SPECIAL RELATIONSHIP

THE HISTORY OF
AMERICAN FOOTBALL
IN THE UNITED KINGDOM

ANDREW GAMBLE

First published by Pitch Publishing, 2022

Pitch Publishing
9 Donnington Park,
85 Birdham Road,
Chichester,
West Sussex,
PO20 7AJ
www.pitchpublishing.co.uk
info@pitchpublishing.co.uk

A CIP catalogue record is available for this book from the British Library.

ISBN 978 1 80150 163 7

Typesetting and origination by Pitch Publishing

Printed and bound in India by Replika Press Pvt. Ltd.

Contents

For Dad, Mum, Christian, and my wonderful friends and family who believed in me …

I would never have had the courage nor the belief to embark on this challenge, let alone complete it, without your consistent love and support. I will forever be indebted.

'Winning is not everything – but making the effort to win is'

– *Vince Lombardi, Green Bay Packers*

Introduction

WILLINGLY OR not, those who know me will be acutely aware that I adore the American sports. Sure, I fell in love with football – soccer in this instance – at a young age. For better or worse, Arsenal were my team. But I thought the United States' major league sports were fascinating. They were emblematic of everything that amazed and intrigued me about American culture: the bright lights, larger than life personalities and exhilarating drama. This feeling was only enhanced as I grew up, and over years my infatuation with these sports now trumps almost every other aspect of my life.

Basketball, ice hockey and baseball are all great, but it was American football and the NFL that ultimately piqued my interest. The hard-hitting, high-octane, physically taxing yet mentally intense gridiron game has simply taken a hold of my conscious self. Like so many modern international fans around the world, I wasn't born into a family that followed American football.

I had certainly never heard of the sport or the NFL as I walked into a second-hand video games shop when visiting my family in Wollongong, Australia. I entered the store and spotted the Madden 2003 case, with Marshall Faulk – the star running back for the St Louis Rams' exciting offence famously known as 'the Greatest Show on Turf' – emblazoned on the cover. Clad in blue and gold, I thought Faulk looked like a superhero. The game was safely packed in my luggage ahead of the long trip home and my life was never the same again.

By playing Madden 2003 on my Nintendo GameCube, I learned the rules and truly fell in love with the sport, absorbing each and every line of captivating, recorded commentary uttered by the great John Madden. An icon, Madden encapsulates everything that is great about American football: the passion, the personality, the delicate knowledge of a sport so profoundly technical it beggars belief. The way the late, great Madden could elucidate any aspect of professional football so any fan, rookie or veteran could follow it was mesmerising, and I will always have the deepest respect and appreciation for him. I can still hear his voice describing the plays that once emanated from my television while playing the game against and alongside my brother, Christian. Madden managed to captivate and educate a young boy so remarkably that it has shaped his life forever. I guarantee I'm not the only one, either.

I've always enjoyed educating people on American football when they express interest, and the sport is wonderfully enriched by a history filled with great personalities, fascinating stories and iconic milestones. The National Football League was founded in 1920 and, like association football, champions were originally determined through end-of-season standings until the playoff system, still in place today, was implemented in 1933 concluding with the NFL Championship Game. Thirty-three years later and the NFL merged with the American Football League (AFL), leading to the birth of the Super Bowl in January 1967. Super Bowl I – billed as the First AFL–NFL World Championship Game – pitted the Green Bay Packers against the Kansas City Chiefs. Led by Bart Starr, the Packers emerged 35-10 winners at the Los Angeles Coliseum, and the Super Bowl has gone on to become one of the leading sporting events in the world. Four decades after the Super Bowl emerged to become the centrepiece of the American sporting landscape, the New York Giants and

Miami Dolphins contested the first International Series clash in London. The National Football League had become international.

The rise of the professional game since the NFL was formed in 1920 has been nothing short of exceptional – but let's rewind once more. The history of American football can be traced to early editions of rugby and association football, the leading sports in the United Kingdom. While undoubtedly taking inspiration from both rugby and football, American football was devised with a number of major differences from the two sports. Walter Camp, a Yale University athlete and coach often referred to as the 'Father of American Football', formulated key rule changes, including the introduction of the line of scrimmage and down-and-distance rules – the key pillars of the sport today. Camp also instituted the forward pass and blocking, clearly leaving a lasting influence on the game. American football continued to develop in the late 19th and early 20th centuries, with college coaches such as Glenn 'Pop' Warner and John Heisman taking advantage of the new passing rule to great success. Their influence led to the explosion of college football, which was the dominant version of the sport until the NFL came to the fore in the 1960s. It was at this time that American football surpassed baseball as the most popular sport in the States, primarily transitioning from Midwestern industrial towns to the sprawling spectacle it is today.

Of course, college football remains incredibly popular to this day, but the professional game is a different beast. Before the formation of the first pro league in the form of the APFA, Pudge Heffelfinger claimed the honour of becoming the first professional American footballer when he agreed a contract worth $500 – $14,445.75 in 2022 – to play for the Allegheny Athletic Association against the Pittsburgh Athletic Club back in 1892. Just 18 years later, American football touched down on British shores for the very first time thanks to the sport's inclusion in military athletic programmes since the Spanish-American War of 1898.

Nowadays, American football is on the cusp of becoming an international phenomenon with London and the United Kingdom at the epicentre of such emerging passion. When the likes of Patrick Mahomes, Aaron Donald and Efe Obada make a sensational play on the other side of the Atlantic, they are notably contributing to the incredible history of this great sport that is unfolding before our very eyes. I hope *The Special Relationship* serves as a comprehensive origins story for American football's triumphant, colourful and widely accepted arrival in the United Kingdom.

SECTION 1:

THE HISTORY OF AMERICAN FOOTBALL IN THE UK

CHAPTER 1

The Silver Cup and a Golden Reception

'North American football has the reputation of being more dangerous than the South American revolution!' – Ernest Prater, *The Graphic*, December 1910

THE UNITED States of America and the United Kingdom have always shared a common history and the 'special relationship' between the countries is unlike most nations in the world. Given the nature of this kinship, it makes sense that America's greatest sport arrived in the UK early in the 20th century – a chaotic but ultimately fortifying period for the Anglo-American bond.

The first taste of American football on these shores came in 1910, during the reign of King George V. The *Daily Mirror*, a British tabloid, sponsored a clash between two teams of US Navy servicemen from the USS *Idaho* and the USS *Michigan*, pitting the Navy's Division III winners against the Division I champions. It was the first time an organised game of the sport was to be played in the country and, beginning a tradition that runs to this day in the National Football League, it was scheduled to be played on 23 November – Thanksgiving Day 1910. In the build-up to the anticipated match, the *Michigan* team were unfortunately forced to pull out due to military commitments. They were quickly replaced by the USS *Vermont*. In front of a crowd of 10,000 awestruck fans, the USS *Idaho* team won 19-0 at Crystal Palace to win the Silver Cup. The trophy was awarded by the Duke of Manchester, William Angus Drogo Montagu.

The USS *Idaho* team had to defend the Silver Cup just 11 days later in the American Navy Football Final against the new challengers, the USS *Connecticut*. The match, organised by Rear Admiral Seaton Schroeder, was once again held at Crystal Palace, but the 12,000-strong crowd were treated to a much tighter affair. USS *Idaho* came out victorious in a gritty 5-0 game to retain the cup, awarded by the Duchess of Marlborough. The second game was deemed to be more serious as word of the first match and its impressive attendance had spread. The fascination surrounding American football was broadening and beginning to take hold on the British Isles.

For the third time in just over a month, the Silver Cup was contested – although this occasion was more muted. Taking place on 21 December 1910, servicemen from the USS *Georgia* and the USS *Rhode Island* competed at Stonebridge Sports Ground in Northfleet, Kent just 25 miles south-east of London. In front of just 4,000 people on the frozen soccer pitch at Stonebridge Road, the team from the USS *Georgia* came away with a 12-0 victory. This was a far cry from the high-octane scoring fans of the modern game are accustomed to, with a lack of a genuine playbook and amateur players leading to fragmented offensive displays. *Georgia*'s star player, Levy, scored two touchdowns, with each point after converted. There was little celebration and no presentation of the trophy to the victorious side, markedly different to the noble affairs at Crystal Palace the month before.

A London reportage artist, Ernest Prater, could reasonably claim to be the first British person to cover an American football game. At any rate, he certainly was the first to do so on British soil, and Prater admitted that British newspapers were initially sceptical of the new, unfamiliar and worryingly violent sport that had arrived from the US. Prater worked for *The Graphic,* a weekly illustrated newspaper that ran from 1869 to 1932, and he equated the physical nature of the new sport to the grim violence of war. Prater stated: 'North American football has the reputation of being more dangerous than the South American revolution!' – a hyperbolic assessment that was rather disingenuous.

However, this comparison wasn't completely wide of the mark for British media. On the same autumnal day that the USS *Idaho* team lifted the first edition of the Silver Cup, a young player from Winsted in Connecticut died playing in an American football match. This was widely reported on in the US and even made it to the desks of British newspapers. Prater mentioned the tragic death in his report of the Silver Cup match, while the *Illustrated London News* provided a more detailed report on the incident. In the 26 November 1910 edition – just three days after the first game on British soil – the newspaper expressed concern with the fact a player could be acquitted on the legal charge of murder if it took place in the course of a game, evidencing how 'rough-and-tumble' the sport of American football can be. On Christmas Eve of 1910, a *Gravesend and Dartford* reporter struggled to grapple with the fact that this sport could share a name with football – a problem many Britons still suffer from – although they were intrigued by the American equivalent: 'The game is interesting to watch, but "football" seems a misnomer, the feet being very seldom used, whilst the match seems to be won more by sheer physical strength than by science.'

After the heyday of the Silver Cup, it was all quiet on the gridiron front in the United Kingdom. The sport was admired by the fans and intrigued servicemen that attended the games in south London and Kent, but British athletes and the general public showed great reluctance to get involved or even remain interested in the sport. The NFL would be formed in September 1920, initially as the American Professional Football Association before switching to its familiar name ahead of the 1922 season, but – aside from the odd footage of college games such as Harvard versus Yale – American football stayed true to its name and clear of the British Isles.

Appropriately, the silence ended when the US Army was drafted in to help the Allied powers in World War Two. The American servicemen returned, bringing with them all sorts of necessary equipment – tanks, artillery and pigskins.

CHAPTER 2

A Spot of Tea and Coffee

'Facetiously labelled the "Tea Bowl Game", the match was voted by observers as comparing favourably with pre-war tilts in Canada and the United States.' – Allan Nickleson, *Canadian Press News,* February 1944

THE UNITED States formally entered World War Two in response to the Japanese attack on Pearl Harbour in December 1941, and American football made its triumphant return to British soil soon after.

The Americans joined up with the Canadian army on British shores as they arrived on 26 January 1942. The first American GIs landed at Dufferin Quay, Belfast in great secrecy although a band of Royal Ulster Rifles serenaded them with 'The Star-Spangled Banner' as the ship docked. Upon arrival, each American serviceman received a 38-page handbook entitled *Instructions for American Serviceman in Britain*, written by the acclaimed author Eric Knight. 'The purpose of this guide is to start getting you acquainted with British companions and understand life and culture,' and so that's what the Americans did, by bonding over their love of sport.

It was 32 years after the third and final edition of the Silver Cup when the next game of American football took place in the UK. Belfast hosted the event and the appetite for the sport had certainly not diminished. In front of 9,000 spectators, Corporal Robert Hopfer and his team, the Yarvards, were defeated by Staff Sergeant Arnold Carpenter and the Hales. The joke behind the name, a portmanteau of Harvard and Yale, was reportedly lost on the crowd, with the *Stars and Stripes* – the military newspaper for the American servicemen – commenting that the fans appeared equally 'puzzled' by both the humour of the captains and the actual sport itself. After the 9-7 win for the Hales on 14 November 1942, the paper lamented that they were unsure whether the onlooking crowd even knew the final score. Ultimately, it was a glorious second coming of the sport. No matter the score or victor, the match raised important funds for the Royal Victoria Hospital in Belfast as well as for the Soldiers, Sailors, Airmen Families Associations.

The clash in Belfast set the tone for things to come and the infectious nature of the sport began to spread throughout the servicemen stationed within the British Isles. Designed and organised by higher powers to keep the travelling Americans busy and out of trouble, games saw companies and regiments pitted against each other, but other matches were scheduled to simply entertain the fascinated spectators.

One game that channelled the true spirit of the sport was played on 8 May 1943. With match times and dates beholden to gaps in combat, White City Stadium in west London hosted an internal college match between the Crimson Tide Artillerymen and the Fighting Irish Engineers. This was essentially a play on the nicknames of the Alabama and Notre Dame football programmes, with Alabama taking on the Crimson Tide moniker in 1907 and Notre Dame becoming the Fighting Irish in 1927 after previously playing as the 'Catholics' and the 'Ramblers'. This match predated the now infamous rivalry between the two iconic colleges since the storied universities played their first official game in the Sugar Bowl of 1973, held in New Orleans. The Crimson Tide team were composed of members of the Field Artillery from Pennsylvania and surrounding states – including Alabama – while the Fighting Irish outfit was filled with engineers from Midwestern states. As this anticipated match between representatives of America's famous colleges took place on the other side of the Atlantic, Private First Class John W. Kennedy and Sergeant Paul W. Dennis, two men from Harrisburg, Pennsylvania, played for the Crimson Tide, with Dennis – who had been stationed in England for the past ten months – scoring his side's third touchdown late in the fourth to give the Tide a comfortable lead en route to a 19-6 victory. Like the match in Belfast before it, the match was played primarily to raise funds for a good cause: the British Red Cross's Pensioners of War Fund, with 25,000 travelling to the west London stadium in support of both charity and gridiron action.

However, perhaps the most prominent of these wartime American football matches was the game known in the annals of both wartime and sporting history as the Tea Bowl. The backstory to the event is particularly interesting, as former quarterback for the Hamilton Tigers of the Canadian Football League (CFL) and then-Major Dennis Whitaker met by chance with a Special Services lieutenant in a London pub. Although conversation covered many topics, they chiefly discussed their favourite pastime: football. Their serendipitous encounter led to the formation of the Tea Bowl, a hybrid match between US and Canadian troops with the first half played under American rules and the second under Canadian rules (three downs rather than four, five points awarded for a touchdown, and an extra player on each side on the pitch). On 13 February 1944, the American troops led by Private Frank Dombrowski formed the Central Base Section Pirates and faced the Canadian Mustangs, which was extraordinarily full of former CFL talent.

To understand the significance of the Tea Bowl it is necessary to explore the background of the Canadian army stationed in the United Kingdom. The Canadians arrived in Britain in December 1939, when the 1st Division touched down at Aldershot in Hampshire. The troops considered themselves naturalised with the British surroundings by the time the Americans arrived, and their original placing at Aldershot was meant to be a favour from the local forces to the Canadians. The Canadian Corps had spent an infamous first winter in the UK under canvas on the flooded Salisbury Plain, swamped by 24 inches of rain in the first four months of their stay during World War One. However, this was quite a cheeky favour as the barracks were rather old, and their mid-Victorian design did not allow for central heating – which naturally coincided with the coldest winter since 1894.

The local population in Aldershot, an old military garrison town, did not welcome their new townmates. The Canadians were struggling too, largely because of the community animosity, but there were also the natural feelings of boredom, homesickness and frustration with bad weather as morale took a dive over the winter. General Andrew McNaughton, the Canadian Army Commander, became slowly overwhelmed with complaints about drunk and disorderly conduct, dangerous driving and theft of army property. The festive season, normally a time of cheer and joy, saw a number of fights break out between British and Canadian troops that led to further animosity between entire units.

In May 1940, the Canadian troops moved to the more welcoming Northampton, where they hit it off with the locals far better than in Aldershot, and misunderstandings were easily overcome. The horrors of the Blitz engendered a shared, collective feeling of dread which united the British and Canadian communities, improving morale immensely. However, morale took a turn for the worse when infantry – predominantly made up of Canadian units – commenced the Dieppe Raid of 19 August 1942.

Operation Jubilee, the amphibious attack on the German-occupied port of Dieppe in France, turned into a disaster for the Allies. Over 6,500 infantry, predominantly Canadian, supported a tank regiment, and were placed ashore by a naval force with Royal Air Force (RAF) support from above. The purpose behind the assault was to capture and hold the port for a short period to test the feasibility of landing and to gather intelligence. Ironically, the raid was intended to boost Allied morale and demonstrate the commitment of the UK to reopen the Western Front.

Between 3.30am and 3.40am – 30 minutes after the initial landings – the main frontal assault was launched by the Essex Scottish and the Royal Hamilton Light infantry. It was intended that they would be supported by Churchill tanks from the 14th Army Tank Regiment landing at the same time. Unfortunately, botched timings led to the tanks landing late, leaving the infantry battalions to attack alone. They faced unrelenting heavy machine-gun fire and suffered heavy losses, with Captain Whitaker of the Royal Hamilton Light Infantry describing a scene of carnage and confusion as his men were unnecessarily killed due to insufficient support.

After less than six hours and casualties rising horrifyingly quickly, the Allied forces called for a retreat. The Dieppe Raid was an infamous ignominy in which just a single landing force, Whitaker's unit, achieved its objective. Within ten hours, 3,623 of the 6,086 men who landed were either killed, wounded or taken as prisoners of war, while the RAF lost 106 aircraft to only 48 casualties for the Luftwaffe. Lieutenant Colonel Peter Young fought in the Royal Hamilton Light Infantry, where Whitaker, despite being his relative youth, successfully led the company towards their objective. 'He demonstrated leadership, and maybe that came from when he was a football quarterback, but he certainly demonstrated absolute leadership in getting his people across that awful beach where they were devastated by fire … It really wasn't well executed in the support that the troops were given, the information they were given, and of course we know the devastating results.'

Soon after the Dieppe Raid, Whitaker – who would eventually become a brigadier general – was furious with how his men and the other infantry were essentially abandoned, and it took time for the wounds to heal. Gail Thompson, Whitaker's daughter, recalled that there was a time during the war in 1944 when the forces were simply waiting for anything to happen and morale continued its downward slump – but, in classic British form, a brilliant idea would come about while having a drink.

Major Whitaker met the lieutenant from the American army and they were both gridiron players so, naturally, were were reminiscing about football and were keen to play the sport amid the wartime scenes. The lieutenant told Whitaker that he had recently been sent enough equipment from the United States to field six teams. After several pints, the two men challenged one another to an international match of football and the Tea Bowl was born. 'My dad said, "Well why don't we have a game between the Americans and the Canadians, maybe we could have it at a big stadium and a lot of people come, that will be fun. Hopefully it'll raise morale of the people,"' said Thompson. The two men subsequently proposed a toast and went their separate ways into the London darkness.

They spoke to the relevant figures, and it was decided – the American army would face their Canadian counterparts in a game of football. Whitaker spoke to Lieutenant General Kenneth Stevart, the Chief of Staff at the Canadian Military Headquarters, as they had attended the Royal Military College together. Lt. General Stuart was a keen football fan and he was enthusiastic about the idea, with Whitaker dubbing his team the 'Mustangs' after they were loaned the equipment. Over at the US Army Central Base Section, Private First Class Frank Dombrowski began to pull together his own team, the 'Pirates'. Meanwhile, a London silversmith received an order for a trophy, an eight-inch silver teapot to be awarded to the winner of the inaugural Tea Bowl.

Whitaker began to search through the ranks for players. He landed on Major Jeff Nicklin, a veteran star receiver of the Winnipeg Blue Bombers; Lieutenant Orville Burke who played quarterback for the Ottawa Rough Riders from 1936–1941; and Captain George Hees, a former Toronto Argonaut. With D-Day still months away, the two teams were granted six weeks when they were relieved of their duties and committed to an intense training programme. They swapped command post exercises for three-cone drills, where the Canadians had no shortage of talent.

Joining the trio of Nicklin, Burke and Hees were the more-than-capable CFL legends Andy Bieber, Nick Papowski and Hall of Famer Paul Papirow. 'Paul was revered because he was just about the best player in his day,' said CFL historian Steve Daniel. 'If there was an equivalent, if you're looking at Liverpool Football Club today, he'd be the Mohamed Salah of that club. Someone you need in your line-up if you're going to win.'

Canadian pipe bands and US European Theatre of Operations Band played a selection of popular songs like 'In the Mood' and 'Chattanooga Choo-Choo' as the Canadian Army Mustangs took to the field against the US Army Central Base Pirates. In many ways, the pageantry surrounding the Tea Bowl resembled the extravaganza of the NFL and CFL's respective showpieces, the Super Bowl and the Grey Cup. The fantastic spectacle was the brainchild of young Whitaker in a pub in Aldershot, highlighting the camaraderie between the North American servicemen posted so far from home.

Why 'bowl'? The term stems from the original Rose Bowl stadium in Pasadena, California, which was the site of the first postseason college football matches. Designed by architect Myron Hunt in 1921, the stadium's name and bowl-shaped design are inspired by the Yale Bowl in New Haven, Connecticut. The Yale

Bowl is considered the prototype of the modern football stadium and has been replicated across the United States.

White City Stadium was the appropriate venue for the Tea Bowl, and the Olympic arena played host for the big event. On the eve of Valentine's Day 1944, 30,000 cheering spectators – each supplied with a programme which included a list of rules to help the Brits understand the game – watched. The BBC broadcasted the event for the American forces network while Captain Sir Edwin Leather sat above the pitch to broadcast the game around the UK.

The first half was played under NFL rules, and at half-time the match was hanging in a scoreless balance. Bands took to the field to deliver a half-time show that, although it would be dwarfed by those of modern-day Super Bowls, thoroughly impressed those in attendance. In the second half, the Mustangs, now with a tactical advantage as the half was played under Canadian rules, stormed away from their American opponents. In just five minutes after the bands left the field, the Mustangs took the lead through a touchdown as a pass was intercepted by an American who in turn fumbled the ball, with Captain Ken Turnbull first to react on the loose ball and take it over the goal line. Whitaker dispatched the conversion in a professional manner. Burke – who displayed one of the greatest performances of his career – then threw a dramatic 40-yard pass to Whitaker, who took it to the house to increase the Canadian lead. However, the extra point was not converted.

The Americans rallied and pressed the Canadians back to bring the score to 11-6, but in the final minute of action, Burke orchestrated a series of successful plays to ensure his side left White City victorious. The former quarterback first intercepted a pass on the 35-yard line before throwing a pass to Nicklin – who was given last-minute leave from the parachute battalion to play – to cross the line and score as the whistle blew to secure a 16-6 victory for the Canadian Army Mustangs over the US Army

Pirates. Lt. General Stuart accepted the silver teapot on behalf of the team as they claimed the win.

Despite the romantic scenes of such a celebrated American pastime breaking ground in London, it was impossible to fully escape the reality of war as several RAF Spitfires took off and flew over the game in case of an attack by the Luftwaffe. However, it was essential that the game continued in order to depict normalcy and improve morale, and it certainly did so. Tens of thousands of servicemen and perplexed citizens wrapped up in scarves and armed themselves with rum to help brave the British winter as they watched – and enjoyed – American football.

The original agreement between Whitaker and the Americans was for a one-off game, but the bitter taste of defeat against their neighbours and fierce rivals at 'their' sport made the Americans hastily organise a rematch. Lt. General Stuart agreed to the second clash, with an American general who had suggested the Mustangs face a team from the US 29th Blue Division. Regrettably, the Canadians were not aware quite how seriously the Americans were taking the rematch – the Americans were already planning to field several NFL-calibre players.

The American Blues ensured they fielded enough star power to match the Canadian professionals who had claimed victory in the Tea Bowl. In fact, while the Americans had strengthened, the Mustangs were depleted as the likes of Whitaker and Nicklin were unavailable, with the latter ruling himself out as he didn't want to risk injury before the Normandy invasion. The rematch would be appropriately named the Coffee Bowl, with a pot of coffee awarded to the victor.

The Coffee Bowl was contested on 19 March 1944 – a mere 36 days after the Tea Bowl – and a crowd of over 50,000 adoring fans packed into White City Stadium. With the same layout as the first game, Sergeant Tommy Thompson put on a show for the ages. Thompson played for the Philadelphia Eagles in the NFL for three seasons before being deployed in the UK, and he was, rather remarkably, legally blind after his sister threw a stone into his eye when they were young children. Thompson dominated proceedings: he threw for a pair of touchdowns, scrambled like a modern NFL quarterback and even returned punts in a truly virtuoso performance that would have been heralded back in the City of Brotherly Love. The Blues, powered by a strong contingent of players from the University of Iowa, won 16-0. Corporal Johnny Bane scored three touchdowns – a British hat-trick – as he hauled in a pair of receiving touchdowns following spectacular passes from Thompson, described by *Stars and Stripes* as a 'one-man-gang'.

As recalled by Captain Hees, it was clear that the Americans had drafted in real talent. 'I came face-to-face with this guy with a deep suntan,' said the former Toronto star. 'Remember, we're in England and this is March. They'd brought this guy in from Hawaii, so we lost. But the first game? We beat those Yanks.' One optimistic Canadian officer managed to find a silver lining, writing in a letter home that the 'fine display put on by the massed bands compensated to some degree for the outcome of the game'. Ultimately, though, the two bowl games were a success regardless of the outcome. Morale improved among servicemen, while the camaraderie and competitiveness shown between both teams inspired the public.

On 6 June 1944, less than three months after the bowl games, the Allies launched the invasion of France. The US 29th Division – victors of the Coffee Bowl – landed on Omaha Beach, where many of those who played that day were killed or wounded. Among the Canadians, Captain Hees was wounded on Walcheren Island in the Netherlands. Fortunately, he fully recovered and went on to serve, first as a distinguished Member of the Canadian Parliament and then as cabinet minister in the Diefenbaker government. Captain Whitaker survived the war to become brigadier general and one of Canada's most established military historians before he passed away in 2001. Captain Nicklin, who had earned promotions since acting as a major, was tragically killed in action on 24 March 1945 while commanding the 1st Canadian Parachute Battalion during the Rhine crossing. Today, the Nicklin Trophy is awarded to the CFL's outstanding rookie.

As for Thompson, the quarterback returned to the NFL to play a further six seasons from 1945. Alongside Hall of Fame running back Steve Van Buren, Thompson and the Eagles won back-to-back championships in 1948 and 1949. He was adored by the Philadelphia faithful as he led the league in touchdowns in 1948 and passer rating across both seasons – but after that fateful day in March 1944, Thompson was immortalised as a legend in west London too.

CHAPTER 3

The GI Bowl and the End of WWII

'Army drew first blood early in the first quarter when, receiving the opening kick-off, they marched to the four-yard line on running plays.'
– Ray Lee, *Stars and Stripes*, November 1944

FOLLOWING THE success of these Bowl games and the continued wartime celebration of American art, culture and sports, more gridiron events were held to raise the morale of stationed troops. On 12 November 1944 – a few months after D-Day – the sport returned to White City as the US Army, named the Eighth Air Force Shuttle-Raders, defeated the US Navy Sea Lions 20-0 in front of 48,000 servicemen and civilians. The game came to be named the 'GI Bowl' as it pitted two of the American military branches against one another in the ETO Army-Navy Grid Classic. After the Canadian Mustangs and US Army Pirates, this game was another example of two teams that donned traditional monikers that are seen in the modern franchises of the NFL.

There's a defining story behind the Shuttle-Raders name. The term 'shuttle' stemmed from the type of missions the Eighth Air Force carried out across Europe – shuttle bombing was a tactic where units flew from their base to bomb their target before continuing to a separate location where they would refuel and rearm. The bomber would then attack a second target en route to their original base, and the team of servicemen paid homage to this common tactic with their team name.

The question remained: Why 'Raders'?

For a long time, people thought this was a misspelling of the word 'Raiders', foretelling the iconic franchise that would reside in Los Angeles, Oakland and now Las Vegas. However, the game programme showed that the Eighth Air Force team were coached by Captain Robert L. Rader, and he simply named the side after his own name. Perhaps it was to stand out amongst the other teams named Shuttle, or perhaps he saw himself as a general manager-like figure. Touchdowns from each of the three starting members of the Army's backfield – including former Wisconsin running back Private Ashley Anderson and ex-Purdue star Private Earl Dosey in the first quarter – helped the Shuttle-Raders secure a dominant win, with Dosey's touchdown coming after Anderson intercepted opposition quarterback Pete Lisec in Navy territory. After the second and third quarters both ended scoreless, Sergeant Tom Baddick scored from close range to complete the rout, although a failed conversion attempt from Private Edward Snow left the final score at 20-0.

The GI Bowl was swiftly followed by a series of matches around the UK. The travelling circus that was American football made a number of stops in new cities – and the naming style of teams had caught on. First, the city of Blackpool on the Irish Sea coast hosted the Air Service Command Warriors' win over the Bearcats of the same company in a match where 30,000 enamoured fans witnessed Ted D'Uva, a New York native, score a remarkable triple lateral touchdown. It's a shame YouTube wasn't an option to record and forever immortalise such a play.

The next stop was Nottingham where, on 23 November 1944, the excellently named Troop Carrier Command Berger's Bouncers defeated Henley's Hurricanes by six points to nil to the cheers of 25,000 people. American football's fanatic tour around Britain continued, choosing Leeds as its final stop before returning to London, its home away from home across the pond. The intrigued northern fanbase turned out in impressive numbers for the bow of gridiron football: 40,000 watched in wonder as the Command Berger's Bouncers – victors in Nottingham – fell to the Air Services Command Bearcats 12-6, who bounced back from their defeat in Blackpool.

A day later, the sport returned to the capital for Tea Bowl II. It was a highly anticipated bout. Fresh after wowing fans in Blackpool, the Air Service Command Warriors battled the Eighth Air Force Shuttle-Raders, winners themselves just 50 days prior. It was set up to be the perfect way to celebrate New Years' Eve – and yet, the expected crowd size never arrived to watch the Warriors' 13-0 win. While there were still 25,000 passionate spectators packed inside White City Stadium, the heyday of British wartime football had seemingly come and gone as the Allied forces increased their tempo of combat to defeat Germany late in 1944 into early 1945.

In fact, New Years' Day of 1945 saw the final two games of American football contested in the UK during World War Two. Belfast – the very place which hosted the first match of this period back in 1942 – was the site as the Navy and Army contested the Potato Bowl with an undisclosed number of fans in attendance. Those that were lucky enough to witness the clash probably wished they hadn't – a 0-0 draw was not exactly the classic that a match between the Army and Navy perhaps might have promised.

Back in London, the second edition of the Coffee Bowl pitted the Army Air Base Bonecrushers against the Army Airway Rams, and the wartime atmosphere had certainly taken a hold of the event. Only 1,200 spectators watched the Bonecrushers win 6-0, with many fans opting not to attend the game as a safety precaution due to the fact that the Luftwaffe had attacked targets in Belgium and the Netherlands and many feared that the British capital would suffer a similar fate.

Coffee Bowl II was the final match of American football played on British soil during World War Two, and while the Americans may have left soon after, the hunger remained. Leagues in the country and around Europe – which had many appropriately named bowl games of their own, such as the Spaghetti Bowl in Florence – endeavoured to play as many games as possible, but the cancellation of one particular contest is emblematic of these struggles. The champions of the Normandy Football League – a name which, quite frankly, is a lawsuit waiting to happen given its acronym – were set to play the Eighth Air Force All-Stars, but the game had to be called off as personnel were required to focus their efforts on a different kind of tactic. Bombing runs in the air were becoming more important than offensive formations on the pitch.

Upon the conclusion of the War, many American servicemen returned home but a few remained in Europe. These US forces stationed in the continent continued their gridiron passion on the other side of the pond. Of course, the Air Forces were instrumental in this process after being active in organising American football matches throughout the UK in the last few years. There were key NFL names associated with the UK during the war, including two-time champion with the Chicago Bears Ken Kavanaugh and iconic head coach Tom Landry. Landry became a second lieutenant at Lubbock Army Field and was based at RAF Debach in Suffolk, where he was assigned to the 493rd Bomb Group before he masterminded 20 consecutive winning seasons in the league.

The end of the War symbolised a key closing of a harrowing chapter in history, and gave people hope for a new beginning. The remaining American servicemen agreed and provided a fix for the intrigued fans: the US Air Force Europe Sports League.

CHAPTER 4

The US Air Force Europe Sports League

'It was a sheer madness and a sight that made strong men turn pale.' – Dennis Dunn, *Stars and Stripes,* December 1952

THE GREAT fight had ended, but the remaining US troops ensured that football fever continued in the UK. Many of the athletes conscripted to join the war effort left their posts to enrol at colleges or sports teams with the help of the GI Bill, a law in place to aid returning veterans. Among them was Tommy Thompson, who returned to the Philadelphia Eagles, and NFL Hall of Fame coach Paul Brown, who progressed from lieutenant in the US Navy to founder of the Cleveland Browns, aptly named after him, and the Cincinnati Bengals.

In 1950s America, football had begun to overthrow baseball as the chief national sport and so its transition to Europe and the UK through the military was rather appropriate. For a while, the only form of the sport was of the touch variety as full squads of players – and complete sets of equipment – were hard to come by. As the Cold War began, morale amongst troops had to be maintained at a high level and so, in 1951, the US Air Force Europe (USAFE)

Sports League was set up to create a competitive division of full contact football between US Air Force servicemen stationed at RAF bases.

The fact that USAFE was correctly pronounced as 'You-Safe' was no coincidence, and the USAFE Football League became the official league for Air Force servicemen stationed at military bases across Europe. Company personnel signed up from bases in Germany, France, Italy, Greece and, of course, the United Kingdom.

The United States Army played in a league of their own, the United States Army Europe, but did so without British involvement as it was more of a continental league. However, the USAFE Football League captured the imagination of the British Isles. As so many domestic RAF bases were in operation, the UK had its own conference hosting teams from different parts of the country.

With the Department of Defense spending billions of dollars defending Western Europe from the threat of the Soviet military, a very small portion was used to fund the USAFE Football League. Russ Crawford, author of *Le Football: A History of American Football in France*, calculated that football – the most expensive sport – was guilty of using approximately one-fifth of the annual athletic budget allocated to the armed forces. Across the 28 teams that formed the USAFE Football League, the cost of operating the league was around $11m.

As part of the European Command's sporting programme, four conferences were initially funded across Europe: the UK Sports Conference (UKSC), the Continental Sports Conference (CSC), the France Sports Conference (FSC) and the Mediterranean Sports Conference (MSC) – although the last two merged with the CSC soon after. The CSC was originally contested by German and French teams before Britain took up the sport, with teams from bases including Rhein-Main, Fürstenfeldbruck, Wiesbaden and Ramstein highlighting the popularity for the sport in Germany while Fontainebleau, Lyon, Toulon and Chaumont suited up in France. The MSC contained outfits from Italy, Greece and Spain. During the league's run from its inception to when it ceased operation in 1993, 12 teams entered to do battle in the UKSC: the Alconbury Spartans, Bentwaters Phantoms, Burtonwood Bullets, Chicksands Fighting Chicks, Fairford Falcons, Greenham Common Pirates, High Wycombe Bucks, Lakenheath Eagles, London Rockets, Mildenhall Marauders, Upper Heyford Sky Kings and the Wethersfield Raiders.

Bases held large-scale try-outs among servicemen in May and June to select a roster of up to 55 men before cutting squads down to 35 in August, and the USAFE base teams were traditionally coached by former players, with former Texas Tech lineman Jim Martin masterminding the London Rockets outfit that dominated the league in the 1950s.

Before the merger that combined three of the conferences into the CSC, the USAFE Football League finals were often played between the champions of the CSC and the UKSC with the final taking place in November after a postseason following a regular season played between August and October. As is sporting tradition, the Germans were a class above on the pitch and their programmes were reportedly comparable to the biggest and best in the United States college game.

The United Kingdom was well represented in the USAFE Football League, and teams from the UKSC won the championship 13 times during its 43-year history. The FSC was victorious on three occasions while the CSC was the home of the champion team for 27 years. The most successful of the British sides were the Upper Heyford Sky Kings, who claimed victory five times – tied for third-most by any team across the USAFE Football League. The Sky Kings enjoyed a dynastic period of success within the British division in the early 1970s, winning the championship in 1970, 1973 and 1974 while falling in the finals of 1971 and 1972 to the Wiesbaden Flyers and Rhein-Main Rockets respectively. In fact, these two teams were the most successful USAFE football teams, with the Flyers winning six championships while the Rockets claimed ten titles.

The Sky Kings were not the only British champions though. The London Rockets, who improved from a 1-5 record in 1952 to finish 9-1 the following year, came agonisingly close as they fell to a devastating 30-21 defeat to the Landstuhl Raiders in the 1953 final at Wembley Stadium. They had defeated French sides Laon and Orly Field in the postseason, with the latter win a 71-0 thumping – the biggest win in USAFE history. The Rockets team had a spine of American stars including Henry Williams and John Hill, who combined for 17 touchdowns heading into their heart-breaking final defeat. The Rockets were 16-0 down at the end of the first quarter following a pair of German touchdowns and a safety, but an inspired second-quarter performance narrowed the gap to just two points at 16-14 before the Raiders pulled away in the third period.

The London Rockets were undeterred by their defeat and bounced back to become the USAFE Football League's first dynasty, winning three straight championships between 1954 and 1956. They were carried largely by running back Tony Small, who hailed from Longview, Texas and scored more than 20 touchdowns for the Rockets across his first three seasons with the team. Their quarterback Warren Doty was also no slouch and showed off his quality after developing at Oregon State in the Pacific Coast Conference.

The Wethersfield Raiders (1963), Bentwaters Phantoms (1968) and Chicksands Fighting Chicks (1986) all were victors of the USAFE Football League, but the Raiders perhaps experienced the most interesting title win. In fact, the 1963 championship was shared between the Bitburg Barons and the Raiders after the final was cancelled following the assassination of John F. Kennedy on 22 November 1963. The Raiders returned to the final in 1965 and

1966 but were emphatically defeated by the Wiesbaden Flyers on both occasions, falling 54-6 and 49-0 respectively.

The Lakenheath Eagles were the other multiple winners of the league, triumphing on two occasions, 1979 and 1990. However, the Eagles were locked in a bitter rivalry with the aforementioned Rhein-Main Rockets as the two teams contested seven straight USAFE Football League finals between 1987 and 1993, with six defeats and several blowout wins for the German outfit.

However, the early days of the USAFE Football League are particularly important regarding British interest. As expected, the German bases wasted no time in proving their might on the field and competed in the first USAFE Football League Final as a unified league (Berlin's Olympic Stadium had hosted the all-German final in 1946). The 1951 final was hosted in Germany as the Rhein-Main Rockets – the league's most successful outfit – defeated the Burtonwood Bullets of Lancashire by an agonising score of 32-31. However, the Bullets would earn an opportunity for revenge next season as they returned to the final and this time, Burtonwood would play in front of a home crowd in the city of London. Just like that, American football was returning to its temporary stomping ground of the years gone by.

The 1952 USAFE Football League Final was hosted on a freezing day at Wembley Stadium, the first, and certainly not the last, time the sport would be welcomed at the 'home of football'. The Burtonwood Bullets had earned the right to return to the final stage after amassing a 7-1 record during the regular season – conceding just one touchdown all season – before prevailing in the semi-finals by a score of 21-0 against the 3-6 Toul-Rosières Tigers of the FSC. They faced the Fürstenfeldbruck Eagles, from the air base in Bavaria, in front of approximately 30,000 fans on 13 December 1952. Pathé News cameras recorded footage of the game, with a posh voiceover claiming: 'The sacred turf of Wembley is invaded by two teams of American Air Force men who are going to play football – well that's what they call it!'

The Bullets scored the first-ever touchdown on Wembley's pitch and thus laid claim to a historic moment, with 22-year-old fullback Lonnie Ward evading a tackle before spectacularly launching a pass to his quarterback Bob Yates, who took the ball 23 yards into the end zone. The crowd went wild, with the Lancs Yanks – the team's cheerleaders – celebrating on the touchline (although they didn't have pompoms). Unfortunately, the fine play was Burtonwood's only score of the day and they were subsequently dismantled by the ruthless, well-drilled Eagles, who scored 26 unanswered points to win the title 26-7. 'The Eagles have won after one of the toughest, craziest matches that ever rocked Wembley,' summarised the newsreel. The unpredictable nature of the game was perhaps encapsulated by the pitch invasion of a stray black Labrador not once but twice, with its return cheered heavily as the dog burst through the line of scrimmage.

The attendance of 30,000 spectators would not have been out of place in the English First Division at Old Trafford or Highbury.

The British press were intrigued and, much like the Silver Cup reports of 1910, they were unnerved, unsettled, and, quite frankly, frightened. The *Stars and Stripes* certainly posted a headline that echoed such feelings. The story screamed 'It's Moider!' and reporter Dennis Dunn insisted that the sport was one that summarised American characteristics, namely a thirst for violence that resembled some sort of illness or disease. He wrote in his report of the USAFE Final that the game 'was a sheer madness and a sight that made strong men turn pale'. A rather famous anecdote that Dunn reported from the game was when he declared that an English soccer journalist turned to him with a bleak expression, echoing the pale-faced sentiment of his report and said, 'I have never seen anything like this. These fellows have something.' Dunn could not agree more: 'I do not think it is curable.'

Another report of the game in the *Sunday Graphic* highlighted the media's insistence to reveal the violent nature of the sport, and the unimpressed onlookers showed no intent to understand the rules: 'At some secret signal, utterly ignoring the ball, the 22 leaped at each other's throats. A whistle blew and the debris was removed ... Stretcher bearers kept carting off bodies and the score apparently depended on a coroner's report – then the final whistle blew and we gave three hearty cheers to the ambulance which had won a fine game.'

The BBC were covering the final and the announcers on the broadcast certainly reflected the general feeling of sheer confusion regarding the rules of the game. The announcer repeatedly insisted, 'You know, I'd like this game a lot, really, if I knew what was going on down there.' Ironically, this is a view still held by many unknowing British sports fans who insist the tactical nature and the stop-start aspect of the game is too much to handle.

However, other newspapers shared the brutal, vicious sentiment conveyed by Dunn and the *Sunday Graphic*. The *Sunday Express* referred to the game as 'Murder in the Midfield' while another publication, *Reynolds News*, was far more restrained and focused on the impressive spectacle of the event. The newspaper, which ran from May 1950 to June 1967, told its readers of 'Mayhem, Hula and Bands', referring of course to the cheerleaders and marching bands that are cemented within the baseline culture of American football. Lt. Colonel John Coffey of the Third Air Force said: 'Bands, yell-leaders, drum-majorettes, all the colour and enthusiasm will be here. You will see the long runs, forward passes, high-soaring punts and the crunching blocking and tackling which are the hallmarks of American football. You will hear the roar and counter-roar of a partisan crowd as the fortunes of their particular favourites rise and wane – you will, in short, see a game of American Football.'

The *Stars and Stripes* reported that present fans were both impressed and disgusted in equal measure. The journalist working the final was Sterling Slappey, an American who specialised in international – mainly European – correspondence. The 35-year-old communicated the feelings of many fans in attendance, including one fan described as a disgruntled Brit, 'a proper cricket type' with a bristling moustache. This particular onlooker felt the game was 'deplorable', while another fan described the game as 'a shame, a complete shame'. In fact, one spectator asked Slappey how many fatalities there are in each game, jibing, 'the battle's a bit rough, isn't it? Your American scrum is a beastly place to be.' While the query may be interpreted as tongue-in-cheek nowadays, it was particularly relevant back then – there were 11 deaths in 1953 and 12 the following year.

Slappey finalised his report by declaring the USAFE Football League Final left a 'general favourable impression' on the British audience, but the chances of American football even becoming a popular sport across the Atlantic were faint: 'It hardly has a chance. England already has its cricket, rugby, and association football (practically no resemblance to the American kind), and those three are enough for any nation.'

Of course, he was ultimately wide of the mark as gridiron football did seep its way back into the British sporting landscape outside of the military – but not for another 30 years. After reports like those in the *Stars and Stripes, Sunday Express* and the *Sunday Graphic,* British athletes would need convincing that American football did not lead to serious injury or death. The USAFE Football League continued to thrive until the league collapsed in 1993 when the 42-year history of competition between USAFE bases drew to a close with Lakenheath named as the final UKSC champions. They wrapped up a seventh successive title with a 16-13 win over the Sky Kings, and the Eagles met with the Rhein-Main Rockets to decide the 43rd and final championship on 28 November 1993, with the British side losing 42-20.

The USAFE Football League had done its job. It had established a fandom and popularity for the sport in the United

Kingdom. The National Football League understood the potential within the British marketplace, and the sport simply needed a home on domestic public-service television. It soon found one in Channel 4.

CHAPTER 5

The 1980s: Greed, Gridiron and Channel 4

'To the outsider it was a disorganised mess. A Big Bore!' – *Sunday Express,* August 1983

WHILE THE USAFE Football League would continue until 1993, gridiron football was by no means a mainstream attraction. This changed in the 1980s and can be attributed to two key reasons, the first of which inspired a generation of fans.

A new television channel, Channel 4, launched on 2 November 1982 and needed vibrant and alternative content to compete with and run alongside BBC1, BBC2 and ITV. Its ambition was to provide entertainment that wasn't covered by the other three channels. It made sense to cover American football – a colourful, dramatic and interesting sport from our neighbours across the Atlantic Ocean. 'It was impossible not to be aware of the NFL in the 1980s because it was very much a part of Channel 4's identity, covering sports that were largely ignored by the established broadcasters,' said Gary Imlach, who became the face of Channel 4's coverage of American football. 'It was more than that, though. There was an element of wanting to present the sports in a context; there was sumo, not just treated as a sport but as a way to look at Japan and its culture – and the sports had to have some cultural cachet themselves, be hip or esoteric or cool.' Imlach, synonymous with American football on this side of the Atlantic in the late 1980s, believes it was a way to illuminate American ideals and culture. 'Of course, you can view the NFL as a mainstream corporate behemoth of a money-making machine, but in the early 1980s, before the internet had shrunk the planet, America – as familiar as it was to people in the UK from films and TV and music – was still properly foreign in many ways. When Channel 4 bought the rights to the NFL, they were buying their way in to a whole idea of America.'

While more dedicated fans may have tuned into the American Forces Radio and Television Network to hear live updates, NFL highlights in the UK were shown during the late 1970s on ITV's *World of Sport*, showing infrequent clips of recent games. These were often simple highlight packages of important postseason or Super Bowl clashes, but the new terrestrial television channel was to be more thorough. 'They used to show Super Bowl highlights around 15 minutes in length on ITV's *World of Sport*,' said Roger Goodgroves, an American football journalist. 'I loved what I saw – I didn't understand but I marvelled at long runs and spectacular passes. Some fandoms predate the 1980s, although Channel 4 was responsible for what we could call the real surge of American football in the country.' Soon after its launch, Channel 4 began broadcasting NFL highlights on a weekly basis and British popularity in the sport surged, with the first show airing on 7 November 1982. It proved to be a turning point for American football, advancing and legitimising the game more in the public eye than ever before. Before the intro credits, the Channel 4 logo transitioned into an American football player with steam gushing from his nostrils – suddenly, the sport was seen in a whole new light. 'I remember an American friend of mine being utterly baffled when he heard the theme tune to the show. What the hell were police sirens doing in the title music to a sports programme? But it made perfect sense to a British audience: cop shows, shoulder pads, glitz, excess, bone-crunching violence – it was all part of a package,' added Imlach.

The show was allocated to run at 5.30pm, dubbed the 'God-slot', as it pitted the highlights against the likes of *Antiques Roadshow* and *Songs of Praise*. The first programmes were highlight packages that ran for 60 minutes, summarising a featured match of the week along with a general round-up of the remaining action around the league. While the 1982 NFL strike, which lasted eight weeks, threatened Channel 4's venture into the sport before it had really begun, channel operators managed to circumnavigate the issue by simply showing highlights of matches from earlier in the season, with up to 750,000 Brits estimated to have tuned in in late 1982. Just three years later, a reported audience of three million watched the show every week on Sunday at 6pm to get the fix of their new favourite type of football and, remarkably, around three times that figure watched the Super Bowl each year.

The second key reason for the surge in popularity was that association football – soccer – was struggling compared to the modern game. Truth be told, it had never been so unpopular. Hooliganism was affecting the sport's popularity following deaths in Birmingham, while run-down stadiums deterred fans and were deemed unsafe following Bradford City's Valley Parade fire on 11 May 1985 which killed 56 and injured more than 250. English clubs were banned from European competition for six years from 1985 due to their actions that contributed to the Heysel disaster in Brussels and a broadcasting strike in 1984–85 meant there were no live games on television, so American football benefitted immensely.

In the early 1970s, the NFL was turning its attentions abroad and began their search for fresh markets. A group of American promoters thought several regions around the world were ready for professional gridiron football, and one of these men was Tex Schramm. Texas Earnest Schramm Jr was an American football executive and the original president and general manager of the Dallas Cowboys. Schramm was known for influencing several changes and innovations that modernised the NFL: instant replay, headsets in the quarterback's helmet to help hear play calls and computer technology in scouting. In fact, Schramm's desire for scouting led to the creation of the NFL Scouting Combine in Indianapolis on an annual basis, and the Cowboys executive's interest in scouting led him to broaden his horizons across international borders. He was interested in building a demand for gridiron football on a global scale, but he zeroed in on Europe and even signed Toni Fritsch, an Austrian association footballer, in 1971. In fact, the league tested Europe's appetite for the game on 27 May 1972 when 42 professional players demonstrated 'Le Rugby Americain' before 8,000 fans in Paris as NFL Bleu defeated NFL Rouge 16-6.

On 5 June 1974, businessmen held a meeting to kickstart the development of the sport in Europe with its first professional league. Bob Kap and West German entrepreneur Adalbert Wetzel – who owned soccer club 1860 Munich – proposed a spring league to be played in the continent, called the 'Intercontinental Football League'. Six teams were planned: the Istanbul Conquerors, Rome Gladiators, Munich Lions, Berlin Bears, Vienna Lippizzaners and the Barcelona Almovogeres. Unfortunately, NFL commissioner Pete Rozelle said in a March 1975 statement that Cold War tensions and economic issues in both the United States and Europe meant the project was impractical at the time and it never truly got off the ground.

Another promoter with global ambitions for America's game was John Marshall, who should be fondly remembered by British gridiron fans. After Super Bowl XVII on 30 January 1983 was watched by four and a half million people in the United Kingdom, Marshall wanted to capitalise on the opportunity before him. He formulated the first NFL game at Wembley Stadium, organising the Minnesota Vikings to clash with the St Louis Cardinals on

6 August 1983. In front of 32,847 spectators – under half the capacity of the famous ground – the Vikings cruised to a 28-10 win. Minnesota dominated from start to finish, with an 18-7 half-time lead stemming from a pair of touchdown passes in the second quarter from Tommy Kramer, a nine-yard pass to Ted Brown and a 31-yarder to Leo Lewis. Rufus Bess closed out the win in the fourth quarter with a 76-yard punt return down the right sideline, his only career touchdown in the NFL. The players were as intrigued by the fans as the locals were with them. Bess recalled that the Brits labelled the players 'gladiators' rather than football players, while Minnesota running back Rickey Young said it was the franchise's name that sparked interest: 'Because we were Vikings, they thought that we were Norsemen, like we were real Vikings from the ship.'

The rules and general mayhem on the field, much like in 1952 with the USAFE Football League Final, confused the fans. 'They didn't really cheer at the appropriate times. When we scored a touchdown, it wasn't a big deal. But when we kicked anything, it was a pretty big deal to them,' running back Darrin Nelson said of the fans that clearly still held soccer and rugby dearest in their hearts. 'They cheered the kick-offs. They cheered the punts. They were pretty silent on touchdowns.' British fan Guy Horchover admitted it was an enjoyable spectacle, but he was perplexed as to why the game took so long: 'It's rather good, isn't it, when they're actually playing, but it's bloody annoying with all those stops between plays. It takes them an hour to play 20 minutes. And why is the referee always dropping yellow dusters on the field?' Flags clearly hadn't caught on yet, either.

However, the media once again offered an underwhelming opinion of the spectacle. The *Sunday Express* led the way, pushing the violent nature of the sport while integrating their own interpretations of cadences, insisting: 'All those endless collisions of outsize flesh and blood … all those baffling hand signals and free-coded rhythm grunts, which only players of their own side could understand … and all those coaches barking orders – to the outsider it was a disorganised mess. A Big Bore!'

While Marshall lost £420,000 and the British press were left mildly disgusted, the exhibition game made a lasting impact – which appeared to be the promoter's goal. 'We never expected to break even, just introduce the game to Britain,' Marshall told a reporter after the match. With the NFL on Channel 4 throughout the season, British people became fans as they were encouraged to try the new game.

Inspired by what they had seen on television – and excited for the upcoming game at Wembley – a group of friends from Harrow Rugby Club founded a team, the London Ravens, with help from USAFE Football League's Chicksands Chicks. They held try-outs with over 200 attending the first session following an advert in the local paper, and the rugby players-turned-gridiron trailblazers cut their roster down to 50 keen players. The Chicks helped them garner support and equipment and even scheduled scrimmages with the Ravens, although several members of the Air Force team thought the request to schedule a practice game was a 'practical joke'. They clashed at Stamford Bridge on 9 July 1983, around a month before Marshall's NFL exhibition, and the Chicks' expectations of a joke quickly became more serious as the Ravens battled hard to lose just 8-0. While they played a second time – a crushing 38-0 Chicks victory in front of 5,000 fans – the Ravens had cemented themselves in British gridiron history as the first British club.

The club certainly were not done making British American football history. The Ravens participated in the first all-British game, taking on the Northwich Spartans – who would later become the Manchester Spartans – at Stamford Bridge in October 1983. After preparing far more effectively than their relatively new opponents, the Ravens crushed the Spartans 48-0, beginning an undefeated domestic streak that would last until 1988. Like any great all-conquering establishment, the Ravens quickly turned their attentions abroad as they faced the Paris Castors in the first international game played in England, tying 6-6 in November 1983, before demolishing Paris Spartacus – the first French American football team after their creation in 1980 – in a resounding 51-0 victory on 30 September 1984. The Ravens were proving their might on the international stage and doing so as they fielded running back Victor Ebubedike, a future star for the London Monarchs.

American football fever was spreading, and the United States Football League (USFL) decided to try to cash in on the rising popularity of the sport with a match at Wembley. The USFL was the NFL's next rival, and while it only lasted three seasons between 1983 and 1985, the league targeted college stars who wanted to get paid as soon as possible. In doing so, future NFL legends such as Steve Young, Jim Kelly and Reggie White all signed on. On 21 July 1984, the USFL came to London as the Philadelphia Stars defeated the Tampa Bay Bandits – owned by Burt Reynolds, with the team name inspired by the actor's successful *Smokey and the Bandit* movie franchise – 24-21 in front of 21,000 fans in the Jetsave Challenge Cup. The Tampa Bay side took a 14-0 lead in the opening quarter before slipping to defeat. One fan, Tony Wells, gave a particularly interesting and relevant reason for his newfound interest in gridiron football and told a reporter, 'American football is a family game. We can take the wife and kids if we want.' This comment truly highlights the prevalent feeling of the time: that association football was being ruined by hooliganism. This was gridiron football's chance.

Ultimately, the match was an attempt to pique the interest of European fans and earn their respect to legitimise the USFL as they attempted to claim the European market from the clutches of the NFL. However, the presence of the NFL on Channel 4 meant that it was a losing battle for the USFL. 'I think an important part of the show's appeal was that we went to the games on behalf of fans who couldn't because they weren't on the same continent as the teams they supported,' said Imlach, who was shocked by the press access and 'different dimension' of American sports compared to the British equivalent. 'Depth charts, TV monitors, play-by-play calls over the PA, full recaps and printed stats distributed at the end of every quarter. The discovery that both winners and losers were obliged to open their locker rooms to anyone with a press pass before the players had had time to get dressed was astonishing.'

The domestic game continued to develop throughout the 1980s, with the London Ravens beginning to establish themselves as a true force, and the need for a league became apparent. Thirty-five teams were now established and the need for an organising body was clear when the teams met in Bedford in February 1984. However, tensions during meetings meant that, like the foundation of the NFL and its numerous rivals until the Super Bowl era, the original British structure was fragmented.

After a meeting at the Baden-Powell House, London on 3 March 1984, at which 26 teams attended, there was no agreement to house all the teams in one league. Seven teams broke away to join the British American Football Federation (BAFF) headed by Mike Lytton while the remaining 19 teams joined the American Football League United Kingdom (AFLUK) with American Gary Hartman at the helm. AFLUK got the ball rolling first, meeting at RAF Chicksands where they decided the first match would take place in April, hosted by the Poole Sharks. Frustratingly, English clubs were at very different stages of their development so notable mismatches were evident during the 1984 season: the Ravens, in the midst of their unprecedented 57-game win streak, defeated Wyton Eagles 27-0, Poole 71-0, Milton Keynes Bucks 46-0, Manchester Spartans 28-0 and 59-0 and thumped Walthamstow Warriors an astounding 87-0. There was also a lack of funding, with teams forced to wait before they were equipped. The Colchester Gladiators were founded in October 1983 but made their debut in a 32-12 defeat to the Streatham Olympians on

20 January 1985. Regardless of these teething issues, attendances were impressive with over 7,000 attending the Milton Keynes Bowl between Poole and Northampton.

Two smaller associations – the UK American Football Association and the Amateur American Football Conference (AAFC) – were born soon after a meeting in Birmingham in 1985 as American football spread throughout the country with over 100 teams entering the formed leagues. In 1985, the Ravens exacted their revenge on the Chicksands Chicks, a 13-12 win, signalling just how far the sport had come in a few years. The Ravens' win showed that the British domestic league could now compete with the USAFE Football League.

The stronger and more established teams, including the Ravens, joined the AFLUK for the 1985 season. With clubs being formed across the country, there were 40 teams in the league for the season, but they were not financially ready to mirror an NFL slate of 16 games in the regular season so, in November 1984, it was decided that 37 teams would split into six divisions, with 16 teams entering playoffs culminating in the British edition of the Super Bowl in August 1985: the Summer Bowl.

The 1985 AFLUK conference consisted of six divisions with between five and seven teams in each. In the Northern Division were the Edinburgh Blue Eagles, Fylde Falcons, Glasgow Diamonds, Glasgow Lions, Leeds Cougars, Manchester Spartans and Tyneside Trojans. The Midland Division saw the Birmingham Bulls, King's Lynn Patriots, Milton Keynes Bucks, Northampton Stormbringers, Nottingham Hoods, Walsall Titans and Warwickshire Bears go head to head. The Capital Division included the dominant London Ravens, Crawley Raiders, Ealing Eagles, Greenwich Bay Mariners, Harlow Warlords and the Stock Exchange Stags. The South-Western Division housed the Dorset Broncos, Heathrow Jets, Oxford Bulldogs, Portsmouth Warriors, Southampton Seahawks, Taunton Wyverns and Thames Valley Chargers while the Southern Division saw the Colchester

Gladiators battle the Rockingham Rebels, Southampton Wolverines, Southend Sabres and Streatham Olympians. Finally, the North Central Division was home to the Leicester Panthers, Manchester All-Stars, Mansfield Express, Newcastle Browns and Staffordshire Stampeders.

The Leicester Panthers proved to be the surprise package of the 1985 campaign after years of careful planning. Alex and Chris McAllister and their friend Pat Joseph placed an ad in the local paper calling for players, while they approached Bruce Cannady, an American stationed at Mildenhall base in Suffolk. It was no coincidence that many of the teams were established near army bases, with teams often borrowing equipment and players. Cannady brought three US servicemen with him to coach the team and they trained three times a week, opting to focus on fitness, tactics and understanding the rules of the game before playing a single match. The Panthers played their first match in March 1985, defeating Northampton 44-7 to kickstart a 10-0 regular season record before they lost in the semi-finals of the playoffs.

The first edition of the Summer Bowl was played on 26 August 1985 at Villa Park, pitting the Ravens against the Streatham Olympians. The Ravens crushed their feeble opposition 45-7, but the attendance of just over 7,000 – well short of expectations – meant the Summer Bowl moniker was unfortunately discontinued. The championship game continued in various formats before landing on the Britbowl, which it is still known as today.

As for the BAFF, 12 teams took part in 1985 with the Cambridge Cats and Brighton B52s storming to 8-0 records before both sides were dumped out of the playoffs in the semi-finals. The final between the Croydon Coyotes and the Rockingham Rebels was played at the Paddington Recreation Ground, with the Rebels triumphing 13-0.

As the domestic 1985 season drew to a close, there was time for one more thrill on British soil as the largest crowd of the year – an estimated 12,500 fans – was in the stands of Brighton's Withdean Stadium to see the B52s face City College from San Francisco in an excellently marketed exhibition game. The match was the first time an American college played in England, and the first time an entirely English team faced a US outfit. The match came about simply from a meeting in early 1985 between David Bentley, the manager of the Manchester All-Stars, and San Francisco coach George Rush to discuss training methods and drills. They organised a two-team tour in which City College would play the All-Stars and the B52s, but postseason play rules for Californian teams meant they could only play once.

It is probably for the best that they faced a single British team, as City College crushed Brighton 76-0 on 8 December 1985. It was decided that the B52s were in a better position to host the game, and it proved to be true as the attendance was almost 4,000 more than the Summer Bowl. The Great Britain Lions also played their first international game, against France, defeating their rivals 7-0 as the country got its first taste of international gridiron action.

However, the NFL remained king and the travel industry was beginning to understand its appeal. Trips were offered to various American cities to watch regular season matches as part of a holiday package. With the lack of live soccer games on TV, the NFL soared in popularity over the 1985 season, culminating in the January showpiece in 1986.

On 26 January 1986, Super Bowl XX took place in New Orleans to crown the champion of the 1985 NFL season, pitting the Chicago Bears against the New England Patriots. The 1985 Bears – led by Walter Payton, their star running back – are considered by many to be the greatest team to have played the game, and Mike Ditka's side duly defeated the Patriots 46-10. An estimated 4 million people in the UK tuned into the Bears' coronation, although some accounts suggest as many as 12 million watched Chicago secure the Lombardi Trophy, and such popularity encouraged the league to return to London despite the financial failure of the first game.

The NFL returned to Wembley for its first official game in London, welcoming the world champion Chicago Bears against 'America's Team', the Dallas Cowboys, on 3 August 1986. NFL commissioner Pete Rozelle penned a message to the growing British fanbase in the game's programme, writing: 'This is a remarkable response when you consider that the victory of the Chicago Bears over the New England Patriots was not concluded until the early hours of the following morning. You British are a hearty bunch!'

The event, billed as the first American Bowl, was attended by 86,000 fans and Chicago head coach Ditka thought the fans enjoyed themselves, but their love for soccer shined through. 'The fans were terrific. They were receptive to the game. They have that soccer mentality and really got into how physical it was,' he said. 'Dallas brought the cheerleaders, but because they were all soccer fans, our kicker Kevin Butler was a hit.' Fans were keen to pay up to £20 for a sideline seat, £10 for the upper terrace and £5 for the lower terrace as the event sold out with 82,699 Brits desperate to watch the newly crowned world champion Bears.

In the pouring rain, Jim McMahon and William 'The Refrigerator' Perry starred as the Bears ran out 17-6 winners. The first touchdown came when Dallas quarterback Danny White's pass was knocked to the floor by Chicago linebacker Wilber Marshall and safety Dave Duerson scooped the ball up to score a 48-yard touchdown following the fumble. The Fridge scored the only offensive touchdown of the game when he powered his way over the line from a yard out – and it was a good thing he did. 'One of the surprising things about the London trip was how popular the Fridge was with the English fans,' said former Chicago Bears photographer Bill Smith. 'The stars of that team were Payton, McMahon and [Richard] Dent. But the rock star to London media and fans was undoubtedly

Perry. They didn't understand much about American football in 1986, but they all knew the Fridge.' Perry became a household name in the British sporting landscape, appearing on BBC One's *Wogan* alongside Dan Marino in 1986 while Payton also made a celebrity appearance on *A Question of Sport*. While his side lost, legendary Cowboys coach Tom Landry joked that the visit to London was better than his last trip, when he was taking a break from embarking on bombing runs over Germany during his stint in the military.

Gary Imlach reported on the first American Bowl, and he believed the clash demonstrated to the NFL that the audience – or market – was worth cultivating. '[It was] a first international bridgehead in their grand plan to sell team merchandise to every man, woman and child on the planet.' Ultimately, the 1986 preseason game was a success and inspired a series of eight American Bowls played in London on an annual basis until 1993, a 13-13 tie between Dallas and the Detroit Lions. The 1987 clash saw the Denver Broncos lose 28-27 to the Los Angeles Rams with the likes of John Elway and Eric Dickerson gracing the Wembley turf, and the Rams won with just 28 seconds remaining thanks to a Charles White rushing touchdown.

In 1988, the American Bowl saw the San Francisco 49ers take on the Miami Dolphins. Billed as Joe Montana against Dan Marino, the two superstar quarterbacks saw limited playing time as Miami stunned the dynastic 49ers 27-21 in front of 70,505 fans at Wembley. '[The American Bowl games] were a fun day out more than anything,' added Roger Goodgroves. 'We knew they were friendlies, we knew the starters would probably not get much airtime, and so it was never seen as anything particularly competitive.' The following year saw the Philadelphia Eagles win 17-13 against the Cleveland Browns in an error-laden performance, and the American Bowl went global in 1990. The NFL organised an International Week, a four-game showcase with matches in Tokyo, Montreal, Berlin and London, where the New Orleans Saints defeated the LA Raiders 17-10 in front of 63,106 fans. The *Daily Telegraph* ran a poll ahead of the 1990 FIFA World Cup which found that American football was more popular than soccer among young British television viewers, with 39 per cent from 25,000 interviewed in the 15–24 age bracket preferring football to soccer. This would soon change with the heroics of Paul Gascoigne and the birth of the FA Premier League in 1992.

The 1991 American Bowl saw the Buffalo Bills defence dominate the Philadelphia Eagles to win 17-13 in front of a record-low attendance of 50,474, while the 1992 edition of the game pitted the 49ers against the Washington Redskins, with San Francisco leaving 17-15 winners.

The regular series that came from a rain-soaked clash between the Super Bowl champion Bears and the famous Cowboys helped the NFL grow, not just in the United Kingdom but around Europe, from an intriguing game to a more mainstream sport. However, Ditka understood just how far the gridiron sport would have to go yet. 'Let's be honest, football is a US sport. Basketball, soccer, even baseball to a certain extent are universal sports. I think it'll be hard for football to become as universal as that.' It also did not help that such games were clearly part of the teams' preseason preparation for their upcoming campaigns, and so were not the full-blooded NFL clashes as seen on Channel 4.

Ditka's comments rang true, as the two domestic leagues – AFLUK and BAFF – were forced to merge after massive losses, and liquidation was imminent. This opened the door for a new league system and, after a lengthy study essentially double-checking whether their investment would be worth it, American beer company Anheuser-Busch were keen for their famous product, Budweiser, to sponsor British American football. They subsequently announced a £300,000 fund to grow the sport in the UK in 1985. Anheuser-Busch simply wanted to give Brits something to relate to, be it football, beer or Bruce Springsteen.

The company originally wanted to sponsor either the AFLUK or BAFF, but instead opted to host their own league, and their sponsorship began to make an impact. 'American football is an expensive sport to play,' Goodgroves commented. 'The sponsorship gave a number of teams the opportunity to subsidise player entry costs which impacted the ability to bring in talented people who weren't just rich enough to be able to do it – a lot of the people we played with were not in the prime of their life, shall we say.'

This led to a division within British American football, as ten teams – including the Brighton B52s and Northampton Stormbringers – signed up instantly while 15 more soon joined. Once the London Ravens and Streatham Olympians announced they were leaving the AFLUK in favour of the Budweiser League, more teams followed suit, although some opted to remain in the reformed British American Football League (BAFL) after AFLUK and BAFF merged. For the inaugural 1986 campaign, there were enough teams to merge American franchise culture with traditional European league structure. The Bud League featured the top 15 teams in the National Division, 48 in the Premier Division (second tier) and 32 more teams in Division One (third tier). The modern structure for the British American Football Association (BAFA) domestic leagues, which is in place today, was taking shape.

There were, naturally, early complications for the new league. The Orpington Owls were banned after two players disrupted a sponsored dinner in London with Budweiser League president Dan Marino in attendance, as the quarterback was in the UK for the kick-off of the league's first season. The European Football League also refused to acknowledge the Budweiser League, instead giving competition places to BAFL, which meant the London Ravens, the Summer Bowl I champions, were ineligible for the 1986 European Club Championship. Their spot was taken by the Birmingham Bulls, who defeated the Leicester Panthers

32-18 in a playoff to book their place in the event in Utrecht, Holland, where the Bulls would finish in a respectable third place after losing to Bologna 40-7 in the semi-finals. The Bulls would go on to win the 1986 BAFL championship, still known as the Summer Bowl, with a 23-2 win over the Glasgow Lions in September 1986.

It was clear early on that the London Ravens and Streatham Olympians were the teams to beat and both finished with 10-0 records as they swept through their respective divisions. The two would meet in the first Budweiser Bowl in August 1986, which was picked up by US television networks with highlights being shown on ABC. The Ravens ran out 20-12 winners, completing their scoring in the first half when touchdowns from Joe St Louis and Victor Ebubedike were accompanied by a sensational 76-yard touchdown pass from Ron Roberts to Tony Taylor. The Olympians came back with two touchdowns in the fourth quarter, but it was a case of too little, too late for Streatham, while London's Ebubedike was named league MVP.

The lack of European prestige hurt the Budweiser League, but the national fight for supremacy would soon end. The BAFL announced it was to fold with over £40,000 worth of debt, only for Budweiser to step in and merge the leagues. The new Budweiser League now housed over 100 clubs across 18 divisions and became the central system for the domestic game.

The year of 1986 is also remembered as a landmark year in British American football as it witnessed the first football game played in the UK between two teams completely composed of female players. In November, the East Coast Sharkettes defeated the Eastbourne Crusaders 30-12 at Bognor Regis. Unfortunately, the women's game would not progress for a while after that, but the groundwork had been laid and they would eventually join the males in playing regular and competitive football.

The London Ravens picked up from where they left off, crushing the Birmingham Bulls 61-8 in week seven as they stormed to the 1987 Budweiser Bowl. The Ravens faced the Luton Flyers in the semi-finals, a team that had attracted headlines when they signed the first player with NFL experience to play for a British team in the form of linebacker Jim Tsarofski. However, the match was notable thanks to the clash between star running backs Ebubedike and Luton's David Munn, who had tallied 1,229 yards and 12 touchdowns. The Ravens won, booking their place in the final against the Manchester All-Stars.

The All-Stars had impressed with American quarterback Rick Bolen under centre, and they surprised with a 27-12 victory over the Olympians in week five en route to finishing 10-0. On 20 September 1987, the All-Stars faced the Ravens at Loftus Road, home of Queens Park Rangers, with Ebubedike once again proving to be the man of the moment. He scored three touchdowns, including a 72-yard run, to lead the Ravens to a 40-23 win and their second successive Budweiser League title.

After Budweiser's takeover of the national leagues, the late 1980s was a period in which a number of North American imports were brought in to elevate the domestic game. Quarterback Bo Hickey – not to be confused with the Denver Broncos fullback from two decades prior – joined the Fylde Falcons in the Northern Division after playing college football for Western Maryland, and he set a passing record of 3,725 yards in the 1988 season that still stands today. The 1988 season was a sensational one. Following another reorganisation to have a National Conference with three divisions (Northern, Central and Southern), the Ravens lost their first-ever game to a British team as the London Olympians secured an enormous win. The Birmingham Bulls were proving to be the team to beat and duly crushed the Ravens 51-13 as the Bulls reached their first Budweiser Bowl. A crowd of 8,972 packed into Loftus Road to watch the Bulls defeat the Olympians 30-6.

The following year was a mixed one for British American football. The GB Lions won their first European Championship – which they retained two years later in 1991 – but the domestic game took a hit when Budweiser announced that they were withdrawing their sponsorship. This opened the door for a new American football league to establish themselves and the Arena Football League (AFL) came to London on 18 November 1989. The idea for the new league stemmed from Jim Foster, a promotions manager with the NFL. Foster devised the notion of indoor football while watching an indoor soccer match at New York City's famous Madison Square Garden in 1981. After presenting ideas to friends within the NFL, he conjured up rules and drew up a business plan before presenting his idea to television networks, and the AFL was up and running for the 1987 season. Two years later the AFL arrived in London, and 12,000 fans turned up at the Docklands Arena to watch the Arenaball Transatlantic Challenge – the first AFL exhibition game in Europe – with Detroit Drive steamrolling the Chicago Bruisers to win 43-14. Foster had a vision to expand the indoor gridiron game within the UK, but nothing came of it after its fleeting moment in the spotlight.

Once again, British American football was in limbo at the end of the 1980s. The National Gridiron League was formed for the 1989 season, with a total of 172 clubs involved, but national press and the game's general popularity was decreasing due to the frustrating backroom politics. Manchester Spartans won the championship in the final Bud Bowl as they defeated the Bulls 21-14, but the damage was done. 'You have to have a product that people will watch and the product was diminished – by the number of splits, team name changes, team location changes – so the stability wasn't there,' Goodgroves revealed.

As the 1990s arrived, a wave of changes swept across society: boy bands replaced synth pop, spandex was usurped by hypercolour T-shirts and Coca-Cola replaced Budweiser as the chief sponsor of the domestic American football leagues. The leadership of the sport continued to evolve and change hands through these early years with BAFL ultimately holding firm until 2010. Since then, BAFA has held its status as the primary league within the country.

The 1980s were a decade that will be remembered for the ushering of gridiron football into the mainstream as the NFL dipped its toe into the market across the pond with more than a dozen professional teams playing on British soil while over 10,000 people took up the sport with over 150 teams founded across the country.

In the 1990s, ambition and an urge to experiment meant that the league would explore their potential new fanbase, with differing levels of success.

CHAPTER 6

The World League of American Football: The Rise and Fall of the Monarchy

'Much of the difficulty appeared to stem from an ambivalence on the part of the NFL owners: they wanted a spring league but did not want to create a rival to the NFL. In the end, they did not create enough of a rival.' – Matt Tench, *The Independent*, September 1992

THE NFL was ready to try and cash in on their potential new marketplace across the Atlantic.

They explored numerous options and looked at previous plans for the proposed all-European league that failed in the 1970s. West German entrepreneur Adal Wetzel joined forces with Bob Kap, a former soccer coach who worked with Lamar Hunt – owner of the North American Soccer League's Dallas Tornado and founder of the Kansas City Chiefs – and the duo put together the blueprint for the Intercontinental Football League (IFL). The league had secured the services of several NFL players for the 1975 campaign, but economic and political issues derailed the league. The IFL would have had teams from around mainland

Europe and, while it ultimately never came to fruition, the seeds had been sown.

The World League of American Football (WLAF) was finally formed in 1989 following a unanimous vote by NFL owners. The league was the dream of commissioner Paul Tagliabue, and garnered support as a spring developmental league in a region that was becoming popular due to the American Bowls held in London, at Wembley Stadium, and abroad. The NFL did consider a spring league in the United States, but they would have been subject to antitrust issues because of the relationship between the players' union and the league if they had additional teams in the country. The board for the WLAF was set up by commissioner Pete Rozelle to include representatives with NFL experience, including Mike Lynn, Dan Rooney, Bill Walsh, Norman Braman and Victor Klam. They were tasked with negotiating television contracts, with the rights being sold to ABC and USA Network in the States and 19 other European channels including Sky's Eurosport channel, while highlights were on Channel 4. The groundbreaking idea to harness the appeal of the sport in Europe was an attempt to increase its popularity across time zones, gridlines and languages as the WLAF was set up as the brainchild of 26 owners and US television networks.

Tex Schramm, the former Dallas Cowboys General Manager, was hired as World League president and chief executive, and he presented the league as a prime-time source of entertainment during the spring and summer while the NFL was in its annual offseason. Schramm helped the league launch international offices and hired league executives before he resigned suddenly on 10 October 1990. He was succeeded by Mike Lynn of the Minnesota Vikings, a fitting replacement as he, like Schramm, had an international vision for the league. Lynn was part of the decision to send the Vikings to face the Cardinals at Wembley in 1983 while Minnesota had also played in the first game on mainland Europe in Stockholm in 1988.

While it was an independent project, 26 of the 28 NFL teams donated $50,000 each to cover start-up costs for the WLAF and, in an attempt to prevent the exorbitant spending that led to the collapse of the USFL, the league office controlled team payrolls and budgets. Base salaries were set at $15,000 for kickers and punters, $20,000 for position players and $25,000 for quarterbacks, each complete with incentive clauses to ensure the prospect appeared attractive. The NFL owned team identities and sold off operating rights for as little as $11m to prospective owners, with the European Division housing the Barcelona Dragons, Frankfurt Galaxy and the London Monarchs, who became the eighth franchise on 3 August 1990. In the States, the North American East Division contained the Montreal Machine, New York/New Jersey Knights, Orlando Thunder and Raleigh-Durham Skyhawks while the West Division included Birmingham Fire, Sacramento Surge and the San Antonio Riders. The WLAF was made up of ten teams across five countries and two continents – it was certainly not the National Football League.

A developmental league, the WLAF was used as a body to test rules upon. The two-point conversion, utilised in the Canadian Football League and college ball, was tested in the WLAF before the NFL adopted it in 1994. To increase diversity and value of European players, at least one non-American player had to participate in every other possession as a minimum.

The WLAF played two seasons in the spring of 1991 and 1992, with each team playing a ten-game regular season leading to playoffs and culminating with the World Bowl championship game. The format of the postseason consisted of four teams – the three divisional champions plus a wildcard team that had the best overall record of the remaining teams. The two victors of the WLAF semi-final playoffs met in the World Bowl.

In these two opening campaigns, the WLAF was barely noticed or even recognised in the United States – but the game was taking off abroad. The three European franchises all surpassed attendance expectations with the trio from across the pond averaging 30,324 fans per game, compared to around 22,000 for the seven North American teams. The London Monarchs were particularly popular and their attendance led the league. WLAF President Mike Lynn, the former general manager for the Minnesota Vikings, couldn't explain the positive reaction in Europe. 'It's an absolute phenomenon,' he said. Lynn was right – European fans in Britain, Germany and Spain had fallen for the sport. In fact, when the Barcelona Dragons returned from a two-week tour of America to play season games, the team was greeted at their hotel by 1,000 fans, a marching band and a fireworks display. American traditions so deeply rooted in the sport were shining through.

An interesting issue was the lack of live television coverage. Despite the success of Channel 4 during the 1980s, the 1991 WLAF season was mostly broadcast on satellite television. Eurosport showed full matches on delay and Super Channel – which would later become NBC Europe – covered the 1991 World Bowl, while Channel 4 showed highlights of Monarchs games on the weekend. Television proved to be a key issue in terms of expanding the sport, and Larry Eichel of the *Philadelphia Inquirer* wrote, 'The only way a Monarchs fan could watch the team's first-round playoff game was to go to Wembley to see it on closed circuit.' While it appeared that the WLAF was succeeding on the field, it was struggling to grow the sport and showcase the new league effectively. Broadcasters were aware of this issue going into the season, and ABC spokesman Mark Mandell said: 'The ratings are, quite frankly, not as high as we would have liked. But we knew going in it was going to have to build and grow. When we went in, there were no teams, stadiums, coaches. We knew it was a good concept. We still know it's a good concept.'

His comments were optimistic, but ultimately there was little to no American infatuation with the WLAF. Chris Dufresne of the *Los Angeles Times* suggested American fans were less likely than Europeans to 'shell out hard-earned dollars for games featuring roster-cut leftovers'. He was right – the WLAF was a novelty to the European audience, but its lack of relative quality when compared to the NFL or the college game meant that stateside fans simply didn't care.

To pique interest in the WLAF, a talent scouting programme was launched named Operation Discovery. Led by former Denver Broncos head coach John Ralston, the idea was to track down top international athletes and integrate them into WLAF rosters. This allowed the league to attract the likes of European Champion sprinter Frank Emmelmann to try out for Frankfurt Galaxy while Victor Ebubedike, the former London Ravens running back who had been training with the New York Jets, joined the London Monarchs.

The Monarchs, for the first two seasons anyway, flew the British flag in the WLAF and they needed to have the appropriate marketing behind them. Billy Hicks, the Monarchs general manager, said the franchise considered names including the Lions and the Royals but they didn't want to clash with the NFL team in Detroit or the Major League Baseball side in Kansas City. The London professional American football team had to be unique. The name 'Monarchs' was suggested, and it stuck. Dave Boss was the corporate vice-president and special projects manager for NFL Properties, and he helped with the design of the helmet of the Monarchs, opting for a monogram 'M' in the shape of a crown. As for the uniform, he decided on a royal blue jersey with red hints to reflect the Union Jack with gold helmet and pants to reinforce the royal theme. Jon Smith, an English soccer agent who set up his own sports marketing company First Artist in 1985, was then named CEO of the Monarchs. Smith had worked with Jarvis Astaire as minority owners of the team as both had originally facilitated the development of the domestic game by sponsoring the British leagues and even helped bring the American Bowl to Wembley in the first place. With their connections, they ensured a deal was struck to allow the Monarchs to play their home games at the iconic stadium.

London's first head coach, Larry Kennan, had experience in the NFL. He was an assistant for the LA Raiders between 1982 and 1987, including acting as quarterbacks coach for their Super Bowl XVIII win in 1984. He was also the receivers coach at the Denver Broncos in 1988 and the Indianapolis Colts' offensive coordinator in 1989 and 1990. As Kennan would learn, team building was a rapid process in the WLAF. He was hired on 1 February 1991 and was quickly jetted to Orlando a week later for the draft, along with his coaching staff. The draft lasted three weeks, with teams picking from 710 available players after watching them work out. The *Orlando Sentinel* described the draft as 'a rather arduous, somewhat monotonous but very innovative 15-day, position-by-position, start-from-scratch process'. It was an extraordinary process and the Monarchs certainly impressed with their picks.

The Monarchs brought in a number of fine players. Cornerback Corris Ervin was a fifth-round pick for the Denver Broncos in 1988, while running back Jeff Alexander was picked up by Denver in the same draft. London also selected defensive stars like linebacker Danny Lockett, who would go on to lead the league in sacks with 15 en route to sharing the Defensive Player of the Year award with Knights corner Anthony Parker, who played 16 games for the Detroit Lions in 1988. Defensive lineman Roy Hart was a second-round pick for the Seattle Seahawks in 1988, but he was cut following a shoulder injury in 1990 to set the wheels in motion for his arrival in the Big Smoke. Hart would register 10.5 sacks in 1991, helping the Monarchs defence during their sensational campaign along with the likes of defensive ends Mike Renna and John Shannon.

Along with linebacker trio Marlon Brown (who was nicknamed 'Space Dog' simply because he wanted it as his nickname), Ken Sale and Rickey Williams, this fierce front seven

– masterminded by defensive coordinator Ray Willsey in his 3-4 formation – became known as the 'Hart Attack'. The defensive backs had their own alias, with Ervin joined by fellow corner Irvin Smith and safety duo Dedrick Dodge and Danny Crossman to form the 'No Goal Patrol'.

It wasn't just the defence that had names for each unit. The Monarchs' physical offensive line became known as the 'Nasty Boyz' after they aggressively scrimmaged with teams during their training camp in Orlando, fighting with opposing defensive linemen. The unit included guards Paul Berardelli and Larry Jones, tackles Theo Adams and Steve Gabbard with centre Doug Marrone – who would become an NFL head coach with the Buffalo Bills and Jacksonville Jaguars – anchoring the line. The Nasty Boyz would look to open gaps for the likes of Ebubedike, Judd Garrett and Jeff Alexander while protecting quarterback Stan Gelbaugh, the jewel in the Monarchs' crown.

Gelbaugh played for the Bills for three seasons without getting into the team due to the success of Buffalo quarterback Jim Kelly. He starred for the Monarchs during the inaugural season of the WLAF, passing for 2,665 yards and 17 touchdowns with a 62.4 per cent completion rate and a league-best 92.8 rating. For his efforts, Gelbaugh was voted offensive MVP and First-Team All-World by his peers and coaches – but he didn't do it without the help of his receiving corps, the 'Bomb Squad'. Gelbaugh's targets were Jon Horton, Andre Riley and Paul Sargent, and the trio would dominate as the offence took the league by storm.

With his team drafted, Kennan trained them in Orlando for around ten days before doing another intense camp in London after roster cuts. The team then travelled to Frankfurt for the first game of the WLAF season in March. The WLAF was not a lot of things, but it was certainly efficient. On 23 March 1991, the Monarchs took to the Waldstadion field to face the Galaxy, with World League president Lynn delivering the game ball via helicopter. Two Brits made an immediate impact on the first play in league history. Norwich City footballer Phil Alexander was the Monarchs kicker and subsequently kicked off to signal the beginning of a new era, and Ebubedike tackled the Frankfurt returner. The Galaxy forced a safety by stopping Garrett in the end zone in the final ten seconds of the first quarter, and a field goal gave them a 5-0 lead before David Smith scored London's first touchdown. A 25-yard field goal from Alexander added to the Monarchs' lead before Gelbaugh hit Horton for a touchdown pass – the first in league history – of 96 yards. Brinson added a third touchdown late to give the Monarchs a 24-11 opening-day win.

If the players enjoyed their season debut, their first match at Wembley was a true celebration. The New York/New Jersey Knights were the opponents as 46,952 fans cheered on, but this was an occasion for the defence and special teams. Gelbaugh found Riley for a 62-yard touchdown, but safety Crossman starred as he blocked a punt and returned it for a score while kicker Alexander made a 40-yard field goal, his longest of the season. The Monarchs, who were trailing 7-3 at half-time, came back with 19 points in the third quarter to win 22-18. On 6 April, the Monarchs added another win with a 35-12 triumph over Orlando Thunder. It was proper British conditions on the rainy Saturday night but Ebubedike starred, and even rushed six straight times for 44 yards and a touchdown to seal the victory.

London kept rolling and crossed the Atlantic to claim their fourth successive win. They beat Birmingham Fire 27-0 in Alabama, with Gelbaugh passing for over 300 yards for the third successive game as he began to stamp his authority on the season. They continued their win streak with a crushing 45-7 victory against Montreal Machine in London in which receiver Brinson scored the first kick-off return touchdown in league history, before defeating the Raleigh-Durham Skyhawks 35-10 in front of 33,997 adoring fans. The Monarchs sat on their throne atop the European Division with a 6-0 record before they embarked on three straight away games stateside. The European Division was not to be sniffed at: the Monarchs were unbeaten ahead of the 5-1 Barcelona Dragons and 4-2 Galaxy, while none of the seven North American teams possessed a winning record.

At this point in the season, the European teams were 11-0 when welcoming American teams, which prompted numerous jet-lag theories to account for the poor performance of visiting sides. These rumours were emphatically put to bed by the London Monarchs, who concluded an 18-day journey that covered 14,237 miles with three straight wins as they defeated the San Antonio Riders 38-15, the Knights 22-7 in New York (with linebacker Brown accounting for 5.5 sacks – a league record – as London tallied 14 sacks in total) and topped the Sacramento Surge 45-21 thanks to a remarkable performance from Horton, who set a WLAF record with 196 receiving yards in the win while Dodge scored a 60-yard pick six. The Monarchs' domination abroad led to suggestions that perhaps it was easier to travel from Europe to American than vice versa, but others began to believe that maybe, just maybe, the Monarchs reigned supreme over all time zones.

London head coach Kennan believed that the European teams were a tighter group than other franchises due to their shared experience of travelling and playing with each other in a foreign setting. Kennan alluded to differing mentalities in the United States and abroad when he said, 'It's a good living, the salaries aren't huge, but it's a fun league to coach. We don't have anybody holding out. That eliminates some of the problems. There are [fewer] prima donnas.'

With a league-leading 40,483 home attendance across their five games at Wembley Stadium, the London Monarchs finished their debut campaign with a stunning 9-1 record, losing only to the Barcelona Dragons by a score of 20-17 in front of a record crowd of 50,835 fans in the final match of the regular season in London. The three Europe-based teams – London, Barcelona and Frankfurt – dominated the WLAF's inaugural campaign, compiling a combined record of 24-6 while no North American team managed to better 5-5. Barcelona needed the win at Wembley to reach the semi-finals, and the Monarchs would soon have the opportunity for revenge, and it would come on the biggest stage of all: the inaugural World Bowl.

Barcelona, who had compiled an 8-2 record, defeated Birmingham 10-3 to book their passage to the World Bowl while the Monarchs were forced to travel to New York to face the Knights once again. A win would guarantee that Wembley would host World Bowl '91, and the Monarchs perhaps felt a little aggrieved after they should have hosted the Knights in London but a scheduling clash with a soccer playoff game between Brighton and Hove Albion and Notts County meant they were forced to travel to the Big Apple and secure the win in their opponents' own backyard. They found themselves 17-0 down early, but Gelbaugh picked out Riley and Garrett for touchdowns each to go into half-time down 20-14. The Monarchs continued to fight back in the third quarter, with Gelbaugh slinging another pair of scores – including a 68-yard bomb to Horton – to take control, but Knights running back Eric Wilkerson scored a touchdown to narrow the lead. Knights quarterback Jeff Graham failed to convert the two-point try, so the Monarchs held a slender 28-26 lead entering the final quarter.

The Monarchs exerted their dominance in the fourth quarter as the 28-year-old quarterback – who finished with five touchdowns and three interceptions – found Horton with a 78-yard rocket while David Smith rushed in to secure a 42-26 win for the Monarchs. After a tumultuous season in which the WLAF lost $7 million running the league, its opening campaign had a fitting ending: two European franchises from major cities meeting in its flagship game. The London Monarchs welcomed the Barcelona Dragons to Wembley Stadium, one week after the English team had flown stateside and ensured an all-European line-up for the 1991 World Bowl was set.

London deserved their time in the spotlight. Coach Kennan was named Coach of the Year, Jeff Alexander led the league in rushing touchdowns, Garrett hauled in the most receptions and Alexander was named best kicker as he and Ebubedike were named to the All-World team as the only non-Americans. In fact, London accounted for 16 players in the first and second teams, with Barcelona the second-best represented team with six. Horton, the team's star receiver, was named British Media Sportsman of the Year.

Ten days after the movie *Silence of the Lambs* was released in the United Kingdom, the WLAF championship game took place at boisterous Wembley Stadium. World Bowl '92 kicked off on 9 June 1991, a Saturday – not a Sunday, as is tradition in America – and it was a fascinating bout in front of 61,108 fans who ignited a scintillating atmosphere to reflect the special occasion. Under the overcast and wet backdrop of the sprawling city, London wide receiver Dana Brinson fumbled the opening kick-off, allowing for Barcelona to start on the Monarchs' 18-yard line. It was the perfect start for the Dragons, but the day had just begun. The Monarchs defence kept the Dragons at bay, and Barcelona's muffed field goal truly set the tone for their performance.

The teams traded possessions early in the game before London took over late in the first quarter. Monarchs quarterback and WLAF offensive MVP Stan Gelbaugh threw a 59-yard bomb to Horton – who led the league with 931 receiving yards – to take the lead 7-0 in front of the British faithful after the wideout had beaten corner Charles Fryar and safety Alex Morris to score. On the very next play to open the second quarter, Dragons quarterback Scott Erney was intercepted for a second time by Crossman but this time the cornerback returned the wayward pass for a touchdown. Crossman would snag a third pick of a dominant first half to set up a 14-yard touchdown pass from Gelbaugh to Garrett – who finished with an astonishing 13 receptions – as London began to dominate. The Monarchs were 21-0 up at half-time, and it was too big a deficit for Barcelona. The Spanish outfit tried, but the raucous London crowd ensured that the home team would shut out their opposition and seal the memorable victory. Gelbaugh finished with 191 passing yards to go with a pair of touchdowns as the Monarchs won the first World Bowl. 'This is tremendous,' said the quarterback. 'I'll never forget this.' The London crowd was deafening, with the partying fans creating a joyous atmosphere on that summer's day as London, even just for a fleeting moment, truly felt like royalty in the American football kingdom.

The World Bowl may have been incomparable to the NFL's Super Bowl, but the British fans certainly enjoyed the occasion. Four men with inflatable sumo wrestlers tied to their back provided some form of entertainment. The half-time show was nothing like Jennifer Lopez or The Weeknd, who have graced such a slot for the Super Bowl in recent memory. Instead, a more traditional act was booked: the Central State University Invincible Marauder Band and Belles from Wilberforce, Ohio took to the Wembley pitch. The maroon-and-gold-cladded entertainment accompanied a mob of young women decked out in white to dance with red and blue paper guitars and fluorescent streamers. This hilariously late-1980s to early-1990s spectacle followed a rather remarkable pre-match dance routine by the Monarchs cheerleaders, the Crown Jewels, to a rap song written especially for the London outfit.

Ultimately, the Monarchs slew their Dragons as Saint George had done before them. The London crowd were particularly thrilled by the entry, late in the game, of Ebubedike, whose three-yard run – the only action he got – sent the crowd into raptures. The Monarchs' triumph would be the only shutout in World Bowl history, cementing London's place in history. Garrett's 13 receptions set a World Bowl record that would never be surpassed, but the day truly belonged to Crossman and the Monarchs defence. His three interceptions earned him the World

Bowl MVP award, and it was the only time that a defensive player would take home the honour.

Monarchs safety Dedrick Dodge used the World Bowl victory to catapult his dwindling professional career, joining the Seattle Seahawks before winning Super Bowls with San Francisco and Denver. Dodge understood that his career owed a lot to his opportunity to play in London, and he used the WLAF league to play his way back into contention for a roster spot in the NFL: 'No amount of money can buy those types of moments that I was fortunate enough to be a part of, but you have to get the opportunity. Where did it come from? It came from when I got the experience to play for the Monarchs, and that's what got me back in the NFL. If not for London, I don't know if I ever get a shot back in the NFL.'

The NFL owners with vested interest in the WLAF voted whether or not to suspend the league in order to re-evaluate the finances. However, one rather demoralising aspect of the league was becoming clear: the success of European teams was nice, but the poor fortunes of the North American teams was hurting domestic interest. 'Our future hangs on one piece of thread – American television,' said WLAF European coordinator Bruce Dworshak before the 1991 vote. 'The real issue here is television.'

There were other issues that clouded the future of the WLAF despite its seemingly successful first season. The blanket contracts that proved so successful in rapidly constructing an entire roster became a glaring problem as, while all contracts were equal, more talented players in more crucial positions were frustrated as they were paid the same as those at the other end of the spectrum. It meant that the future of the WLAF was confirmed on 23 October 1991, six months before it kicked off. Players decided to try their luck in the NFL after starring in the opening campaign, and many joined practice rosters to never return. Uneasy lies the head that wears the crown – the defending champion Monarchs were hurt the most by the exodus and embarked on a miserable

1992 season. Head coach Kennan left for Seattle to work under Tom Flores in the NFL, while players were poached too: apart from Dedrick Dodge joining the Seahawks, Roy Hart joined the Raiders, Steve Gabbard went to the Packers and Mike Renna to the Eagles. Corris Ervin joined the Hamilton Tiger-Cats in the Canadian Football League while Marlon Brown was traded to Ohio Glory.

Kennan was replaced prior to the season by Ray Willsey, the defensive coordinator of 1991, and while he had the necessary experience – he won two Super Bowl rings with the Los Angeles Raiders – and tactical nous, he allegedly lacked the charisma or personality to truly dominate and control a locker room. There was turmoil at the top, too. Jon Smith, CEO and minority owner of the team, left his post following a dispute with the WLAF prior to the 1992 season, citing his frustrations with the league's attempts to manipulate rosters to include more American players to appeal to the United States market.

It proved to be a tough season for the Monarchs, who won two of their ten matches as they lost seven and secured the first draw in league history, a 17-17 contest against Birmingham Fire at Wembley in April 1992. The Monarchs' World Bowl title defence got off to a great start when, on 21 March, they defeated the Knights 26-20 in overtime, but it would be their only win at Wembley all year as the team – whose other win came in Montreal against the Machine when London were already mathematically eliminated from World Bowl contention – slipped to a 2-7-1 record. None of the three European teams had winning seasons and the Monarchs finished bottom of the European Division.

Gelbaugh struggled in 1992 as he finished the year with 11 touchdowns and 12 interceptions, and the team was eliminated from postseason contention in week eight after suffering defeat in Orlando. Perhaps the reason for Gelbaugh's struggles was the absence of his favourite target Horton, who endured a murky year. He signed with the NFL's Cardinals but returned to the

Monarchs for the 1992 campaign only to be handed a year-long suspension with no official reason disclosed. He was replaced by former University of Central Florida receiver Bernard Ford, who did well enough as he qualified for the All-World Second Team alongside Marrone as the Monarchs' sole representatives. Another bright spot was Danny Lockett, whose 14 sacks led the WLAF in 1992.

Despite the poor showing by their teams during the 1992 season, the European fans remained loyal and attendances were still reasonably high even if they declined from the previous year; the Monarchs' attendance actually dipped below 20,000 for the first time at Wembley. The North American teams performed better as Sacramento Surge defeated Orlando Thunder 21-17 to win World Bowl 1992, but the WLAF was suspended after its second campaign, as NFL owners refused to invest more funds after successive financial losses. On 13 September 1992, the league was officially on ice following a unanimous vote by league owners. Matt Tench claimed that the owners didn't truly care whether the league continued, and the 'razzmatazz' that captured the attention of the British public had not rubbed off on its American equivalents. '[The NFL owners] wanted a spring league but did not want to create a rival to the NFL. In the end, they did not create enough of a rival.' After the WLAF was suspended, Hicks resigned as general manager of the London Monarchs.

NFL Commissioner Paul Tagliabue suggested that there were plans in place to resurrect the league in 1994 or 1995, but optimism for such an outcome was low. With the Monarchs struggling in 1992 before the WLAF was suspended, the calendar year was topped off by the folding of the London Ravens. The pioneering domestic franchise were demoted to the third tier of domestic gridiron football and after just three wins in the previous two seasons, the Ravens ceased existence.

London's love affair with American football had struck a fresh obstacle, but the city – and the WLAF – would be given a lifeline.

CHAPTER 7

NFL Europe

'There are strong similarities between the National Football League and God. Both are inflexible, make decisions from on high, have millions of followers, generate more income than most countries, but still worry about money. Both face strong competition from other sources. And both move in mysterious ways. Especially the NFL.' – Keith Elliott, *The Independent*, March 1993

KEITH ELLIOTT'S summary of the NFL's handling of their general operations and the World League is hilariously accurate. As the league was locked in an antitrust and free-agency lawsuit with the National Football League Players Association, the NFL decided – again – that it needed another pro football league. The European director of the World League, Nick Priestnall, stood firm about the future of the league when its outlook was unclear. 'I have heard it said that their avowed intention is to bring back the World League bigger and stronger,' he said. Priestnall was partly right: the World League of American Football was suspended for two years after the 1992 season, but its return was announced after a successful vote on 26 October 1993. This time, things would be different. Jerry Vainisi, the WLAF vice-president of operations, understood that the success of the newly reformed league would depend on how the product was distributed around Europe. 'Some of our people will probably shoot me for saying this, but the US market is not really our concern,' he told the *New York Times*. This time, there were no North American teams.

When the WLAF returned on 8 April 1995, the North American teams were no more. In July 1994, it was instead announced that the London Monarchs, Barcelona Dragons and Frankfurt Galaxy were to be joined by the Amsterdam Admirals, Rhein Fire and a new British outfit, the Scottish Claymores. There were no more divisions – all six teams played in a single conference, facing each other twice (home and away) over a ten-game season. With this new format, the World Bowl would match the first-half league leader – who would host the game – against the end-of-season league leader (or runner-up if the first-half champion had the best record). Does that format sound ridiculous? It certainly was – the process was abandoned after the 1997 World Bowl.

New wacky match rules were added, too. With association football and rugby being more popular sports in Europe, the rules were altered to encourage the kicking element of the game and pander to the new audience. The league awarded four points to field goals of more than 50 yards – a single point more than in the NFL – which meant that the total score of a touchdown and an extra point could be matched by two field goals, provided one was longer than 50, as both amounted to seven points.

While coverage was an issue during the first run of the WLAF, the NFL had an idea for the relaunch of the league – Fox penned a new deal to broadcast NFL matches and negotiated to become a co-owner and major financial contributor to the WLAF in return for broadcasting rights. The WLAF also signed a merchandising deal with Reebok, who had exclusive rights to manufacture team uniforms and apparel.

It felt like the last-gasp, Hail Mary effort by the NFL to finally get into the real end zone – the lucrative embrace of the British and European mainstream. The World League's relaunch was the NFL's new attempt to expand the lure of gridiron football beyond the States and firmly into their transatlantic neighbours. At this stage, American football was certainly not unheard of in the UK and the sport actually seemed to suffer from some sort of fatigue. With the birth of the Premier League reinvigorating soccer, its gridiron equivalent had a distinct 1980s feel to it. Its popularity had peaked a decade earlier, with Channel 4 commanding a record average audience of 3.1 million during the 1985–86 season. Heading into the 1995 season, Gareth Moores, the new general manager of the London Monarchs, was aware of the challenge that the Monarchs faced – influencing and attracting fans beyond the hardcore American football faithful. 'The UK has the most educated American football audience outside America,' Moores said. 'But most fans don't have proper access to the NFL and yearn for top-quality American football. That's what the World League will offer.'

Unfortunately, dwindling interest – despite an invented rivalry with the Scottish Claymores – meant that the London Monarchs were forced to leave Wembley Stadium, turning instead to Tottenham Hotspur's White Hart Lane. The Monarchs would reside there for the 1995 and 1996 seasons after securing an exemption from the WLAF, as the pitch was only 93 yards long, some 27 yards shy of a regulation-size 120-yard field when accounting for end zones. These scoring areas, which run off each end of the field, were only six yards deep with the last yard of turf sloping worryingly downwards. Monarchs quarterback Brad Johnson, who would later throw a pair of touchdowns for the Tampa Bay Buccaneers in Super Bowl XXXVII, spoke about the troubles that some of his team-mates had with the White

Hart Lane pitch. 'We did have a quarterback, Kevin McDougal, he dropped back at the end of the season on the one-yard line and he fell out of the end zone and ended up taking a safety on a five-yard drop,' he said. 'It was kind of awkward.'

Notwithstanding these problems, the relationship between gridiron football and Tottenham Hotspur had been struck – two matches in the 2019 NFL International Series were played at their new stadium with more set to be played on an annual basis – and the Monarchs embarked on their attempt to return to the World Bowl in a new stadium with new management and coaching staff under head coach Bobby Hammond. Hammond employed Bill Walsh's West Coast offence, utilising short passes to limit turnovers. He would also have NFL-calibre talent on his roster; as part of the invigorated project, NFL teams could now allocate players directly to a WLAF franchise of choice with each team able to receive recruits on loan.

Quarterback Johnson, who returned to the Minnesota Vikings after his year in London before leaving the franchise in 1998, was one of the new recruits, as was fellow signal-caller Jim Ballard of the Cincinnati Bengals. The New York Jets sent tight end LaVar Ball and offensive guard Terrence Wisdom to London, while the Monarchs also brought in offensive tackle Mike Moody and receiver Terrence Warren from the Seattle Seahawks. The Claymores' first roster also housed NFL players including quarterbacks Matt Blundin from the Kansas City Chiefs and the Houston Oiler Lee Williamson. As with all teams, the Claymores had seven 'national' players, including wide receiver Scott Couper.

The Monarchs got off to a poor start, losing 45-22 at Frankfurt, but they bounced back with a 23-7 win at Rhein Fire where Johnson threw for 181 yards and the defence starred with a pair of interceptions and fumble recoveries. London would come crashing back down to earth in their home opener against the World Bowl runners-up Amsterdam Admirals, losing 17-7 with only 8,763 in attendance at White Hart Lane. In fact, attendances would be an issue all year. The Monarchs tried to rectify the problem by slashing prices by 50 per cent but, from their five home games of the 1995 season, the Monarchs averaged just 10,417 fans per match.

London's highlight of the 1995 WLAF season didn't come at their new home. Exactly 250 years after the last attempt by the Scottish to overthrow the monarchy, the Claymores welcomed the Monarchs to Edinburgh for the Battle of Britain on 15 May 1995. Like the Calcutta Cup in rugby, there was a trophy awarded to the winners of the match. The coveted Budweiser Cup was contested on eight occasions between 1995 and 1998, with each team collecting four wins. It was a rivalry for the ages and the first contest – an 11-10 win for the Monarchs at Murrayfield – was remarkably close and suitably controversial. The two teams combined for 12 turnovers and Monarchs kicker Don Silvestri was at the centre of the drama. With seconds remaining and the Claymores leading 10-7, he missed his 48-yard field goal attempt, but the play clock had expired before the unsuspecting Silvestri swung at it. The Monarchs subsequently took the delay-of-game penalty, moving five yards back for a 53-yard attempt. Silvestri made it and, with the new four-point rule, the Monarchs left Edinburgh the victors by a single point.

The win over the Monarchs left them with a 2-3 record. A new era was set to begin as the 5-0 Admirals were guaranteed to host World Bowl '95 in June 1995. London lost to Frankfurt but triumphed in Barcelona and at home to Rhein Fire, their only home win of the season, to sit at 2-1 for the second half of the season, but their slim hopes of facing the Admirals in the season finale were crushed in week nine as the Monarchs lost 17-10 in Amsterdam. Johnson was intercepted three times and conceded a fumble in the agonising defeat.

The team's poor performances mirrored the drop in attendance that corresponded with the move from Wembley, and the franchise even closed one half of the stadium for matches as they struggled to attract fans. In their home clash against the Claymores, London were soundly defeated 22-9 as they went 1-4 at home and 4-6 on the dismal 1995 year. Johnson finished with 2,227 yards and threw for 13 touchdowns compared to 14 interceptions.

As for the Claymores, they went 2-8 in 1995 with their highlight being the win over the Monarchs in that final game of the season. They played their first-ever game in Edinburgh on 9 April 1995, a 19-17 loss to the Rhein Fire, and their first win came two weeks later with a 20-14 triumph over the Galaxy in Frankfurt. However, six straight defeats followed – including a 31-0 shutout against the Admirals and an overtime defeat to the Fire – before their win over their British rivals. The Claymores finished rock bottom of the six-team division, but there were bright spots including Siran Stacy rushing for 785 yards and five touchdowns while also collecting 324 receiving yards. Their attendances at Murrayfield started brightly with over 10,000 but slumped to 6,800 for the final home game against Frankfurt.

In the end, the Monarchs' attendance was some 12,000 less than the average turnout at Wembley in 1992. On top of this, the atmosphere was flat and nothing like the rowdy vibe of three years earlier. British journalist Simon O'Hagan believed the new, revamped World League had lost the shine, glitz and glamour the league had when it launched in 1991 and it was affecting the fragile domestic fanbase. 'American football is entertainment as much as sport, intended to appeal as much to the party animal as the family audience,' O'Hagan wrote. 'If English football feels a little threatened by the return of the transatlantic variety, then perhaps the leisure centre and the theme park should be threatened more.' O'Hagan's mockery of the World League was becoming the norm in the UK and Europe, although Germany was firmly infatuated with the sport. League officials and frustrated fans alike were asking questions and attempting to understand why the WLAF was struggling, but the answer was simple: it was American football, sure, but it was not the NFL.

In the build-up to the 1995 World Bowl, the 1996 WLAF season was confirmed to go ahead. With league officials becoming increasingly desperate to gain a foothold in the European market, the NFL decided to change its marketing strategy. Riding a hopeful wave of Americanisation, the league opted to draft in some high-profile and mainstream personalities, including the arrival of William 'The Refrigerator' Perry in London. To say the former Bear had lost his effectiveness would be putting it lightly, but Perry – a 33-year-old who weighed 350lbs – was still a household name that could get butts into seats, something that the Monarchs desperately needed as their popularity waned with the move to White Hart Lane. The Scottish Claymores bagged a big name of their own and secured the services of Scotland rugby union captain Gavin Hastings as kicker. His signing was part of an aggressive marketing push under general manager Mike Keller, which included a roster featuring more NFL players. Quarterback Steve Matthews arrived on loan from the Kansas City Chiefs and he opened the season, but when Jim Ballard returned and showed greater consistency to replace the injured starter, he secured the role for the rest of the campaign.

Hastings may or may not have been the missing piece, but the 1996 season belonged to the Claymores. They topped the World League with a 7-3 record, winning all five regular season matches at Murrayfield, and even defeated the London Monarchs at White Hart Lane in the opening match of the season on 14 April 1996. Yo Murphy scored a touchdown with Hastings converting the extra point only for the Monarchs to lead 21-7 after scores from Tony Vinson, Gaston Green and safety Darren Studstill. The Claymores levelled the game through rushing back Siran Stacey and receiver Sean LaChappelle – who would be named the offensive MVP after registering over 1,000 receiving yards – before Monarchs kicker David Gordon missed a 39-yard potentially game-winning field goal. Claymores kicker Paul McCallum didn't make the same mistake as he slotted his attempt to secure a 24-21 overtime win. Gordon was cut immediately after the game.

The Claymores followed up with home wins over the Barcelona Dragons (23-13) and Amsterdam Admirals (21-14) before suffering their first loss, a 15-14 defeat in Germany to Rhein Fire. Under the kooky and bizarre WLAF rules, the Claymores went into their mid-season battle with the unbeaten Frankfurt Galaxy knowing that the winner would host the World Bowl. The Claymores dominated, winning 20-0 to bring the championship game to Scotland.

The Monarchs, under head coach Bobby Hammond, struggled in 1995. Running backs coach Tony Allen was a former player with the London Ravens and he led the Olympians to five British championships in the 1990s. With the likes of Russell White, Gaston Green (an All-Pro with the Los Angeles Raiders in 1991) and Tony Vinson – on loan from Atlanta – the Monarchs had the second-best rushing attack in the WLAF with all three in the top ten players in terms of rushing yards. After losing to the Claymores, the Monarchs lost 37-3 in Frankfurt to the reigning champions. General manager Moores had had enough. Hammond was fired and offensive coordinator Lionel Taylor took his place; he possessed over 40 years of NFL experience, an All-Star four times with the Denver Broncos as a player and a two-time Super Bowl champion as an offensive assistant, before arriving in London in 1995. He got off to a good start with a 27-20 win over Rhein Fire, but it was short-lived. A last-gasp Barcelona field goal condemned the Monarchs to a 9-7 defeat before London were dismantled 28-9 in Amsterdam.

With the Claymores securing their World Bowl spot from their first half of the season performance, the Monarchs were hoping to join them with an impressive second-half showing. A 27-7 win at home to Frankfurt, headlined by the scoring return of Vinson after he had fallen out with former coach Hammond, was followed up by a 16-13 win over Amsterdam at White Hart Lane. It all came crashing down in Catalonia, with the Dragons defeating the Monarchs 7-6 as the offence struggled immensely. After the game, Perry announced his season was over with a nagging knee injury, although his absence would not be felt as hard as it perhaps should have been with the Fridge failing to recapture his old form. The Claymores defeated the Monarchs for a second time, winning 33-28 in Edinburgh before London ended their season on a high. They secured a 17-14 win over Rhein at Chelsea FC's Stamford Bridge to finish their 1996 season with a 4-6 record, the second of three successive years with such a record.

The Monarchs' rivals were the toast of Britain. The Claymores made Scotland a fortress, winning each of their five matches at Murrayfield and only losing in Rhein, Amsterdam and Barcelona. On 23 June 1996, the Scottish Claymores welcomed Frankfurt Galaxy to Edinburgh for World Bowl '96. As 38,982 fans piled into Murrayfield, the Fox Sports announcer introduced the teams: 'For a millennia, the tattoo and the bagpipe has called Scotland's heroes to defend her land, and her honour. Now a new challenge presents itself as a Germanic horde invades the Scottish midlands. The Frankfurt Galaxy and the Scottish Claymores clash in World Bowl '96 as a season's worth of emotion and sweat will rise to a crescendo and determine who will conquer the world.'

Eat your heart out, Braveheart. The World Bowl lived up to that epic billing, and the match was entertaining from the opening kick-off. Claymore safety George Coghill, who had registered five interceptions including a pick six on the season, stripped the ball from returner Mario Bailey's arms. With the ball loose, running back Markus Thomas scooped possession and returned it 25 yards to score on the opening play. The Claymores scored a touchdown and national rugby captain Hastings came out to kick a successful extra point to the cheers of the home fans, who definitely were not mistaking the show for the Six Nations.

The Galaxy responded to the fast start and the defending World Bowl champions calmly drove 80 yards in 11 plays that culminated with Jay Kearney scoring a 16-yard touchdown on a reverse play that allowed the receiver to waltz into the end zone untouched. In the second quarter, Galaxy quarterback Steve Pelluer was the architect of a short 30-yard drive that ended with a two-yard touchdown pass to Mario Bailey, who made amends for his earlier fumble. Frankfurt were in front for the first time, but it was a brief moment. With the game edging towards half-time, Claymore signal-caller Ballard led two successful drives late in the second quarter to turn the tide of the championship clash. A six-yard touchdown pass to Yo Murphy cut the deficit but an error meant that the extra point was missed, so a 16-yard touchdown pass from Ballard to Murphy allowed the Claymores to regain the lead. The home team failed on their two-point try after the Galaxy's pass-rush overwhelmed the special teams unit, and the two teams went back to the locker room with the Claymores leading 19-14.

Scotland increased their lead with a 46-yard field goal early in the third quarter, but the Galaxy responded with a four-play, 74-yard drive that ended with a 32-yard touchdown pass to Bailey. Like the Claymores earlier in the game, the two-point conversion failed to leave the score at 22-20 in favour of the Claymores. However, the Scottish team bounced back themselves with a 71-yard touchdown pass to Murphy. A 50-yard field goal worth four points by Paul McCallum gave them a 32-20 lead. Frankfurt quarterback Pelluer drove downfield to score with a five-yard pass to Mike Bellamy, but the Galaxy needed a turnover. They got one to set up the chance to defend their World League title with under a minute remaining. With a tense onlooking crowd, the atmosphere began to turn from a vibrant roar in support of the battling Claymores to one of anxious dread. Pelluer completed a series of short passes to move past midfield and into Scottish territory before the season came to a head with the Galaxy on fourth and short. After the snap, the hand-off to running back Ingo Scibert was fumbled. Against all odds, Pelluer recovered the ball and picked up a crucial first down before a late flag was thrown. After much discussion, the officiating team stated that the fourth down rule had come into effect. Since another player recovered the ball, the original play was blown dead. This meant that the Claymores earned a turnover on downs and held on to win the 1996 World Bowl. Three touchdown passes from Ballard to World Bowl MVP Yo Murphy inspired a 32-27 win for the Claymores. Their triumph was the WLAF's first worst-to-first turnaround after they finished sixth in the six-team league a year prior. While dramatic, the Fox announcer was ultimately right: Scotland's heroes defended their land from the Germans and they had conquered the world.

The defending champions opened the 1997 campaign with a 16-3 win in Amsterdam, but back-to-back home defeats to Barcelona and Rhein Fire left the Claymores with a 1-2 record. They won in Frankfurt but suffered a difficult 16-8 loss to the Monarchs at Stamford Bridge before a three-game winning run against Amsterdam (10-6), Rhein (23-20) and the Galaxy (24-7) placed the Claymores right back in World Bowl contention. However, a crushing 10-9 home defeat to the Monarchs derailed their hopes before they were completely obliterated by a 46-18 loss in Barcelona. The Claymores finished with a better record than their British rivals, but 5-5 was just not good enough for a World Bowl berth; while the Barcelona Dragons had the same record, they were the winners of the first half of the season and named as World Bowl hosts. The Dragons went on to win the fifth World Bowl as they defeated Rhein Fire 38-24 in Spain.

As for the Monarchs, the 1997 WLAF campaign was more of the same. Even with the signing of 1995 WLAF Defensive Player of the Year Malcolm Showell, poor performances and declining popularity ensured it was a miserable season. The team were embroiled in a public dispute with Spurs manager Gerry Francis over the state of the White Hart Lane pitch, so new general manager Alton Byrd – who was selected in the tenth round of the NBA draft by the Boston Celtics in 1979 before a knee injury saw him cut – opted to permanently move to Stamford Bridge. Former soccer player Clive Allen, who scored over 200 goals for the likes of QPR, Spurs, Manchester City and Chelsea, was brought in to much uproar in a move similar to Hastings' Claymores adventure. He was designated to kick efforts within 40 yards and made 100 per cent of his field goals, but the figure slipped to only 70 per cent when it came to points after touchdowns. There were bright spots in London's 4-6 1997 season: they did the double over the defending World Bowl champions and British rival Claymores, while Showell led the league with 9.5 sacks.

However, there were low points too. On 4 May 1997, the Monarchs slipped up to the Dragons in what was the largest comeback in WLAF history. London's suffocating defence and performing offence – a rarity in 1997, it must be said – gave them a commanding 30-7 lead at half-time. It all came crashing down in the second half, with the Dragons cutting the score to 32-29 before a botched snap led to an ugly safety and quarterback Jon Kitna dived over the line to score and seal an unlikely 37-30 Barcelona win.

In 1998, everything changed. The World League of American Football was renamed NFL Europe to reflect the stature of the professional league and add some sort of desperate shine or value to an idea that was rapidly depreciating in value. Qualification for the World Bowl also changed, pitting the two teams with the best overall record against one another in the championship game at a predetermined site. These changes were made to combat instances like the Barcelona Dragons, eventual 1997 World Bowl champions, after they secured a place in the World Bowl with a 4-1 first-half record. With qualification to the big game secured, the Spanish franchise opted to rest players and play lethargic, low-intensity football to close the season with a 5-5 record.

In the United Kingdom, the Monarchs continued to downgrade and rebranded as the England Monarchs in October 1997 ahead of the new season. Sporting a new colour scheme of red, white and black as well as a new uniform and logo to reflect the St George cross, the team opted to play home matches in a number of cities, echoing the travelling matches played by the Air Service Command Warriors and others back in 1944. It was decided that the Monarchs would play home fixtures in Bristol's Ashton Gate Stadium, Birmingham's Alexander Stadium and London, although the games in the capital were now played at the Crystal Palace National Sports Centre. 'It makes sense to take the Monarchs to the country, and I think that's a trend you'll see continuing,' remarked WLAF president Oliver Luck. 'It is a move aimed at responding to the many fans we know live outside of the greater London area.' While this was an optimistic take on the rebranding by Luck – father of former Indianapolis Colts quarterback, Andrew – the move was a hopeful attempt to raise attendances at Monarchs home games. The average attendances had hovered around 10,000 since the league returned in 1995, despite Wembley drawing regular crowds of 40,000 in the Monarchs' championship-winning season of 1991. Such attendances were unrealistic at this stage, particularly as a winning team would help attract fans and the Monarchs were certainly not that. After three seasons of mediocrity, the England Monarchs went 3-7 during the 1998 season. The Scottish Claymores fell from first to worst almost as quickly as they had risen to World Bowl glory, with the Monarchs' northern rivals finishing with a 2-8 record to sit bottom of NFL Europe. They faced each other at one of the Monarch's three home stadiums, Alexander Stadium in Birmingham, in week four with each British team winless. The Monarchs scored two touchdowns to win 14-10, but the Claymores got their revenge three weeks later with a dramatic 27-24 win over their English neighbours.

Ultimately, British gridiron fans had little to shout about in 1998. The two British representatives in NFL Europe occupied the bottom two spaces in the six-team league. Both teams were in real trouble. Leaked information came to light that suggested a third German team was to be added to the league's stable, popular and ever-growing market in the heart of Europe. After another uninspiring season, the Monarchs were shut down and replaced by the Berlin Thunder. Despite NFL Europe president Luck claiming attendances were less vital to revenues than the cash-strapped pre-1998 WLAF, London fans were alienated by the Monarchs' rebranding and not enough fans were attracted in Bristol or Birmingham. The risk had not paid off. The Monarchs left NFL Europe with the Battle of Britain rivalry against the Claymores tied at 4-4.

Memories of the championship of 1991 were fading but the Monarchs closed down with a number of records worth celebrating. They were the first European team announced ahead of the 1991 season and showed the developmental potential of the league. In Brad Johnson, they had the first former quarterback start in the NFL and win a Super Bowl while the likes of Dedrick Dodge, James Parrish, Ted Popson and Obademi Ayanbadejo won championship rings themselves. The legacy of the Monarchs as a whole was less impressive though. The team became the first to have six successive losing seasons and was the only side to never reach multiple World Bowls. Ultimately, London finished with a record of 28-23-1 across 52 matches, although a third of those wins came in that magical debut campaign.

With the Monarchs abolished, the fragile mirage that was NFL Europe began to fade but British interest clung on through their rivals north of the border. The Claymores played at Hampden Park for the first time in a week eight loss to the Galaxy, but 1998 was a tough year for Scotland as they finished bottom of NFL Europe. They improved in 1999 with head coach Jim Criner, in his fifth season at the team, leading them to a

4-6 record. Truth be told, there was little to shout about in 1999 as the team finished second last ahead of the Thunder, but the Claymores did cement themselves in American football history when quarterback Dameyune Craig, on loan from the Carolina Panthers, threw for a mammoth 611 yards in the road win over Frankfurt, setting a new record passing total in pro football. His helmet and the number two jersey Craig wore that night are displayed at the Pro Football Hall of Fame in Canton.

As for the Claymores, the 2000 season saw the team return to impressive heights. They finished the regular season in second place with a 6-4 record, qualifying for the World Bowl for the second time after their 1996 triumph. The Claymores started well with wins against Amsterdam and in Frankfurt before a 42-3 demolition of the Berlin Thunder sent them to 3-1, but a pair of losses left World Bowl qualification in the balance. Naturally, the Scots recovered with sensational wins over Barcelona (28-0), Amsterdam (42-10) and Rhein (31-24) to book their place in the World Bowl, which would be held at the Fire's Waldstadion.

At World Bowl 2000 – the eighth edition of the European championship game – on 25 June, 35,860 fans watched in Frankfurt as the Claymores faced the 7-3 Fire. The home side struck first when they orchestrated a 51-yard, 11-play drive capped off by a 21-yard field goal from Manfred Burgsmüller, but the Claymores hit back to take the lead on their own opening drive. They travelled 75 yards in just three plays, with Aaron Stecker's 36-yard rush finishing in the end zone, before the teams exchanged field goals for Scotland to go in at half-time 10-6 leaders. Unfortunately for the British side, Rhein quarterback Danny Wuerffel led a match-winning drive with just over five minutes remaining, draining the clock as Pepe Pearson scored from a yard out. The Claymores got the ball back but their barefoot kicker Rob Hart's 40-yard attempt to tie the game sailed wide left. The Fire were champions and it would prove to be

Criner's last game in charge of the Claymores as he departed to take charge of the XFL's Las Vegas Outlaws.

The 2001 campaign was the first under new head coach Gene Dahlquist, with each of their home games played at Hampden Park, and the Claymores won four clashes in Glasgow. Unfortunately, they lost each of their other games to finish 4-6 and secure another losing season, their third in five years. It was a tough year. The Claymores, with a margin of victory or defeat no more than ten points in each of the opening six games, held a 3-3 record and harboured faint hopes of qualifying for the World Bowl. However, defeats in Berlin and Barcelona either side of their lone home loss to the Dragons condemned them to a fourth-place finish. Dante Hall, nicknamed the 'Human Joystick' in the NFL due to his agility and ability to juke defenders out of their cleats, scored five touchdowns during his one season in NFL Europe before he went on to be named as a First-Team All-Pro (2003) and to successive Pro Bowls (2002 and 2003).

The Claymores started the 2002 season with their fifth quarterback in as many years, with Scott Driesbach of the Detroit Lions honoured with the role. He started very well. His first play in a Claymores jersey was a touchdown pass to Scott McCready as Scotland romped to a 45-17 win over the Dragons at Hampden Park. It would be somewhat of a false dawn as the Claymores slipped to a 1-3 record with narrow losses to Rhein and Frankfurt. Once again, their matches were agonisingly close and back-to-back defeats to the Berlin Thunder ended their World Bowl chances. However, the team's first-ever victory in Barcelona – a 27-24 triumph at the Estadi Olímpic de Montjuïc – secured a 5-5 record for the Claymores. Hart, who had missed the all-important World Bowl kick two years earlier, went a perfect 10-10 in field goals as he shared kicking snaps with future two-time Super Bowl champion Lawrence Tynes.

The following year was heartbreaking as the Claymores finished 6-4 and missed out on a place in World Bowl XI on a tiebreaker with Rhein and Frankfurt, the eventual champions. It was particularly disappointing as the championship game was held at Hampden Park and, despite their impressive season on paper, Dahlquist was fired after the campaign. Elsewhere in NFL Europe, the Barcelona Dragons – who had a brief fling with soccer juggernaut FC Barcelona to become the FC Barcelona Dragons in 2002 before they dropped the sponsorship after a single year – experienced a sharp decline in popularity, and economic trouble. They were relocated and replaced by the Cologne Centurions.

The 2004 campaign was the Scottish Claymores' tenth and final season in NFL Europe. After arriving in the league along with two other teams amidst much fanfare back in 1995, they were discontinued with a whimper. Four consecutive losses to open the season was hardly ideal. A tight 13-12 win ensured the team picked up a win from the first half of the campaign, but their form was mirrored in the second period to complete a 2-8 season for the Claymores – tied for the worst in their history as they propped up the table.

On 21 October 2004, the Claymores were no more and were swiftly replaced by the Hamburg Sea Devils for the 2005 season. Five of the six teams left in NFL Europe were German due to the competitive market there; the Amsterdam Admirals were the sole non-German franchise. Scotland's average attendance of 11,306 across their decade-long life was comparable to Scottish Premier League clubs, but Germany was able to consistently bring in more fans and, crucially, revenue. Critics joked that the league should be renamed 'NFL Deutschland' or 'NFL Germany' as their franchises claimed all seven World Bowl titles between 1998 and 2004. Like the British public in the 1980s and 1990s, enthusiasm for gridiron football in Germany stemmed less from the sport of American football itself, but on the spectacle that came with it. 'Certainly a lot of fans come primarily because of the show, but we don't care,' admitted Rhein Fire assistant coach Jörn Maier.

'It gives us the chance to develop football in Germany further.' Journalist Andreas Kröner echoed this sentiment, although in less optimistic terms than Maier: 'Even during the match, spare ribs, cheeseburgers and hot dogs are more important to most fans than touchdowns, field goals and interceptions.'

From the beginning of the new millennium, it became apparent that NFL Europe was on borrowed time but some figures remained stubborn in their support. Patrick Venzke, a former Jacksonville Jaguar plying his trade in Frankfurt, claimed that players dreaming of the NFL no longer need to go to college and could use NFL Europe as a path to the big time. 'A college career is no longer mandatory,' Venzke stated. 'The quality of NFL Europe is so great that you can make it from there.' Venzke could not have been more wrong. Sure, there were a couple of successful examples: Hall of Fame quarterback Kurt Warner played for the Amsterdam Admirals in 1998 before taking the NFL by storm with the St Louis Rams and their infamous offence dubbed 'the Greatest Show on Turf', winning Super Bowl XXXIV; Jake Delhomme, defeated in Super Bowl XXXVIII, was Warner's backup in Amsterdam. He went on to actually win the 1999 World Bowl with Frankfurt Galaxy before making his name in the NFL. However, these stories were few and far between as the novelty of NFL Europe began to wear thin and, with the league reportedly losing $30 million a season, it made sense to abolish it, after 16 years.

Regardless of the declining success of NFL Europe or the American Bowls that ended in 2005, the NFL has always had eyes abroad. The international market possesses much potential, and for as long as the league exists there will be questions asked about its presence in Europe, Asia or Central America. NFL Commissioner Paul Tagliabue was the architect of a ground-breaking move, placing emphasis on the international matches by making them meaningful to franchises, players and fans alike. On 2 October 2005, the NFL made the short trip across the United States' southern border to Mexico City where the Estadio Azteca hosted the first regular season clash held outside of America. Under the name NFL Fútbol Americano, the Arizona Cardinals defeated the San Francisco 49ers 31-14 in front of 103,467 fans. The NFL captured the vibrant Latin American culture.

However, the question still remains: why did a professional European edition of the NFL fail? Various reasons were put forward when NFL Europe collapsed, with many citing the limited appeal of gridiron football outside of North America. John Williams, an academic from the University of Leicester's Department of Sociology, believed that British and European fans may have suffered from the oversaturated presentation of the sport due to its regular breaks. 'One of the tensions for the English audience is our favoured sports have an element of flow,' said Williams. 'Play is not broken for tactical talks or timeouts. That's always been a mystery for British fans, who think the games are too contrived and made for TV and too brutal.'

The Hail Mary pass that was the revamped World League of American Football and NFL Europe may have ultimately fallen incomplete, but the stage was set for the future. After the Claymores folded in 2004, the European money-losing child of the NFL featured the Amsterdam Admirals and five German teams. The Hamburg Sea Devils defeated Frankfurt Galaxy 37-28 at World Bowl XV, and the championship game proved to be the final match in the league's relatively short history. Just six days later, NFL officials announced that NFL Europa, as it was now called, would be disbanded – yet all was not lost. NFL Europe managing director Uwe Bergheim was confident the experiment had succeeded in establishing a fanbase for gridiron football in the European market. 'Despite the great support of fans, business partners and the cities, we were active, we decided that it was time to change the strategy,' he said. Bergheim was right – the strategy had most certainly changed. Just four months later, Wembley Stadium was the site of American football once more as the International Series began.

Mark Waller, senior vice president of NFL International, echoed the sentiment of Bergheim ahead of London's arrival on the NFL's landscape. 'NFL Europa has created thousands of passionate fans who have supported our sport for many years,' he said. 'And we look forward to building on this foundation as we begin this new phase of our international development.' Some 35,404 days after the USS *Idaho* won the Silver Cup in the first game of American football on British shores, the New York Giants clashed with the Miami Dolphins at Wembley under the banner of the NFL.

The modern and international National Football League was born.

SECTION 2:

THE INTERNATIONAL SERIES

2007

The Dawn of a New Era

NFL REGULAR SEASON WEEK SEVEN
28 October 2007
NEW YORK GIANTS 13
MIAMI DOLPHINS 10
Wembley Stadium

THE WEATHER was an appropriate introduction to the United Kingdom for the NFL. Instead of travelling to sunny Florida, the 5-2 New York Giants made the transatlantic trip to London to face the winless, 'home' Miami Dolphins in front of 81,176 rain-soaked fans at the iconic Wembley Stadium. The conditions were grim, and the freshly laid turf at the recently opened stadium was loose and poor – and it showed immediately. Miami receiver Tedd Ginn Jr barely returned the opening kick-off as he slipped and stumbled to the ground at the 25. Dolphins quarterback Cleo Lemon led his offence into New York territory and his ten-yard scramble put his side in kicking distance where the Giants defence would hold them. The abysmally British conditions claimed their first victim in the first quarter, with Miami kicker Jay Feely missing the 48-yard attempt to ensure the first opening drive in NFL history outside of North America went scoreless.

It was now New York's turn to impress. The Giants travelled downfield, serving up a combination of effective run and pass plays to dice through their hapless opponents as easily as their own cleats tore up the shoddy turf. Thanks to an unnecessary roughness call against Miami, the Giants found themselves on the opposition four-yard line. A rush from Brandon Jacobs earned only a yard before two incomplete passes were thrown by quarterback Eli Manning, including one where the probable future Hall of Famer missed a wide-open Amani Toomer in the end zone. New York were forced to settle for a 20-yard field goal attempt to take the lead and forge history by scoring the first competitive professional points in the United Kingdom. It was poetic that the first points were scored by New York kicker Lawrence Tynes. A former Scottish Claymore in NFL Europe, the 29-year-old hailed from Greenock, a small town in Scotland. Playing in his maiden campaign with the Giants after three seasons in Kansas City, Tynes was still trying to win over his new employers. While other players were struggling amid the pouring rain, Tynes was more accustomed to the British weather and confidently stepped up to kick the field goal through the posts. It felt right: a Scot giving the Giants a 3-0 lead beneath British rainclouds and the Wembley arch to the cheers of the adoring home crowd. The moment felt like a dream, but it was a remarkable reality.

Ironically, the journey that took the NFL to the London International Series game of 2007 was relatively short. While the dream of NFL Europe became a nightmare, the powers-that-be were piecing together their greatest plan yet: a regular season match in either Germany or the United Kingdom. In October 2006, the league owners approved a plan to play annual regular season games in Europe, Canada or Mexico, with the latter two options removed from consideration in early 2007. The NFL emphasised that it would choose the teams in line with the scheduling process, rather than by teams putting themselves forward, and it became apparent that the San Francisco 49ers,

Seattle Seahawks and Miami Dolphins were on the list to 'host' a match in Europe, ahead of the Buffalo Bills, Kansas City Chiefs and New Orleans Saints. The home team's opponent, which would not necessarily be one of the other five teams, was set to be announced during the week of Super Bowl XLI, where the Indianapolis Colts defeated the Chicago Bears 29-17. 'It is preliminary, but we certainly are putting resources into pulling that together,' said Mark Waller, the senior vice president of NFL International when asked about the prospect of an International Series. 'We now have an international committee of owners and we talked it through with them, and they asked us to do some groundwork.'

The groundwork that Waller spoke of – the logistics of scheduling an international game to account for travel implications on player fatigue during an NFL season – were completed and NFL commissioner Roger Goodell, who had only just finished his first year in the role after replacing Paul Tagliabue, announced that London had beaten out Germany as the selected city. The new Wembley Stadium was to be the site of the clash; a reconstructed, modern version of the historic ground that hosted the USAFE Football League Final back in 1952. It was built to be the home of English association football, a music venue and host of other sporting events like the NFL, following on from the old Wembley which hosted a preseason game in 1983 and eight American Bowl games between 1986 and 1993. Commissioner Goodell, like each of his predecessors, was desperate to break into the European market and stay there.

Despite the appetite for American football being seemingly larger in Germany than Britain due to their dominance in NFL Europe, London was chosen thanks to its worldwide prestige. 'The international popularity of the NFL grows every year,' said Goodell when he announced that the Miami Dolphins were chosen to welcome the New York Giants in the first NFL regular season game played outside of North America. 'London and its international stature adds to the impact of the game.' Miami owner Wayne Huiznega, who would later sell the franchise to Stephen M. Ross for $550m in February 2008, was thrilled that the Dolphins were chosen to host the game. He suggested Dolphins matches were popular among British fans, with the team's fame undoubtedly stemming from Dan Marino's popularity in the 1980s.

The Giants ownership were equally enthused about the prospect of playing in London. New York's president and CEO John Mara insisted the Giants were ready to play in the epicentre of overseas NFL fandom. Mr Mara, whose grandfather Tim Mara founded the Giants in 1925, was quick to point out that the week seven matchup would give fans the opportunity to not only see a regular season game, but one with weight behind it: 'It will signal the beginning of the second half of the season when teams begin their playoff run.' The Giants would go on a historic surge of form that culminated in a monumental Super Bowl triumph over the previously undefeated New England Patriots in one of the NFL's great upsets – but at the start of the season, there was only one thing the front office was focused on: putting on a show in London that left enough of a mark to inspire a legacy.

It wasn't just the franchises that were looking forward to the event, with the mayor of London, Ken Livingstone, pleased that storied franchises like the Miami Dolphins and New York Giants were coming to the city. He claimed that while 10,000 American fans were expected to travel over for the game, the event was staged primarily for the enjoyment of the local population. London had won the right to host the 2012 Olympic and Paralympic Games, while the Tour de France was also set to start in the United Kingdom. The Big Smoke was cementing itself as a sporting powerhouse.

During the NFL regular season of 2007, over 97 per cent of matches were sold out to achieve a then-record average attendance of 67,775, so league executives were hoping the London game would be of similar popularity. Their hopes became reality. In the 72 hours following the announcement in Super Bowl week, over half a million ticket requests were submitted. On 17 May 2007, the first batch of tickets were made available to randomly selected individuals who initially expressed interest and all 40,000 tickets were sold inside 90 minutes. All available tickets, including hospitality and tailgate passes, were sold in two days. Studies after the game claimed that only 3 per cent of attendees were Americans, with 22 per cent being the Londoners that Livingstone alluded to while 60 per cent were Brits who lived elsewhere and were willing to make the short trip to the capital for the game. Fans were encouraged to wear the colours of their favourite team rather than the two on show, creating a sea of colour labelled a 'Rainbow Coalition' by NFL UK managing director Alastair Kirkwood. The NFL had well and truly arrived from America, and the United Kingdom loved it.

Tynes's field goal put the first points on the board and the Giants took control after the dismal conditions took another victim clad in aqua and orange. On third down, receiver Marty Booker motioned into the quarterback position with Lemon sat back in shotgun formation. Booker fumbled the snap and Giants safety Gibril Wilson subsequently recovered to give his team excellent field position, but the Dolphins defence held strong and forced a punt. With Miami struggling to get anything going offensively, New York finally found their groove late in the second quarter and meticulously moved downfield with a 13-play, 59-yard drive to find themselves on the opposition ten-yard line. With conditions deteriorating, the Giants ran the ball frequently and efficiently. The run was so effective on this dismal British afternoon that even Manning, not particularly renowned for an ability to make plays with his legs, decided to have a go. Facing first-and-goal with just over a minute remaining in the first half, Manning faked the hand-off to Jacobs and, with the Miami defence focused on stopping any receiving options, the quarterback saw his chance.

Manning rushed towards the end zone in an instant, darting to the corner and evading the last-ditch diving tackle by Miami defensive lineman Jason Taylor to score the first regular season touchdown outside of North America.

After Tynes's extra point, the Giants held a commanding 10-0 lead – and then the brutal conditions took yet another casualty. After Lemon guided the Dolphins to a new set of downs on their own 48-yard line, the quarterback scanned the field for possible options that could take Miami into New York territory before the ball slipped out of his hand, allowing Hall of Fame defensive end Michael Strahan to recover possession firmly in Miami territory. Starting their drive on the Miami 35-yard line with 30 seconds remaining in the first half, Manning had two passes fall incomplete before Giants offensive coordinator Kevin Gilbride moved back to the reliable run game, with Manning handing the ball off to Jacobs. The running back picked up a first down thanks to a 12-yard rush to take the Giants to the Miami 23. New York brought out Tynes to once again kick despite the pitch being well and truly torn up at this stage. Holder Jeff Feagles moved some of the shredded grass from the prime spot and Tynes nailed the 41-yard kick to give the Giants a 13-0 lead at the break.

Conditions hardly improved for the start of the third quarter, which the Giants began with possession. The Miami defence looked far stouter and they almost scored a defensive touchdown on the very first play as Manning's swing pass aimed at Jacobs narrowly avoided the clutches of Taylor, only to fall incomplete. The two franchises then traded possession with the punters and kickers ironically getting utilised on European soil. The gloomy conditions meant the ball was slippery and therefore easily fumbled, with Jacobs doing so after a hit by Miami cornerback Jason Allen, who forced the ball to pop into the air before New York centre Rich Seubert recovered. The play ultimately meant very little, as offensive efficiency was at a low given the conditions. On Miami's next possession, quarterback Lemon threw a wayward pass that perhaps, in a drier situation, would have been intercepted by Giants safety Wilson but the ball slipped from his clutches and fell incomplete to the relief of the Miami fans.

Big Blue got to the Miami 40 when, on second down following another incomplete pass by Manning, Miami earned themselves a lifeline. Manning dropped back and looked towards Plaxico Burress, New York's star receiver on the right-hand side of the field, before Miami defensive end Matt Roth crushed the quarterback from his blind side. The hit, which frankly might have been felt back in Manhattan, knocked the ball loose and Miami crucially recovered. Lemon leaned on his legs and the run game to take the Dolphins into Giants territory, with Jesse Chatman's 24-yard run downed at the 21-yard line. Miami tasted blood, so they ran the ball hard and often to find themselves just two yards from the end zone on second and goal. Masters of their own undoing, Lemon muffed a snap and was forced to improvise, rolling right down the throat of linebacker Kawika Mitchell for a sack and loss of nine yards. Now third-and-goal, Lemon's high pass towards the right-hand corner of the end zone was broken up by Giants cornerback Sam Madison. With Miami forced to kick a 29-yard field goal, Feely – who had missed his earlier attempt – made no mistake to put the Dolphins on the board with just over a minute remaining in the quarter. It would be the only score of the third period, but the Giants were able to quickly reach the Miami 40-yard line on their drive thanks to impressive runs by Jacobs and Manning.

In the fourth quarter, Manning hit tight end Jeremy Shockey for a 22-yard gain to advance to the Miami 13. While a touchdown would have surely secured the win, a pair of incomplete passes and a short rush by Jacobs meant it was fourth down. Out came Tynes to kick for three points and extend the lead to 13 with just 12 minutes remaining, but the Scot couldn't best the conditions on this occasion. He hooked the attempt left and kicked the tattered turf in frustration. A quick Miami three-and-out, inflicted chiefly by a Fred Robbins sack on third down, was followed up by a long but ultimately scoreless New York drive. Miami needed to drive down the pitch and score to have any chance of winning their first match of the season. They did just that, with a series of short plays culminating in Lemon finding rookie Ginn Jr in the end zone to score both the first touchdown of his career and the first receiving NFL touchdown in the United Kingdom. The 21-yard score was followed by an extra point by Feely, making it a three-point game.

With the match on the line, Feely skidded an onside kick all the way across the wet surface and straight out of bounds. Manning ensured the Giants would get the win by kneeling three times, running out the clock to a chorus of boos from many fans who may not have quite understood the formulaic nature of what was unfolding before them.

Despite the consistent substandard and miserable conditions that undoubtedly affected the offensive effectiveness of either franchise, the Giants secured their sixth consecutive win of the season after starting with two defeats. Jacobs had a career-high 131 yards on 23 carries, while Mitchell and Robbins also stood out on the box score with a sack apiece, but it was a rough day for Manning. The quarterback, who would retire in 2019 as a two-time Super Bowl champion, completed just eight of his 22 attempts for 59 yards. With such a poor performance, the British conditions had a pretty solid argument to be International Series MVP. Giants head coach Tom Coughlin was frustrated by his team's lacklustre ending to the game as they went scoreless in the second half while Miami put up their ten points in the same period. He certainly did not mind the result though, as it meant the Giants had won six matches in a row for the first time since 1994. The franchise would go on to claim their seventh championship when they defeated the 18-0 New England Patriots at Super Bowl XLII in February 2008.

In the 'home' locker room, the Miami Dolphins were on the other end of the spectrum. The loss at Wembley was their

11th straight defeat, to leave the franchise with a record of 0-8 heading into their bye week. Rookie head coach Cam Cameron, previously the offensive coordinator and mastermind behind the high-flying San Diego Chargers between 2002 and 2006, was clearly frustrated by the loss and the catalogue of offensive errors from Miami. However, Cameron praised the city of London and the debut of the International Series: 'I can't imagine a game being put together better than this. The hospitality was like none I've ever seen.' The 2007 Dolphins continued the opposite trajectory of their Wembley opponents and won just one match all season – a 22-16 home triumph over the Baltimore Ravens in week 15. The Dolphins' 1-15 record was the worst in the NFL that season and the worst in the iconic franchise's 40-year history. Cameron was subsequently fired after the conclusion of the dismal campaign, ending his brief career as an NFL head coach.

The NFL's venture outside of North America and into Europe was, despite the weather-induced quality on display, a monumental success and backed up commissioner Goodell's pre-match claims that the league's flagship event, the Super Bowl, could be held in London. Goodell singled out Wembley Stadium as a prime candidate for the biggest match in football due to the British enthusiasm for the sport.

The league also looked towards other countries as viable candidates to host regular season matches moving forwards. Ultimately, these would not come to be. The NFL only had eyes for London and the United Kingdom.

2008

Big Easy Win in the Big Smoke

NFL REGULAR SEASON WEEK EIGHT
26 October 2008
SAN DIEGO CHARGERS 32
NEW ORLEANS SAINTS 37
Wembley Stadium

AS THE New Orleans Saints and the San Diego Chargers took to the Wembley pitch, conditions were very different to the scenes of 364 days before. It was a chilly, dry London evening with both teams hoping to bounce back from road losses. Saints quarterback Drew Brees was outclassed by former NFL Europe quarterback Jake Delhomme in a 30-7 defeat to the Panthers in Carolina while San Diego fell 23-14 to the Buffalo Bills in upstate New York. The match, which pitted Brees against the team that selected him in the 2001 NFL Draft, was played in front of an enthusiastic crowd of 83,226 British fans with many spectators donning their favourite jerseys.

Brees and the Saints started with the ball and the 29-year-old quarterback moved the sticks for the first time in the match with a fine drag pass to tight end Billy Miller. Running back Deuce McAllister was heavily involved in the opening drive, picking up several first downs as the Saints marched deep into

San Diego territory. After New Orleans took an offensive holding penalty, they found themselves held up in the red zone and kicker Taylor Mehlhaff made the 23-yard field goal to give the Saints the lead. The Chargers responded well: Hall of Fame running back LaDainian Tomlinson juking left and picking up 26 yards – but their drive ended in similar fashion. Philip Rivers's intended pass to receiver Malcolm Floyd on third down was well broken up by Saints cornerback and future Detroit Lions defensive coordinator Aaron Glenn. Nate Kaeding levelled the score at three points apiece with a 33-yard field goal.

In the second quarter, Brees truly found his rhythm. He completed a clutch third down pass to Miller to earn a new set of downs before firing a perfect ball into the arms of Lance Moore. The 31-yard gain by the receiver put the Saints in the Chargers' red zone, and further rushes placed Brees on his former team's 12-yard line. With 11 minutes remaining in the first half, the legendary quarterback dropped back and faked a release towards Miller, who was darting towards the corner of the end zone. Instead, Brees juked inside to evade San Diego linebacker Tim Dobbins – drafted by the Chargers in 2006, the year Brees left for New Orleans – before floating a perfect pass to Devery Henderson all alone in the back of the end zone. The crowd erupted around Henderson, who celebrated with the rest of the offence while Brees jogged to the sidelines. The quarterback was aware his former team would not just sit back and let the Saints dominate. He knew more plays would have to be made, particularly after Mehlhaff hit the post from his extra point attempt. Brees's revenge game against the Chargers was indeed about to explode into a masterclass of offensive firepower.

While the match itself was of rather low quality – largely due to the awful conditions – the 2007 debut of the NFL International Series in London was incredibly successful. The league quickly confirmed that it would return for another regular season game in 2008, with commissioner Roger Goodell claiming that viewing figures in the United Kingdom had grown by 40 per cent since the Giants and Dolphins clashed. 'The game in London was undoubtedly one of the highlights of the entire 2007 season,' said Goodell. 'The fan interest was tremendous. We had an overwhelmingly positive response to the event from all involved – the teams, our sponsors and business partners and, of course, the fans themselves.' The commissioner's announcement hardly veiled the financial benefits of the International Series, but the passionate fanbase was what made the trip to London so successful. 'Playing a limited number of regular season games internationally will help build and grow an already passionate international fanbase,' Goodell added at a Super Bowl press conference in downtown Phoenix before the Giants' unlikely win over the Patriots. 'We look forward to another spectacular event in 2008.'

On this occasion, the match did not include the future Super Bowl champion for the 2008 campaign, but the Saints – who triumphed in the Super Bowl for the first time in franchise history the following year – and the Chargers certainly put on a spectacular show. It was a highly anticipated game as it was the first time Brees would face his former team after leaving for New Orleans prior to the 2006 season.

Before Brees won the Super Bowl and became the NFL's all-time passing yards leader as a Saint, he was drafted by the Chargers in 2001. San Diego offered Brees a five-year contract worth $50m as he neared the end of his rookie deal, but it was heavily incentivised as the quarterback was coming off arthroscopic surgery. In the final game of the season, Brees tore his labrum and suffered rotator cuff damage after being hit by Gerald Warren while trying to pick up his fumble against the Denver Broncos. The Chargers refused to raise their offer – so the future Hall of Famer met with other franchises, namely the Miami Dolphins and the Saints.

Miami were uncertain whether Brees's shoulder would ever fully heal, and their medical staff advised against signing him in favour of trading for Minnesota quarterback Daunte Culpepper instead. Brees inked a six-year, $60m deal with the Saints and the rest is history. 'I just felt that energy in New Orleans,' Brees said after signing with the team in March 2006. 'From the very beginning there was a genuine feeling that they wanted me there. They believe I can come back from this shoulder injury and lead them to a championship.' The Saints put more money – guaranteed and incentive-based – on the table for Brees as they wanted to position the signal-caller as the marquee attraction to boost ticket sales after Hurricane Katrina. The Saints got their man and Brees found what he was looking for. Now he was set to face his former team, and Chargers owner and chairman Dean Spanos understood the implications of such a fixture being chosen to go across the pond: 'This is another positive step in the effort to globalise our great sport. It's an opportunity for the NFL to show off two of their marquee teams and some of their best players.'

The players were equally excited to travel to London. Chargers linebacker Shawne Merriman said he had spoken to Giants defensive end Michael Strahan about the spectacle of playing in the United Kingdom: 'He just told me about the excitement and the media coverage.' Last year's Wembley matchup pitted two of the most iconic and popular franchises, particularly in the United Kingdom, against one another. By pairing two smaller market teams from New Orleans and San Diego, the league was using the 2008 clash to truly gauge the sport's popularity in Britain.

The Chargers requested to play on the East Coast the week before crossing the Atlantic to help acclimatise to the time zone difference from San Diego. The Chargers therefore played and lost in Buffalo on 19 October 2008 before travelling to London. Spanos quashed any talk that the international travel may unfavourably affect the Chargers' season by referencing the fact that the Giants were reigning Super Bowl champions. The last time the Chargers went to the Super Bowl back in the 1994 campaign, the franchise had played a preseason game in Berlin the previous summer – perhaps it was on the cards again.

The match in London was ultimately an opportunity for Brees to show his former team what they were missing – and he took every chance. Immediately after Mehlhaff's missed extra point, the kicker picked out Chargers return specialist Darren Sproles, who made moves downfield. Upon reaching the 30-yard line, the ball was ripped from his clutches by Usama Young and suddenly New Orleans found themselves with the opportunity to increase their six-point lead in London. McAllister earned three yards with a short run before Brees found tight end Mark Campbell for an important first down. Another pair of short passes left the Saints on the Chargers three-yard line, and New Orleans head coach Sean Payton called a timeout. They were going for it on fourth down. With nine minutes remaining in the second quarter, Brees handed it off to McAllister who burst into the end zone for the 51st time in his career to make it 16-3 in favour of New Orleans. The touchdown was memorable for McAllister; the score moved him into second place on the Saints all-time touchdown list.

San Diego wasted no time in hitting back. On the very first play of their drive, Rivers faked a hand-off to Tomlinson, evaded the rush of Saints defensive end Will Smith and threw a perfectly placed yet wobbly ball to the left touchline into the clutches of receiver Vincent Jackson for a 13-yard gain. A pair of short plays meant the Chargers faced third-and-one on the New Orleans 44. It was too far to kick, so Tomlinson – or LT as he was famously referred to – had to pick up the yard to keep the drive going. Lined up in I-formation, Tomlinson spun out of a tackle and rushed through a gap created by rookie fullback Mike Tolbert. Tomlinson delivered not one but two fierce stiff arms on defensive backs Kevin Kaesviharn and Randall Gay before going out of bounds at the New Orleans four-yard line. The Chargers were looking to score with their new set of downs, but a Tomlinson rush was telegraphed and the Saints defence forced the star running backwards. A false start penalty pushed the Chargers to third down from the 12 – a theme of San Diego's trip to Wembley. The Chargers were flagged 14 times for 134 yards. After taking the five-yard penalty, Rivers snapped the ball from shotgun and stepped up in the pocket to complete an underneath pass to Tomlinson. The Hall of Famer juked inside Saints linebacker Jonathan Vilma before powering through a pair of defensive backs to dive over the goal line. At 16-10, it was game on between the Saints and Chargers in London.

It took just two minutes for the Saints to retaliate. Brees completed a deep ball to Henderson for 20 yards with additional gains coming from a roughing the passer call against the Chargers. It was a classic pass from Brees: he evaded pressure before throwing across his body into the arms of his receiver. On the very next play, Brees faked the hand-off and looked left towards his first read, Lance Moore. The receiver had burned away from the double coverage he was facing and Brees popped the perfect floated 30-yard pass inches from where the defensive backs could reach. Moore hauled it in and the Saints were back with a 13-point lead after Mehlhaff nailed the extra point. British fans could scarcely believe their eyes – was this what gridiron football was supposed to be like? The offensive firepower on display in 2008 certainly trumped the year prior.

The Chargers answered in style to close the second quarter. Rivers found legendary tight end Antonio Gates and receiver Jackson for solid gains. At the two-minute warning, the Chargers were just inside the Saints half and Rivers took a deep calming breath as he walked towards the line of scrimmage. The quarterback, then just 26 years of age, called a play action pass. Rivers went through the motions, faked the hand-off to Tomlinson before delivering a pump fake that preceded an inch-perfect dime to Gates. The bruising tight end was challenged by two defensive backs before going down at the Saints 12-yard line.

With New Orleans perhaps expecting a Tomlinson run, Rivers once again faked the hand-off and delivered a perfect pass over Saints safety Young and into the arms of Gates for the touchdown. Kaeding kicked the extra point and the Chargers were within a score of taking the lead. The San Diego defence held strong to end a streak of five straight touchdown drives, and the two franchises went into half-time with the Saints holding onto a slender 23-17 lead.

Beginning the third quarter in similar fashion to the first, Brees continued his vengeful run against his former employers. The Saints started on their own 13-yard line but moved into dangerous territory thanks to one play. Brees looked right at Moore before pump faking and swivelling left. He saw Marques Colston, the franchise leader in receiving yards, bursting through a gap in coverage between the trifecta of linebacker, cornerback and safety. Brees delivered the ball perfectly, and Colston showed off his elusiveness to break away from Chargers safety Eric Weddle. The receiver was stopped illegally, as Antonio Cromartie committed a horse collar tackle to try and stop Colston. With the Chargers defence standing strong, the Saints were forced into a third-and-long situation on the Chargers' 24-yard line. Brees displayed his ice-cold demeanour with a pass to tight end Miller – but it wasn't enough for a first down after Stephen Cooper and Quentin Jammer stopped him short. Payton and Brees conversed and went for it on fourth down, with the quarterback faking a toss to Aaron Stecker before spinning and picking out Miller, who muscled his way over the marker. Brees then completed a shovel pass to fullback Mike Karney to place the Saints on the one-yard line. As the British fans held their breath, Brees nailed the execution of the goal-line play. He faked the give to McAllister before wheeling right and throwing towards the back of the end zone, where Mark Campbell was waiting to score.

Rivers solemnly looked up towards the Wembley arch before he encouraged his offence and returned to the field. Leaning on the dual threat posed by Tomlinson, the Chargers perambulated downfield to find themselves five yards short of the end zone. Rivers could smell his chance to draw the Saints closer and keep the game alive late in the third quarter, and he found Samoan tight end Brandon Manumaleuna for the score – but it was all for naught. Offensive lineman Kris Dielman was deemed guilty of holding, which not only nullified the touchdown but also sent the Chargers back ten yards. Now on the 15, Rivers found Tomlinson on a short route to the right-hand side of the pitch before the running back was stopped at the six-yard line. Kaeding kicked the 24-yard field goal attempt between the posts, and the score read 30-20 in favour of New Orleans.

The Saints offence continued to roll, with Brees finding Miller for a 20-yard gain before several defensive penalties – including a dubious pass interference call on third down against San Diego cornerback Cletis Gordon – once again took New Orleans to the Chargers' one-yard line. Saints fullback Karney rushed into the end zone to give his team a 17-point lead that was surely insurmountable as the game entered the fourth and final quarter. Rivers responded well, but another offensive penalty – against Rivers for delaying the game – conceded deep in New Orleans territory meant the Chargers had to settle for a frustrating field goal, which Kaeding converted. However, head coach Norv Turner wasn't done yet. With 9:35 remaining, kicker Kaeding attempted an onside kick and, true to his surroundings, passed the ball like a soccer player. Kaeding's perfectly weighted pass, hit with the inside of his right boot, meant the ball's bounce was unpredictable. It ricocheted off the questionable Wembley turf and bounced over Saints safety Young before Chargers receiver Kassim Osgood recovered the loose ball. San Diego were in a position where they could tie the game but would need two converted touchdowns either side of a defensive stop.

Rivers immediately guided the Chargers offence downfield as he hit Chris Chambers and Jackson for two completions each.

The second pass to the latter receiver, Jackson, was the crucial one. With his offensive line protecting him, Rivers launched a dime towards the corner of the end zone. It found Jackson, who sprinted and dived for the ball. At first glance, the play appeared incomplete as Jackson slid over the thick white line that represents the boundaries of the pitch – but as he did, the receiver's knees were down in the end zone. The Chargers had scored the 14-yard touchdown and made it a seven-point game in London.

The Saints offence punted as the San Diego defensive backs made some excellent plays. With four minutes remaining in the match, the Chargers began the crucial drive from their own 12-yard line following an offensive holding penalty against tackle Jeromey Clary. Rivers wheeled right, eyeing receiver Jackson on a streak downfield. Instead, Rivers showed tremendous pocket presence to evade pressure from the outside before picking out Tomlinson, who had swung left near to the line of scrimmage. Tomlinson was in acres of space, and he duly turned a short pass into a 32-yard gain. The Chargers continued to pluck away, and a fourth down conversion by Rivers – a pass to Gates for 11 yards – suggested San Diego were all set to tie the pulsating match. On third-and-15 with 78 seconds remaining, Rivers snapped the ball out of a pro set formation and stepped up to avoid pressure. He moved right to avoid another New Orleans defender before launching a jump ball towards his reliable target Gates. The ball was tipped and deflected up into the air, allowing for Jonathan Vilma to make the interception and surely end the Chargers' hopes of a comeback.

The Saints simply had to hold the ball. McAllister rushed several times and the Chargers responded with timeouts until Sean Payton called a peculiar play on fourth down. Instead of Ben Graham punting the ball, the Saints head coach – renowned for his gutsy calls that would lead to a converted onside kick early in Super Bowl XLIV – made Brees run backwards to take as much time as he could off the clock before conceding a safety, worth two points. 'It was a bit of a clock management issue,' said Payton. 'That became more important than the two points.' The Chargers started on the halfway line and had one crack to save the match. Rivers duly launched a Hail Mary into the end zone but it was ultimately batted down by Saints cornerback Mike McKenzie, sealing the win for New Orleans. Drew Brees had defeated his former team at the first time of asking.

The Saints went into their bye week perfectly balanced at 4-4 en route to an 8-8 final record. While New Orleans couldn't continue the form that saw New York triumph in the Super Bowl after winning in London, the franchise only had to wait an extra year before Brees got his hands on the Lombardi Trophy. The former Chargers quarterback had torched his old team for 339 yards and three touchdowns without a turnover at Wembley. His box score was similar to Rivers's own performance, who passed for 341 yards and three touchdowns but did throw an interception, and defeat left the Chargers with a record of 3-5 heading into their bye. They would go on to also finish 8-8, but San Diego remarkably made the playoffs. The Chargers defeated Peyton Manning and the Indianapolis Colts on Wildcard Weekend before their postseason run was ended by Ben Roethlisberger and the Steelers, who came away 35-24 winners in Pittsburgh.

The International Series was playing an instrumental role in attracting more fans outside the United States. Commissioner Goodell announced a plan for the Buffalo Bills to play an annual regular season game in Toronto from the 2009 season and had declared the league would return to Mexico City. These two ventures would be unsuccessful and unreliable respectively, but the matches in London were a hit. Goodell suggested not only would a regular season game be played in the capital of England for another three years, but there was an overwhelming response from franchises wanting to play abroad. 'Maybe it's because the Giants played in London and they went to the Super Bowl,' he added.

Maybe that was the case, but London's arrival as a regular site for the NFL was proving to be appealing for the biggest and best teams throughout the league.

2009

New England Conquer Old England

NFL REGULAR SEASON WEEK SEVEN
25 October 2009
NEW ENGLAND PATRIOTS 35
TAMPA BAY BUCCANEERS 7
Wembley Stadium

THE ATMOSPHERE at Wembley Stadium in 2009 was the best an International Series game had yet produced, and there was a reason why. Before Tom Brady cemented his status as the 'GOAT' – the greatest player of all time – he arrived in London as a three-time Super Bowl champion and a former MVP. He had narrowly missed out on a perfect season with the New England Patriots in 2007 when they were defeated in the Super Bowl by the New York Giants. Brady came into the 2009 season after recovering from a torn ACL and MCL sustained in the opening game of the 2008 campaign, but he was back to his best – and the bubbly crowd knew it. On the CBS broadcast, analyst Phil Sims predicted an 'outstanding game' ahead. While the match may not have been outstanding, the 84,254 fans – a record for the London games at that point – certainly left the stadium feeling satisfied as they watched a 32-year-old Brady work his magic from the comfort of their own country.

For British fans, the prospect of Brady and the Patriots was tantalising, but the Tampa Bay Buccaneers were sliding towards mediocrity. The Bucs won their first Super Bowl in the 2002 season and were hoping to challenge for their third NFC South title in the past four years. They even harboured dreams of becoming the first franchise to lift the Lombardi Trophy at their home arena as Super Bowl XLIII was set to be played at the Raymond James Stadium in Tampa. 'The Tampa Bay Buccaneers organisation is extremely excited and honoured to be chosen to participate in the NFL International Series,' said Buccaneers executive vice president and Manchester United owner Joel Glazer. 'We look forward to being part of the NFL's global outreach and playing our great game in front of Buccaneers fans overseas.' While Glazer was referring to the sport of American football as 'great', the performances of his franchise in 2009 were anything but. Following a defeat to the Carolina Panthers in Tampa, the Buccaneers were winless through six matches for the first time since their 2-14 1985 campaign, their worst season since 1976 when the franchise debuted with a record of 0-14.

The Patriots were at the opposite end of the spectrum. New England were an established threat when they arrived in London: champions in three of the last seven years, which would and perhaps should have been more but for the pesky New York Giants. They were the NFL's defining franchise across the first two decades of the 21st century. Brady's injury in 2008 should have ended the Patriots' season, yet they impressively finished with a record of 11-5, narrowly missing out on the AFC East title to the Miami Dolphins – the only time that New England failed to win the division between 2003 and 2019. The NFL had never seen dominance like this before and in 2009, before Brady and Belichick would collect another three rings, the sport's latest dynasty touched down in the United Kingdom.

New England left Massachusetts in fine fettle. They recovered from an overtime defeat to the Denver Broncos with an emphatic win over the Tennessee Titans, in which the Patriots led 45-0 at half-time – the largest lead at the interval in league history. Brady recorded five passing touchdowns in the second quarter alone, setting another NFL record as New England won the match 59-0 to tie the largest post-merger shutout and margin of victory in league history with the Los Angeles' Rams win over the Atlanta Falcons in 1976 by the same score.

The Patriots flew to Wembley with a 4-2 record ahead of their week seven clash with the winless Buccaneers and New England wasted no time in impressing the international fans. Tampa Bay received the first possession and, just five plays into the game, the Patriots led. Buccaneers quarterback Josh Johnson, a sophomore drafted in the fifth round of the 2008 NFL Draft, tossed a low pass into the arms of the onrushing Patriots safety Brandon Meriweather. The 25-year-old had anticipated the throw and picked off Johnson to return a 39-yard interception for a touchdown. 'I just happened to have a good break on the ball,' Meriweather said. 'I think the quarterback and receiver were on two different pages, and he just happened to throw it to me. Any big play sets the mood.' Tampa Bay's offence, ranked 28th throughout the NFL for the 2009 season, continued to struggle in the face of the New England defence.

On the ensuing drive, it became clear that the rendition of 'God Save the Queen' that preceded kick-off perhaps should have been altered. Her Majesty did not need saving nor rescuing, but the Buccaneers certainly did. Tampa Bay moved downfield thanks to an 11-yard rush and 19-yard reception by running back Cadillac Williams before Johnson hit rookie receiver Sammie Stroughter to advance to the New England 33. Johnson then stepped up to avoid edge pressure before he threw a deep ball towards wideout Michael Clayton. Meriweather was there again, deflecting the ball up in the air before intercepting Johnson for a second time just six minutes into the match. A 31-yard return from the safety allowed the Patriots to start on their own 46, but they struggled to get going on offence as two short passes from Brady were not enough for a first down. Luckily enough for the New England offence, they were almost granted a slow start due to the sheer inadequacy of their opponents. Following a Bucs three-and-out, the Patriots began their second drive of the match with a smart end-around to rookie receiver Brandon Tate. Tate was playing in his first NFL match after spending the first six weeks of the campaign on the Physically Unable to Perform list, and the first play of his professional career went for 11 yards. Brady then hit legendary wideout Randy Moss on a pair of plays, with the latter going for 37 yards as Moss embarked on an inside cross to take the Patriots to the Tampa Bay 11. Two plays later, the New England offence was on the board as Brady faked a hand-off to running back Kevin Faulk and found Wes Welker on a screen pass, and the veteran receiver weaved his way through tackles to score. Stephen Gostkowski added the extra point to increase the Pats' lead to 14-0 with 2:16 remaining in the first quarter.

The match may well have been over after just one quarter, but the fans inside Wembley Stadium didn't care one bit. The Buccaneers could not advance even a single yard before punting the ball back to Welker. The wideout, who led the NFL in receptions in 2007, 2009 and 2011, returned the ball 24 yards to give Brady and the hungry offence incredible field position. The Patriots started on the Buccaneers 30-yard line and got to work as Brady threw a pair of short passes to tight end Chris Baker and Moss. Laurence Maroney edged the ball forwards with a short gain to bring New England 11 yards from the end zone before Brady showed signs of mortality. Looking for Moss and the touchdown, Brady threw a deep ball towards the left-hand sideline only for Bucs safety Tanard Jackson to pick off the lofted pass. The crowd was left stunned, almost disappointed, that the man who would become the GOAT threw a pass more befitting of a sacrificial lamb.

Unfortunately, the Buccaneers could not take advantage as they immediately went three-and-out, paving the way for Brady to make amends for his error. The quarterback did not disappoint. He stepped up to perfectly evade the pressure on his right from defensive end Tim Crowder before unleashing a short throw to Sam Aiken, a fourth-round selection by New England's AFC East rivals, the Buffalo Bills, in the 2003 NFL Draft. Primarily a special teams player, Aiken slipped a tackle by Tampa Bay linebacker Barrett Ruud and took the short pass all 54 yards to score the first receiving touchdown of his career. After stiff-arming Jackson to cross the line for the third touchdown of the game, Aiken made the score 21-0 with 11:18 left in the second quarter.

Another punt by the Buccaneers ensured the Patriots started on their own 33. Welker took a six-yard rush before Brady was intercepted for the second time in just four passes when his deep throw towards Tate was snagged by sophomore cornerback Aqib Talib, who would later play for the Patriots, Broncos and Rams, winning a Super Bowl in Denver. The performance of New England's quarterback, particularly after he dominated Tennessee a week earlier, was particularly unlike his normal, effective self. Brady throwing the pigskin to Tampa Bay players would actually become a familiar sight 11 seasons after the clash at Wembley.

Following the 2019 NFL season, there were substantial rumours of unrest between Brady – a Super Bowl champion on two occasions in the last three years – and the franchise he had called home for nearly 20 years. Brady had been the quarterback in Foxborough for 285 regular season matches and 41 playoff clashes over two decades, winning six Super Bowl championships, four Super Bowl MVPs and three NFL MVP awards, but his contract was set to expire in March 2020. With free agency rapidly approaching, the day most feared by Patriots fans came to fruition. On 17 March 2020, the day before his contract with the Patriots expired, Brady announced he would not re-sign with the franchise. Suddenly, the biggest fish since Peyton Manning entered the free agency pool – and it was a short-lived chase. On 20 March, Brady signed with the Tampa Bay Buccaneers. The two-year contract was worth $50m in guaranteed money, with up to $4.5m available annually through incentives as well as the inclusion of a no-trade and no-franchise tag clause. Brady announced the deal on Instagram with the following message:

'Excited, humble and hungry … if there is one thing I have learned about football, it's that nobody cares what you did last year or the year before that … you earn the trust and respect of those around through your commitment every single day. I'm starting a new football journey and thankful for the Buccaneers for giving me an opportunity to do what I love to do. I look forward to meeting all my new team-mates and coaches and proving to them that they can believe and trust in me … I have always believed that well done is better than well said, so I'm not going to say much more – I'm just gonna get to work!'

The three-time MVP had joined a team ready to compete. His receiving weapons – headlined by receivers Mike Evans and Chris Godwin – were the best that the 42-year-old had at his disposal in years, and favoured weapon Rob Gronkowski even came out of retirement to head to Florida. Brady had joined a coach in Bruce Arians who, while never winning the championship, had found success with the likes of Manning, Ben Roethlisberger and Carson Palmer, and Arians knew the gravity of acquiring a player of Brady's calibre. 'Tom is the most successful quarterback in the history of our league, but what makes him so special is his ability to make those around him better,' said Arians. 'He is a proven winner who will provide the leadership, accountability and work ethic necessary to lead us to our goal of winning another championship.' The Buccaneers were almost crowned champions before a down had been played, and Tampa Bay's official website announced the signing by stating: 'All in! Tom Brady, Bucs team up to pursue championships.' The plural nature of the final word left readers questioning whether the hype for a team that hadn't made the playoffs since 2007 was too much. In the end, Brady and the crew lived up to it.

The 2020 regular season was rather unspectacular for the Buccaneers, with Brady suffering the most lopsided loss of his career in a week nine blowout 38-9 defeat to Drew Brees and the New Orleans Saints. Tampa Bay settled for a wildcard spot – the first of Brady's career – in order to punch their ticket to the postseason as the Saints won the NFC South. Brady and the Bucs came alive in the playoffs, throwing for 381 yards and two touchdowns to comfortably defeat the Washington Football Team and set up a Divisional Round clash with the Saints. Brady threw for 199 yards and two touchdowns while rushing for a score in the 30-20 win, which proved to be Brees's final game of his historic career. With the win, Brady extended his record of Conference Championship game appearances to 14, having reached 13 AFC title games in New England. In his first NFC Championship clash, Brady and the Bucs travelled to Lambeau Field to face Aaron Rodgers and the Green Bay Packers, the number one seed in the conference. Leaning on an incredible first-half display from Brady, the Buccaneers defeated the Packers 31-26 to become the first team to reach the Super Bowl in its home stadium. In Super Bowl LV, Brady threw for 201 yards and three touchdowns as the Buccaneers thumped the defending champions, the Kansas City Chiefs, 31-9. Brady took home the game's MVP award for the fifth time, extending his own record, and he became the second quarterback after Manning to lead two different teams to Super Bowl glory – and the first to do it with teams from different conferences. Brady has proved time and time again that success follows him wherever he goes, be it in Massachusetts, Florida or London.

Despite Talib's brilliant interception, the Buccaneers failed to cross midfield and were forced into a quick three-and-out. The Patriots came back and attempted a fake punt on fourth down, but a penalty negated the play, so New England punter Chris

Hanson thumped possession back without any trickery. After an insipid passing performance, the Buccaneers attempted to flip the script. They drove into New England territory as Johnson threw a pair of deep passes to Antonio Bryant, the second of which was a 33-yard touchdown to make it 21-7 as Bryant beat Patriots cornerback Darius Butler down the right sideline. Butler would get his revenge just six plays after the Bucs had put points on the board, intercepting Johnson at the New England 11 to end the first half.

The Patriots began the second half with a ten-play, 73-yard drive orchestrated by Brady and finished off with a 35-yard touchdown laser over linebacker Geno Hayes to tight end Benjamin Watson. With New England's three-score lead restored at 28-7, the game began to stagnate as defences found momentum. The two teams exchanged punts until early in the fourth quarter when Brady and running back Maroney drove the Pats from their own 11-yard line. For the second time in the second half, the Patriots embarked on a ten-play drive to score, capped off by Maroney's touchdown run from a yard out to make it 35-7. The two franchises exchanged punts again until the Buccaneers found themselves on their own 23-yard line facing fourth down. With nothing to lose, Bucs head coach Raheem Morris went for it with backup quarterback Josh Freeman, but the rookie was strip-sacked by Derrick Burgess to seal the game. The win meant New England had bettered their record to 5-2 entering the bye week, but the Buccaneers were left winless at 0-7. The defeat extended their losing streak to 11 games, their longest since 1976–77 when they endured an NFL record 26 straight defeats.

Ultimately, the Buccaneers had no answer for Brady over four quarters, and their future quarterback drilled Tampa Bay for 308 yards and three touchdowns. 'Tom, he's the guy that changed the game. He's the guy you worry about constantly,' said Bucs head coach Morris. 'When you have a great quarterback like that, that's what he does and that's what he will do for you.' Unfortunately for

Morris and the Buccaneers, Johnson was not a great quarterback – although his career was particularly astonishing. He had 19 separate stints at 16 different teams across varying professional levels, but he suffered on that October night in London. Johnson finished with 35 per cent pass completion for 156 yards, a touchdown and three interceptions before being withdrawn for rookie Freeman.

While New England were not quite as dominant as their crushing win over Tennessee, they finally got their first road win of the season. It took a trip across the Atlantic to get such a victory, so perhaps the change of scenery had helped Belichick's side. 'It's been an enjoyable couple days here and glad we could end it on a positive note,' the legendary coach said. Both Belichick and Brady – renowned as the greatest quarterback–head coach tandem in NFL history – were clearly impressed by the spectacle of the International Series, but they ensured the team got the win first and foremost. 'We had plenty of distractions coming over here, but everybody was really energised,' said Brady. The quarterback, already a two-time Super Bowl MVP by this point, enjoyed the trip to the UK and commented on the remarkable effort made by the country in hosting: 'All the flashbulbs were going off before kick-off. I think it's a privilege to come over here and get to enjoy this type of experience. It will probably never happen again for us, so we'll retire 1-0 internationally.'

While Brady and the Patriots would indeed return just three years later, they had left a permanent mark on the sport's international fanbase to boost New England's rapidly rising popularity in the United Kingdom. The GOAT had grazed on British soil – and he would come for seconds in 2012.

2010

Two Historic Franchises Ignite Wembley

NFL REGULAR SEASON WEEK EIGHT
31 October 2010
DENVER BRONCOS 16
SAN FRANCISCO 49ERS 24
Wembley Stadium

NO OTHER position influences the game quite like the quarterback. The quarterback leads the offence to score points and is the on-field leader of their organisation. The quarterback touches the ball on every offensive snap, and no other player can do more to win or lose a football game. The San Francisco 49ers and the Denver Broncos understand the position's importance better than most, with the likes of Joe Montana and Steve Young dominating the NFL with San Francisco in the 1980s and 1990s while John Elway and Peyton Manning led Denver to glory in the 1990s and 2010s.

Unfortunately, both franchises were lacking quality at quarterback in 2010. Alex Smith, the first overall pick in the 2005 NFL Draft, suffered an injured shoulder in the previous week's 23-20 loss to the previously winless Carolina Panthers.

Smith was ruled out and replaced by his backup, Troy Smith, for the game at Wembley. He had just 14 games of experience in the NFL and was set to take on Kyle Orton, a backup himself for much of his career who had just suffered a 59-14 loss to the Oakland Raiders. San Francisco's head coach Mike Singletary – more familiar with hitting quarterbacks as a mean linebacker on the legendary 1985 Chicago Bears – was going to have to work some magic to get Smith up to speed. In just his third season as a head coach, Singletary had already deployed JT O'Sullivan, Sean Hill, David Carr and his project Alex Smith at quarterback. Now, it was the turn of Troy.

Regardless of their form on the field, the *Guardian* referred to the clash as 'something of a coup' for the British audience. The 49ers gained a large following in the UK during the 1980s – the Channel 4 heyday of gridiron football – as San Francisco won four Super Bowls thanks to iconic figures like Montana and Jerry Rice. In fact, the duo even led the 49ers to a Super Bowl win over the Denver Broncos in 1990. Super Bowl XXIV was the most lopsided match in Super Bowl history. The 49ers stormed to a 55-10 victory over the Broncos, and Montana became just the third player in league history to win both the Super Bowl MVP and the league MVP in the same season after Bart Starr and Terry Bradshaw did so in 1966 and 1978 respectively.

Montana and the 49ers looked to win a third consecutive Super Bowl the following season and stormed to the best record in the NFL at 14-2. In the NFC Championship Game, San Francisco's quarterback was sacked from his blind side by Leonard Marshall, and the hit forced Montana out of the game as the New York Giants went on to defeat the 49ers with a field goal as time expired.

The four-time champion suffered numerous injuries, including a broken finger, bruised back and a concussion. Montana also injured his throwing elbow in the game, which resulted in him missing the entire 1991 season to recover. These nagging physical issues saw Montana miss 15 games in 1992 as well, leading Steve Young to assume the role of starting quarterback for the 49ers on a permanent basis. Montana was traded to the Kansas City Chiefs in 1993 while Young led San Francisco to another Super Bowl win in 1995. Unfortunately for 'Niners fans, the team visiting London was unrecognisable from the dominant dynasty of the 1980s and 1990s.

It was confirmed on Friday, 10 January 2010 that two of the most celebrated and storied franchises in NFL history, the Broncos and the 49ers, were scheduled to meet in London. There were even talks held for Wembley to host a monumental second match, with the Chiefs and Seattle Seahawks pegged to contest the unprecedented game but officials dropped the plan, citing the economy and the ongoing negotiations, which would lead to the 2011 Collective Bargaining Agreement after a brief lockout.

The Broncos have a rich history of their own and have cultivated a brand synonymous with success, which is particularly impressive given the team's bumpy start. The Broncos were founded as an AFL franchise on 14 August 1959 and they became the first AFL team to ever defeat an NFL team when they beat the Detroit Lions 13-7 in 1967. However, the Broncos were unsuccessful in the 1960s. Denver won more than five games in a season only once, going 7-7 in 1962 and compiling an overall record of 39-97-4 across the decade. After joining the NFL as part of the AFL–NFL merger of 1970, the Broncos reached Super Bowl XII in 1977 but fell 27-10 to the mighty Dallas Cowboys.

The franchise tasted further defeat in Super Bowl XXIV against the 49ers – Denver's fourth loss in as many trips to the big game – before quarterback Elway and the Broncos declined in the 1990 season as their 5-11 record secured bottom spot in the AFC West. Denver returned to the playoffs in 1991 only to fall short in the AFC Championship Game to the Buffalo Bills. The Broncos found form in 1996 as they stormed to an NFL-best 13-3 record but lost in the first round of the postseason to the Jacksonville Jaguars. It would be the final playoff defeat in Elway's career.

After three defeats in the Super Bowl for the legendary quarterback, he finally got his hands on the Vince Lombardi Trophy in Super Bowl XXXII. Elway led the Broncos to a maiden Super Bowl victory with a 31-24 win over the Green Bay Packers, and he followed it up a year later as Denver won Super Bowl XXXIII. The 34-19 triumph over the Atlanta Falcons proved to be Elway's final match in the NFL as he retired at the top, a fairy-tale ending to a storied career that Manning would imitate in 2015 when the five-time MVP led Denver to their third championship win at Super Bowl 50.

Broncos President and Chief Executive Pat Bowlen was excited about the opportunity to return to London. 'Our organisation has been fortunate to play in several American Bowls in previous years, including one in London, but to play a regular season game overseas is truly special,' said Bowlen. Broncos head coach Josh McDaniels – now a six-time Super Bowl champion as a position coach and offensive coordinator for the New England Patriots across two different stints – welcomed the 'privilege' of playing in the United Kingdom: 'The previous games [in London] have had a playoff-like atmosphere to them. We'll be ready for the challenge.'

When the match kicked off in front of 83,941 screaming fans, it certainly felt like the 49ers were back in San Francisco. Elway took to the field along with Jerry Rice for the coin toss to rapturous applause, but that was about as welcoming as it got for Denver. The 49ers ensured they took advantage of the support and struck first when veteran kicker Joe Nedney made a 34-yard field goal before the end of the first quarter following a seven-minute drive led by Smith. Making his first NFL start since 2007, Smith made plays behind a protective offensive line led by All-Pro Joe Staley. 'I've never been to London, but I've always wanted to go,' the offensive tackle said ahead of the match. 'I couldn't think of a better way to get to visit England than to go there doing something I love to do.'

Nedney's field goal was followed by a remarkable run of six straight punts as possession after possession led to no score. Broncos quarterback Orton, ranked second in the NFL in terms of passing yards, could not lead his team downfield while the partisan crowd booed Denver at every opportunity. The fans soon became restless as the third quarter got underway, before the Broncos finally engineered a response of their own.

Just six minutes into the second half at his own 28, Orton launched a deep ball to receiver Brandon Lloyd down the right-hand sideline. The former 49er hauled in the pass before he was tackled by rookie safety Taylor Mays at the one-yard line, presenting Denver with the best opportunity of the game so far to score a touchdown – and head coach McDaniels ensured the chance would not go begging. Divisive quarterback Tim Tebow, the first-round pick for the Broncos earlier in the year, took to the field and executed a sneak to score his second career touchdown run and give Denver a 7-3 lead after Matt Prater's extra point conversion.

While the lead was certainly not insurmountable, the 49ers were in a difficult position. Their offence was incredibly one-dimensional and predictable, relying on the run game – spearheaded by Frank Gore – to make progress after influential tight end Vernon Davis was withdrawn at half-time due to an ankle injury. 'I've been waiting for this opportunity since they started playing games over in London,' said Davis when the 49ers were confirmed to take part in the International Series. 'I've always wanted to go overseas and now I get to go over with my team-mates and play football. I can't wait to go over there and show all of Europe what 49ers football is all about.' Unfortunately, Davis could not showcase the football he wanted to due to his injury, and his team struggled in his absence. After a promising drive broke down inside Denver territory, Nedney thumped a

52-yard field goal – which would have reduced the score to a one-point game – agonisingly against the post.

The Broncos looked to take advantage of Nedney's miss and almost did exactly that. Orton threw a deep right pass to Lloyd for 25 yards to set up at the San Francisco 38, and Denver attempted to flex their offensive playbook with a flea flicker. The play was executed to near-perfection with Orton throwing a touchdown pass to wide receiver Gaffney, but the play was unfortunately nullified due to a chop block penalty on running back Knowshon Moreno. Even with this heartbreaking hiccup, the Broncos were in the ascendency and had the 49ers on the ropes as Orton hit rookie receiver Demaryius Thomas – who would go on to set multiple receiving records with the franchise as well as triumphing in Super Bowl 50 – for a 31-yard play. However, three straight Orton incompletions meant the Broncos would have to be satisfied with just three points on this drive, and Prater obliged from 32 yards to extend Denver's lead to 10-3 as the fourth quarter began.

For the hordes of San Francisco fans within Wembley Stadium, it appeared as though there was no way back for the Bay Area outfit. Stand-in quarterback Smith was struggling immensely; the 2006 Heisman Trophy winner had completed just four passes from nine attempts for a measly 37 yards in the first half and all appeared lost when influential target Davis went off injured. Suddenly, something clicked for Smith – and the momentum sensationally shifted in favour of the 49ers.

The drive started poorly as an incomplete pass was compounded by an offensive holding penalty against tight end Delanie Walker. The 24-year-old made amends almost immediately, collecting a deep Smith pass for a 27-yard gain into Denver territory. Walker wasn't done there as he caught a speculative 38-yard pass after an impressive scramble from Smith to keep the play alive. The dramatic reception placed the 49ers on the one-yard line, allowing Smith to complete the drive with a run into the end zone and level the score at 10-10 with 11:57 remaining.

With the British crowd jubilant, rejuvenated and, frankly, relieved that a touchdown had been scored, the 49ers began to feed off the spirited atmosphere. Under five minutes later, Smith threw a 20-yard pass to the left-hand side of the field, picking out Michael Crabtree who brilliantly evaded André Goodman to turn and rush into the end zone. After trailing for so long, the 49ers were in front.

San Francisco applied the finishing touches to Denver on the next series. In Broncos territory, 49ers linebacker Manny Lawson stripped the ball, allowing for team-mate Takeo Spikes to recover to great applause. Smith picked out Walker on a four-yard pass, and then Gore did the rest. Five successive run plays later, Gore celebrated a touchdown that made the score 24-10 in favour of the 49ers with just under four minutes remaining.

The Broncos fought back instantaneously as Orton relied on his receiver duo of Eddie Royal and Lloyd to quickly move the chains. The quarterback finished the drive with a short pass to Lloyd in the end zone, but Prater – to the amusement of the San Francisco-supporting crowd – shanked the following extra point, firing wide left. The miss meant the Broncos needed a touchdown and a two-point conversion to tie the game.

The 49ers ran down the clock on their next possession before Andy Lee punted back to Royal, who returned the kick to the house. His celebrations unfortunately were cut short after reserve linebacker Jarvis Moss was penalised for an illegal block above the waist, and Denver were forced to go again from their own 19-yard line with just 96 seconds remaining. Orton led the Broncos into 'Niner territory, but his deep pass intended for Jabar Gaffney was intercepted by cornerback Shawntae Spencer to seal the win for San Francisco.

All in all, it proved to be a successful venture across the pond for the 49ers. 'We got to get an NFL team over here,' said Spencer after the match. 'The energy is unbelievable. The fans, the wave, the flags. It really felt like a home game tonight.' Head coach Singletary echoed his cornerback's praise for the British support: 'The people here in London are incredible, and the fans obviously love football just as much as we do.' Big words from Singletary, but there was no doubt the 2010 clash truly had an electric atmosphere. Even Denver head coach McDaniels agreed: 'It was a very pro-San Francisco crowd and we were fine with that. We wouldn't change a single thing about this trip.'

The Bay Area franchise left London following the huge win to move to 2-6 while Denver suffered their fourth successive loss to sit bottom of the AFC West with the same record. Smith was a successful replacement, throwing for 196 yards while Gore was productive on the ground as he went for 118 yards on 29 carries. The Broncos mirrored their record to finish 4-12 and the 49ers didn't fare much better, struggling for consistency in the latter half of the season to record a 6-10 season.

While it may not have been a clash of superstar quarterbacks, the Broncos and 49ers' clash at Wembley Stadium came alive in the fourth quarter and it will be fondly remembered by each of the 83,941 fans that witnessed it – unless they were a Denver fan.

2011

The Bears' Welcome Return to London

NFL REGULAR SEASON WEEK SEVEN
23 October 2011
CHICAGO BEARS 24
TAMPA BAY BUCCANEERS 18
Wembley Stadium

THERE WAS a sense of familiarity surrounding the fifth instalment of the International Series. Not only were the Tampa Bay Buccaneers arriving for their second trip in three years, but the Chicago Bears were back at Wembley Stadium after 9,213 days.

Back in 1986, the Bears came to London and defeated the Dallas Cowboys 17-6 just months after Chicago had claimed the franchise's first and only Super Bowl championship. When head coach Lovie Smith and his 2011 Bears outfit rolled into London, they were a shadow of the 1985 team, but it was a shadow cast from their greatest season since the 2006 run to the Super Bowl. Smith and quarterback Jay Cutler had taken Chicago to the 2010 NFC Championship Game before suffering defeat to their bitter divisional rivals, the Green Bay Packers. The Bears licked their wounds and harboured playoff hopes coming into the season, but they arrived in London with a 3-3 record following a win over the Minnesota Vikings the previous Sunday night. The 39-10 victory came after Cutler threw for 267 yards and a pair of touchdowns without a turnover – a rarity for a 28-year-old who chucked 26 interceptions in 2009 alone.

In the red corner, the Buccaneers defeated the New Orleans Saints thanks to quarterback Josh Freeman's 303 passing yards and two touchdowns, leading his team to a 26-20 win before jetting to London. Tampa were cautiously optimistic for the 2011 season after missing the 2010 postseason on tiebreakers as they posted an impressive 10-6 record. The Bucs had not been to the playoffs since 2007 and, even though they were dominated by the Patriots in 2009, there was an air of apprehensive optimism surrounding the team. In Raheem Morris – who labelled the team 'youngry' – the Bucs had the youngest head coach leading the youngest 53-man roster in the NFL. While the Bucs got off to a slow start with a narrow loss to Detroit on the opening day, they embarked on a three-game winning streak to see off the Vikings, Atlanta Falcons and Colts to help the franchise take command of the NFC South. With a 4-2 record, Tampa Bay made the eight-and-a-half-hour flight from Florida to London.

There is something to be said about the travel plans for each team. Morris decided to fly the day after the win over New Orleans, touching down in London on Monday morning. He wanted to give the team plenty of time to adjust and counteract any potential jet lag, ensuring the Bucs would acclimatise to the new time zone and be at their swashbuckling best at Wembley Stadium on Sunday. The Bears went a different route and decided to wait until Thursday night to fly to London, with Smith hoping his players would sleep on the plane and treat the excursion as any other road game.

The 2011 International Series was the fifth regular season clash to be played at Wembley in as many seasons, but there would be an unwanted first: with an attendance of 76,981, it was not a sell-out contest. This was due to the 2011 NFL player lockout, a work stoppage imposed by the 32 owners from 12 March to 25 July 2011. It transpired when the owners and the NFL players, represented by the National Football League Players Association, failed to come to an agreement surrounding the new collective bargaining agreement (CBA) with disputes concerning financial issues such as rookie salaries, free agency guidelines, revenue sharing and television contracts as well as health benefits and season length. During the 130-day period, the owners essentially 'locked out' the players from team facilities. There was no free agency or training camp, and players were even restricted from communicating with coaches and doctors. The new CBA was agreed before the 2011 regular season, and football life resumed.

London organisers blamed the NFL lockout for the failure to sell out the 2011 International Series as the game was unconfirmed for a while and tickets were put on sale very late in the year – September rather than December of the previous year, as was tradition. Still, the game provided plenty of action for the marginally more intimate British crowd. The clash between the Bears and Buccaneers saw turnovers, penalties and fan-related antics – namely the overexcited fan that took to the field, ripped his shirt in half and high-fived players before being tackled to the turf by security guards. Chicago receiver Roy Williams summarised the atmosphere at the game particularly succinctly: 'We had a squirrel and a streaker on the field, so it was a great experience.'

The match at Wembley was the Bears' first match abroad since the 1997 American Bowl at Croke Park in Dublin, where they lost 30-17 to the Pittsburgh Steelers – but it didn't take long for Chicago to start on the front foot in London. Just over six minutes into the game, star running back Matt Forte followed up a 22-yard run to score an exhilarating 32-yard touchdown on the game's fifth play. The back burst to the right-hand side of the field and excellently weaved his way through the defence, almost juking Bucs defensive tackle Frank Okam back to Florida. 'When you get the opportunity to make a big play you've got to make the most of it,' said Forte. 'I've got to take advantage of every time I get into open field to make a play.'

A multi-faceted back, Forte arrived in London with a league-leading 908 combined yards rushing and receiving through the first six games of the year. Forte was the latest in a long line of great running backs to don the Bears jersey over the years, from Harold 'Red' Grange – a two-time All-Pro and two-time NFL champion – to the legendary Walter Payton, a five-time All-Pro, an MVP and the face of the historic 1985 Bears. While Forte wasn't quite the bruising force of Payton, he was a modern take on the position, as useful in the passing game as on the ground. His individual quality lived up to his franchise's famous name and stature within the sport: the Bears are one of two remaining franchises from the NFL's founding in 1920 along with the Arizona Cardinals, who were also originally from Chicago.

Forte helped the Bears return to form with two winning seasons in the three since he was drafted by the franchise in 2008 after just three such campaigns in the previous 12 years. While the Bears have tasted Super Bowl success just once, they have won more matches than any other NFL franchise in the league's history. Their lack of success, particularly in the modern era, has led to the franchise's overall decline in prominence, but the Bears are a powerful, influential team with an iconic name that has truly stood the test of time. When founders George Halas and Edward 'Dutch' Sternaman paid the $100 fee to officially own the rights to the Chicago team back in 1922 – a franchise worth an estimated $3.525 billion a century later – the small matter of what to name the team remained. Replicating the name of the city's baseball team was common practice, so Halas and Sternaman considered the Cubs to mirror the two-time World Series winners. However, Halas uttered a sentence that would change the course of the franchise forever: 'Football players are bigger than baseball players so, if baseball players are cubs, then football players must be bears.' In 1922, the franchise became the Chicago Bears we recognise today in name and in appearance, as Halas adopted the orange and blue colours of the University of Illinois.

With runs like the opening touchdown at Wembley, the Bears looked like the team of old. Unfortunately, the sentiment didn't last long, perhaps an all-too-familiar feeling for Chicago fans. Less than four minutes after Forte had found the end zone and the Bears defence had forced a punt, Cutler threw an interception. He panicked in the face of linebacker Geno Hayes and tossed a pass that ricocheted out the hands of running back Marion Barber and into the arms of Tanard Jackson. The safety collected the interception without breaking stride and took it all the way to the 12-yard line, giving the Bucs excellent field position to great applause from the Wembley faithful. The youthful Bucs immediately showed their inexperience on the very next play as Freeman was picked off by safety Chris Conte on his own two-yard line. The brief death of offensive football continued on the next snap as Forte was stopped in his tracks. The back bounced off a big hit from Quincy Black and the two-point safety was secured when Ronde Barber – a veteran cornerback of 15 years – wrapped up Forte and forced him down. It was a defensive play that reflected the culture of Tampa Bay's greatest season, nine years prior.

The play from Barber was a throwback to the Buccaneers defence that stood atop the NFL in 2002. While perhaps not as renowned as the Bears, the Buccaneers have a claim to plenty of history in their own right and have won two Super Bowls, one more than their 2011 opponents. The first success came in 2002, with the Bucs topping the Oakland Raiders to win Super Bowl XXXVII on the back of their excellent defence which featured a remarkable five All-Pro players including defensive tackle

Warren Sapp, safety John Lynch and Barber himself. The unit established themselves as one of the most potent pass defences ever seen and cemented their place in league history thanks to the 48-21 win over the Raiders. The Buccaneers therefore became the first team from the 1976 expansion to lift the Lombardi Trophy, beating out the Seattle Seahawks, who would taste success themselves in 2013.

The expansion of the NFL from 26 to 28 teams was agreed as part of the AFL–NFL merger of 1970, but it was not carried out until after the 1973 season. Tampa were the first city to receive an expansion franchise for $16m– some way off the fee paid by Halas and Dutch just over 50 years prior – and the team was awarded to Tom McCloskey, a construction owner from Philadelphia. McCloskey didn't agree to the finances surrounding the deal and backed out, so Hugh Culverhouse, a tax attorney from nearby Jacksonville, acted as owner from the Bucs' inception to his death in 1994. A name-the-team contest led to the branding of the franchise as the Buccaneers, referencing the pirates who often travelled around Florida's Gulf Coast during the 17th century. Not quite as epic as the immortal quote spoken by Halas of the Bears, but a cool allusion nonetheless.

Unlike the pirates from whom the Bucs take their name, Tampa Bay failed to conquer new lands on distant shores. Three punts followed the two-point safety before the Bears landed the next blow. In the second quarter, a seven-play drive culminated in Cutler throwing a deep pass to Roy Williams, with the receiver excellently collecting the pass on the turn. Williams was too fast for EJ Biggers and too strong for Sean Jones, powering through the defensive duo to score the touchdown and give the Bears a 14-2 lead. The Buccaneers improved to finish the first half in fine fashion themselves as Freeman completed six straight passes for 62 yards to ultimately take the Bucs to the Bears' 16 with four seconds left, and Connor Barth drilled the field goal to put offensive points on the board.

Tampa Bay failed to carry what little momentum they built before half-time into the third quarter. Freeman threw two incomplete passes either side of a Kregg Lumpkin run that was repelled and lost ground. The Bears kicked off their drive with Cutler immediately going after Bucs star corner Aqib Talib, throwing a deep pass down the middle to Johnny Knox for 23 yards. Forte took Chicago to the Tampa 12, and the defence far too easily allowed Barber to waltz into the end zone to make it 21-5.

Both franchises struggled offensively for the remainder of the third quarter. Freeman was intercepted for the second time in the game with a poor pass intended for Kellen Winslow. The play was easily read by linebacker Lance Briggs, whose return to the one-yard line was brought back following an illegal block penalty. Bears kicker Robbie Gould missed a 41-yard field goal wide right after both franchises punted and, just under five minutes later, Freeman was picked off for the third time when his pass to Winslow was nicked by Hall of Fame linebacker Brian Urlacher at Chicago's nine-yard line. If there was anything the London crowd could say they saw plenty of on that late autumnal night in 2011, it was interceptions. Twelve seconds after Freeman's erroneous throw, Cutler followed suit. Tampa's defensive end Michael Bennett had eased through protection and Cutler, under duress, threw an awful pass off his back foot into the clutches of safety Corey Lynch. Amid deteriorating hopes of an unlikely comeback, the throw reinvigorated the young Bucs.

The Bucs began their drive at the Chicago 21 following Lynch's interception return and four plays later the deficit had been reduced. Freeman picked out Winslow in the right-hand corner of the end zone to make it a ten-point game. After another Chicago punt, Freeman and the offence continued to roll downfield. Operating out of shotgun at the Bears' 24-yard line, Freeman evaded Julius Peppers and launched a terrific pass to Dezmon Briscoe for the touchdown. Suddenly, it was 21-18 with just over seven minutes remaining.

The Bears began their crucial drive. After earning a first down, Cutler hit Williams who juggled the ball but spectacularly brought it in for a 15-yard gain. When a false start penalty set the Bears back, Cutler threw a swing pass to Forte and, after collecting the ball at the line of scrimmage, he burst down the touchline before he was tackled by a combination of Elbert Mack and Sean Jones at the Tampa four-yard line. The Bears somehow couldn't find a way into the end zone as the Bucs held strong, so Gould extended Chicago's lead to 24-18 with two minutes remaining.

Despite three interceptions and a catalogue of errors, Tampa Bay were in control of their destiny at Wembley. A pair of passes took Freeman and co. into Chicago territory, 39 yards from the win. He lined up in shotgun formation for three straight plays, with the first two falling incomplete before the killer blow was struck. With 37 seconds remaining on third down, Freeman surveyed the field but Peppers – who tallied 159.5 sacks across a distinguished career – charged through the offensive line untouched before the quarterback could finish his reads. Freeman panicked and launched a pass towards Preston Parker, but DJ Moore was there to secure a fourth Chicago interception of the day and add another win to their record. 'I was pretty much where I was supposed to be,' Moore said. 'Ball is up for grabs, you go for it.' Moore snagged the pick and ran out of bounds, ensuring the Bears would return to the Windy City with a win.

It was a different story for the Buccaneers, who were dealt their second loss at Wembley in three years. It was a second defeat of the day for the Glazer family as the owners had taken a helicopter to London after watching their soccer team, Manchester United, suffer an excruciating 6-1 loss to rivals Manchester City at Old Trafford, United's home stadium. Red Devils defender Rio Ferdinand was scheduled to join the Glazers and take to the Wembley field as the Bucs' honorary captain, but he chose to stay home after the earlier embarrassment. It turned out to be a shrewd decision.

Freeman threw four interceptions and the Bucs lost one fumble for five total turnovers. 'The problem with us is we're too young,' coach Raheem Morris said after the game. 'We're foolish. There's no excuses, no explanations, no travel excuses, no time zone excuses, whatever you want to call it.' It seems the early flight to London was the wrong call, and it would get much worse for the team back in the States. After their impressive 4-2 start to go top of the NFC South, the Bucs didn't win a single game for the rest of the season. Their inexperience and naivety became horrifyingly apparent, with self-inflicted troubles – turnovers, penalties and generally bad defence – derailing their campaign. The defence ranked 30th in the NFL in total yards and the unit allowed the most points in the league, while Freeman tossed 22 interceptions – more than triple his total from the season before – a total that was second-worst across all quarterbacks.

The Bears improved to 4-3 with the London win. Forte showed off his class as he inspired the offence, and Urlacher, who played his entire legendary career in Chicago, heaped praise on his star team-mate: 'He's the best player in the NFL right now. The guy's a complete football player – production every week. You look at everything he's done this year and it's amazing.' Unfortunately, Forte's season ended prematurely in week 13 when he sprained his MCL in a 10-3 loss to the Kansas City Chiefs. Forte ended his 2011 campaign with 997 rushing yards, three rushing touchdowns, 490 receiving yards and one score through the air. He was named to the NFC Pro Bowl roster, becoming the first Bears running back to be named to the Pro Bowl since Neal Anderson in 1991.

Despite starting the season with a 7-3 record, the Bears would finish 1-5 to close a disappointing 8-8 season in which they missed the playoffs. This would kickstart a rather lengthy playoff drought for the franchise; they would not return to the postseason until

2018. All too brief flashes of quality aside, Chicago's football team have since certainly better resembled cubs than the bears they were expected to emulate.

2012

The GOAT Against the Rams

NFL REGULAR SEASON WEEK EIGHT
28 October 2012
NEW ENGLAND PATRIOTS 45
ST LOUIS RAMS 7
Wembley Stadium

OCTOBER 2012 was a landmark month in the relationship between the NFL and the United Kingdom. Amidst the hype and anticipation of the New England Patriots – defeated once again by the New York Giants, this time in Super Bowl XLVI – returning to London to face the St Louis Rams, the NFL announced it would play not one but two regular season games at Wembley in 2013. NFL UK's managing director Alistair Kirkwood was committed to growing the sport's popularity on this side of the Atlantic and have it stick around this time, rather than the trend of the 1980s. Naturally, rumours started to swirl regarding the possibility of a London-based franchise. Unlike the London Monarchs, this would be a team competing in the National Football League.

Ultimately, there was still a way to go. Ahead of the Rams' clash with the Patriots, quarterback Sam Bradford met budding young fans near Arsenal's training ground in an attempt to entice the next generation into following the other football. Bradford suddenly realised the enormity of the task he had ascribed himself. 'It was surprising just how little they knew about our game,' the St Louis quarterback said. 'Some of the kids, it was the first time they'd ever seen an American football.' While Bradford expressed shock at the lack of football knowledge among the British youth, Wembley was rocking on 28 October 2012.

The clash with the Rams was to be the 11th regular season game played outside of the United States in NFL history, following the five preceding London games. It was the second time the Patriots had played under the Wembley arch after their 35-7 drubbing of the Tampa Bay Buccaneers just over three years prior.

Both teams had experienced solid starts to the season. The Patriots sat at 4-3 after defeating the New York Jets while St Louis had just suffered a narrow 14-13 loss to the Green Bay Packers, their first home defeat of the season. Like the Bears and Buccaneers of the year before, the Patriots and Rams had differing plans for crossing the Atlantic to contest their clash. While New England arrived on the Friday, the Rams imitated the Bucs and landed on Tuesday to give themselves an extra three days to adjust to the time difference ahead of their Super Bowl XXXVI rematch in London. Unfortunately, the Rams appeared far more jet-lagged than their opponents and the final score was certainly more lopsided than the decade-old championship clash.

The Rams were already on the back foot before the game had even kicked off, as wide receiver Danny Amendola – who would win a pair of Super Bowl rings in New England as a favourite target of Tom Brady – was ruled out for the third straight game with a right shoulder injury. It didn't seem to affect Bradford and the Rams offence on the opening drive as short passes to Steven Jackson and Austin Pettis helped move the Rams to midfield against the favoured New England defence. Bradford faked a hand-off to running back Jackson and, with defensive pressure backing off, picked out Chris Givens to give the Rams an early 7-0 lead. For a brief, fleeting moment, the Rams looked like the Greatest Show on Turf – one of the elite offences in NFL history.

The comparisons between the 2012 Rams and the Greatest Show on Turf lasted one drive too many. 'You can't ask for a better start to the game. First time we touched the ball we go down and score,' Bradford said. 'It just all fell apart from there.' While St Louis enjoyed a fine start to the game, it was time for the Patriots to show the British public what the NFL's top-ranked offence looked like.

Although the nominal road team, the Patriots were certainly well supported by the 84,005 in attendance and the British fans made their presence known as New England marched downfield. In just eight plays, Brady covered 77 yards as short passes to the likes of Julian Edelman and Wes Welker were interchanged with rushes from Steven Ridley. The incisive drive was capped off with a score as Brady threw a strike to Brandon Lloyd for a 19-yard touchdown after the former Ram created separation from the leaky St Louis defence. Brady had extended his run of consecutive games with a touchdown pass to 40, the third-longest streak in NFL history behind Drew Brees and Jonny Unitas. Unitas', record stood at 47, while Brees was ongoing at 49. Brady's streak would end at 52 matches as the Patriots offence struggled against Cincinnati in 2013 with the legendary quarterback finishing two games shy of Brees's record of 54, which ended on Christmas Day against the Atlanta Falcons in 2012.

New England took control from that moment on. Brady surgically cut through the Rams defence with a mixture of short and intermediate passes combining perfectly with a stable run game; it was a microcosm of the Patriots' 20-year dynasty. After Brady picked out legendary tight end Rob Gronkowski – who would go on to win four Super Bowls and form the greatest quarterback–receiver tandem in NFL playoff history – for a second 25-yard gain of the drive, the Pats found themselves on the Rams' one-yard line. St Louis did their best to keep New England at bay, stopping two runs and forcing an incomplete pass to take it to fourth down but the Patriots were undeterred, and Shane Vereen found a gap to burst across the line and score. With under a minute played in the second quarter, New England led 14-7.

The Patriots soon scored again as they tried to put the game to bed before half-time. Starting on their own 22, New England romped to the end zone in nine plays, with Brady picking out Gronkowski on three passes: a 17-yard gain, a screen on third down that went for 32 yards, and a seven-yard touchdown dagger right down the middle of the pitch to increase the lead to 21-7. The enigmatic Gronkowski celebrated the touchdown by imitating a Buckingham Palace guard before doing his signature spike. 'That was a "Palace Guard", that little nutcracker dude that's guarding the house,' said Gronk of his celebration. Brady, though, wasn't the biggest fan of Gronkowski's end zone moves: 'I don't know what the hell he was doing on that first one. I was trying to get out of the way. He needs some work on that.'

As the Rams were trying to get their offence back on track, Bradford found some rhythm, spreading the ball to Jackson, Givens, Brandon Gibson, Daryl Richardson and Lance Kendricks to lead his team to the Patriots 35. Facing fourth down, head coach Jeff Fisher tried to play his trump card – and Pats mastermind Bill Belichick saw it coming. The Rams lined up in field goal formation and Jonny Hekker held the ball while kicker Greg Zuerlein sold an attempt as well as he could. The Pats defence was ready: three players swallowed the punter-turned-quarterback for a turnover on downs with two minutes remaining in the first half.

The Patriots wasted no time in scoring before the break. A combination of passes to Welker and Woodhead – as well as a pair of defensive pass interference penalties – allowed New England to cover 56 yards in nine plays. Ridley ran in a one-yard touchdown with just ten seconds remaining to make the half-time score read

28-7 in favour of the Patriots. It appeared they were the team deserving of the 'Greatest Show on Turf' tag.

It didn't get better for the sorry St Louis team in the second half. Immediately after receiving Zuerlein's second-half kick, Brady picked out his fullback Michael Hoomanawanui for an 18-yard gain while Ridley rushed for 30 yards to take the Pats to the Rams 32-yard line. Four plays later, Brady picked out Lloyd with a nine-yard score for his second touchdown reception of the game.

At 35-7, the Rams offence continued to be a sad imitation of what an attacking unit in the NFL should look like, with yet another three-and-out. While the Rams offence remained consistent in their inadequacy, the Pats stayed true to their excellence and immediately drove 58 yards to the Rams 35, allowing Stephen Gostkowski to kick a 53-yard field goal and increase the lead to 38-7.

The next two drives were particularly forgettable as the two franchises exchanged punts, with the Pats' punt actually being their first of the game with 2:36 left in the third quarter. New England returned to form soon after, moving 55 yards in six plays which was capped off by a 14-yard touchdown pass to Gronkowski to make it 45-7. The pass to the tight end was Brady's last piece of action in the Big Smoke as he was withdrawn for backup quarterback Ryan Mallett.

The Rams reached the Pats 25 on their next drive, but it ended in frustratingly predictable fashion as a wayward Bradford pass was picked off by cornerback Alfonzo Dennard. The Patriots punted with Mallett under centre, allowing the Rams to move to the New England 15 – but Rams backup quarterback Kellen Clemens, brought in for Bradford after head coach Fisher had seen enough, was intercepted by safety Tavon Wilson, who took it 45 yards to the Pats 46. Mallett took three knees to see out the clock and secure the win for New England, and he was booed as the British crowd clearly didn't appreciate the underwhelming climax. Pats head coach Bill Belichick typically didn't complain about the Wembley atmosphere: 'The stadium was great. Playing on grass is always good … It's good to see the jerseys muddy, grass stains. Guys picking up dirt out of their facemasks, stuff like that. We don't see a lot of that back in the States.'

New England became the first team to win multiple games in London. While it wasn't totally out of the blue, the Patriots certainly had the majority of the support inside the iconic stadium despite the Rams being the designated home team. The win ensured the Pats went into their bye week at 5-3, while St Louis sat at 3-5. New England were defensively sound, allowing just 326 total yards of Rams offence while forcing two interceptions, and they held St Louis to just three of nine on third down conversions. Brady threw for 304 yards and four touchdowns in the dominant display, two each to Lloyd and Gronkowski, who caught eight passes for 146 yards. Along with Ridley's 127 yards, New England had at least 350 yards of total offence for the 17th straight game, ironically breaking the NFL record set by the Kurt Warner-led Rams in 1999/2000 when the Hall of Famer quarterbacked the famous 'Greatest Show on Turf' offence.

The Patriots finished the 2012 season with a 12-4 record, earning a bye to the Divisional Round where they defeated the Houston Texans 41-28. Their quest to return to the Super Bowl ended at the final hurdle, losing to the eventual champions, the Baltimore Ravens, in the AFC Championship Game; the first time Brady had lost a home game when leading at half-time. As for the Rams, they went on to finish 7-8-1 to secure their sixth straight losing season and their ninth consecutive non-winning season since 2004.

The 2012 instalment to the International Series was monumental. It was the last time a single regular season match was played in London on an annual basis. From 2013 onwards, the NFL hosted at least two such games in London, which was quickly becoming a permanent and celebrated fixture on the league's calendar.

2013

Wembley Double-Header

NFL REGULAR SEASON WEEK FOUR
29 September 2013
PITTSBURGH STEELERS 27
MINNESOTA VIKINGS 34
Wembley Stadium

VIKINGS FIRST invaded British shores in AD 793, raiding the coastal island of Lindisfarne. The Norsemen remained until 1066, when William the Conqueror emerged from the Battle of Hastings triumphant. Fast forward to 2013, and Vikings were back in the United Kingdom, although they faced very different opposition in the Pittsburgh Steelers and this occupation only lasted a day.

The NFL-organised tailgate party proved to be a success, with the crowd arriving for food up to six hours before the game to soak in the atmosphere. Celebrities flocked to the game with the likes of former world heavyweight champion David Haye among a selection of Brits joining fans in attendance to cheer on Pittsburgh and Minnesota in London. Gene Simmons of Kiss sang a unique version of the American national anthem to kick off the pre-match festivities while Haye blew the Vikings' giant horn as the team ran onto the field. The crowd didn't seem to care that both teams came into the match winless after each carrying lofty preseason expectations, with the Steelers suffering a 40-23 home defeat at Heinz Field to the Chicago Bears while Minnesota's defence could not stop the Cleveland Browns in a 31-27 loss at the Mall of America field – not the best way to start the final season at the stadium before the franchise moved into the US Bank Stadium in 2016.

The 83,519 in attendance loudly cheered for the best players throughout, including Steelers quarterback Ben Roethlisberger and reigning NFL MVP Adrian Peterson. The savvy crowd cheered for lesser-known players, too – there was a rather loud 'Heath' chant following each of the six catches Pittsburgh tight end Heath Miller made. 'They were just full of energy,' Minnesota's Peterson said of the Brits. 'The fans were crazy. It was a great atmosphere to play in.'

With quarterback Christian Ponder ruled out due to injury, the Vikings named Matt Cassel as the starter in London and he got off to a productive start. On the Pittsburgh 38, Cassel launched a deep ball towards rookie receiver Cordarrelle Patterson. His pass appeared to be intercepted by Ike Taylor for the first turnover of the match, but Patterson showed an impressive football IQ to knock the ball loose from the cornerback's hands. As the drive stalled out, Blair Walsh thumped a 54-yard field goal through the uprights to give Minnesota a 3-0 lead.

Following a Pittsburgh punt, Cassel hit Jerome Simpson for a six-yard gain as the Vikings sat on their own 30. The quarterback signalled for a hitch route on third down, which would ordinarily earn a short gain to move the sticks, but Greg Jennings had other ideas. The receiver spectacularly spun past corner Cortez Allen and juked past a diving William Gay before bursting through the middle of the Pittsburgh defence after fellow receiver Jarius Wright made a crucial block. Jennings sprinted 70 yards to take the ball into the end zone, narrowly avoiding a last-ditch attempt to tackle him from legendary safety Troy Polamalu. The sensational touchdown would kick off Jennings's best outing in purple and gold since he joined from their bitter NFC North rivals, the Green Bay Packers, where he enjoyed success with both Brett Favre and Aaron Rodgers hurling him touchdown passes. On this September night in London, Cassel was playing like one of the greats Jennings was accustomed to – but this play was all about the receiver. 'You throw a five-yard hitch, and he goes 70 yards,' said Cassel. 'It makes your job a lot easier. Those guys made plays all night.' The spectacular play was Jennings's seventh 70-yard touchdown reception of his career, moving him one closer to Jerry Rice's all-time record of nine.

The Steelers responded perfectly as Roethlisberger used his bevvy of receiver talent, including Antonio Brown – a future two-time NFL leader in receptions and receiving yards – and Emmanuel Sanders, who hauled in a deep pass for a 36-yard gain. Pittsburgh got off the mark when rookie running back Le'Veon Bell scored on an eight-yard rush, juking around the outside before acrobatically diving over the pylon for the first touchdown of his career. It was Bell's debut for the Steelers after he was drafted in the second round of the 2013 NFL Draft and suffered a mid-foot sprain, an injury that kept him out of action for the first three weeks of the season. His spectacular somersault touchdown would give the Pittsburgh fans a taste of what was to come: Bell holds franchise records for the most scrimmage yards in a season (2,215 in 2014) as well as the most receiving yards by a running back (854 in 2014). More importantly, the Steelers had scored and reduced the deficit to 10-7.

After that whirlwind start, the two teams struggled to get going offensively before Peterson blew the roof off Wembley. On first down at their own 40, Peterson burst through a gap created by tackle Phil Loadholt and hurdled Taylor before using his incredible pace and power to burn away from the Pittsburgh defence. The crowd went wild, much to the 2012 MVP's delight: 'It was electric. There was a good mix of purple and yellow, but I think the purple trumped it. It felt like a home game.' Peterson had sprinted 70 yards to score and extend the Vikings' lead to 17-7, but his journey to get to this point – doing his trademark celebration in front of a packed Wembley Stadium – was far longer.

Some 646 days before the Vikings and Steelers clashed under the arch in London, Peterson suffered a torn ACL and MCL, an injury that traditionally derails or even prematurely ends the career of a running back. After a long offseason of rehabilitation, Peterson tallied 2,097 rushing yards and 12 touchdowns, becoming the seventh player to eclipse 2,000 rushing yards in a single season. Peterson was named NFL Most Valuable Player for his heroics, becoming the first running back to win the award since LaDainian Tomlinson in 2006. After the season concluded, Peterson underwent surgery for a sports hernia and it was reportedly known he had played through the injury for at least a quarter of the season. Ahead of the clash with Pittsburgh in London, the superhuman MVP was trying to prove he could get it done on both sides of the Atlantic – and he did exactly that.

After Peterson's incredible touchdown, Shaun Suisham dragged the Steelers back within a touchdown as he sunk a 26-yard field goal before Walsh nailed a 37-yard attempt to make it 20-10 at half-time.

In the third quarter, Big Ben – Roethlisberger, not the clock tower – got the offence rolling with short passes to Sanders and Jerricho Cotchery. Roethlisberger then went deep down the middle and Brown looked set to haul it in for a touchdown when Minnesota corner Josh Robinson tripped him from behind. Flags were thrown in abundance; the penalty moved the Steelers to the Minnesota one-yard line, and Bell would not be denied. The rookie burst through a gap created by guard David DeCastro to score and make it 20-17. However, Pittsburgh's defence – a unit heralded in league lore as being particularly indomitable – was uncharacteristically leaky in the Big Smoke. Cassel threw a deep pass into the clutches of Simpson, and the sixth-year receiver –

who found viral fame when he flipped over a defender to score a touchdown while playing for the Cincinnati Bengals – burst forwards to complete a 51-yard gain for Minnesota. Peterson then rushed for four successive plays, and he excellently juked inside Polamalu to waltz into the end zone for a seven-yard touchdown, pushing the lead to 27-17.

Minnesota were back in control of possession just four plays later as Roethlisberger missed receiver Sanders and fired a pass into the grateful arms of linebacker Chad Greenway. An unnecessary roughness penalty against LaMarr Woodley took the Vikings to the Pittsburgh 16, and Cassel responded as he faked a pass before throwing a dart to Jennings, who leaped into the air to score and make the lead 34-17. Like the warriors of centuries past, the Vikings were conquering abroad.

The Steelers weren't quite done yet, though. With just under 13 minutes remaining, Roethlisberger completed a nine-yard drive by picking out Cotchery to stroll into the end zone. The Vikings then settled for a field goal but Walsh sliced his 44-yard effort wide left to the dismay of British fans. On the following drive, Roethlisberger led a series of short plays to advance to the Minnesota 11 before it stalled out. Up stepped Suisham and, unlike Walsh, he didn't fluff his lines. He thumped the 28-yard chip shot down the middle to make it a one-score game.

The Steelers defence then forced a punt, giving their team one final chance to tie the game. Starting the crucial drive on their own 22 with 1:43 left and no timeouts, Roethlisberger diced the Minnesota defence, completing six passes to Cotchery, Brown and Miller to reach the six-yard line before spiking the ball and stopping the clock. On third down with 19 seconds remaining, Minnesota came up with the game-clinching play as Roethlisberger was sacked by Everson Griffen – the fifth sack on the day by the Vikings defence – to force a fumble that was scooped up by defensive tackle Kevin Williams. Seconds later, 'Purple Rain' by Prince blasted from the speakers around

Wembley Stadium while players clad in purple embraced. Their trip to Britain was a success.

Jennings and Peterson proved to be key for Minnesota as each player scored a pair of touchdowns to help the previously winless Vikings to a 34-27 victory. The 2012 MVP ran for 140 yards on 23 carries while Jennings collected three passes for 92 yards. 'It would have been a long flight back to take after a loss,' the wideout, signed in the offseason, said. 'To do this at Wembley Stadium is a once in a lifetime experience.' Cassel finished with 16 completed passes on 25 attempts for 248 yards and two touchdowns to go with zero turnovers – a statement of intent as he eyed usurping Ponder on a permanent basis. Head coach Leslie Frazier spoke highly of London following the win: 'I think I'll always have a special place in my heart for Wembley Stadium. With all the noise, we felt at times like we were back at home.' The Vikings struggled in 2013, finishing bottom of the NFC North with a record of 5-10-1 while Cassel would go on to start nine games as Ponder suffered from recurring injuries.

As for the Steelers, Roethlisberger finished with 383 yards as well as a touchdown and an interception apiece – and the exasperated quarterback was not happy: 'We are in uncharted territories and the water is dangerous right now, so we have to stick together and get out of it. Right now, you could say we're the worst team in the league. That hurts.' While Pittsburgh may not have been the worst of the 32 NFL franchises, his words rang true to a certain extent. The Steelers were off to their worst start to a season since the AFL–NFL merger; the last time they went 0-4 was back in 1968 when they recorded six games without a win. The franchise had contested three of the previous eight Super Bowls, but their defensive unit – traditionally dubbed the 'Steel Curtain' – were yet to force a turnover on the season. Their struggles were summarised when Cassel fumbled in the second quarter, and the ball was somehow recovered by receiver Simpson for a ten-yard gain. The Steelers would come out swinging after their bye week, winning five of their following seven matches before finishing the season 8-8 to narrowly miss out on a playoff berth.

The two teams that had arrived in London winless – a fact that threatened to quash the pre-match hype among domestic media outlets – put on a touchdown-filled, big-play spectacle in a game that has gone down in the annals of history as one of the great clashes of the International Series thus far, if not the best. The best part for British fans? There was another game to come in 2013.

NFL REGULAR SEASON WEEK EIGHT
27 October 2013
SAN FRANCISCO 49ERS 42
JACKSONVILLE JAGUARS 10
Wembley Stadium

For British American football fans, a second NFL regular season match in London sounded like a dream. For Jaguars fans residing in Florida, it was a very different story.

The Jacksonville Jaguars are a relatively new NFL franchise. An expansion team in 1995, the Jaguars surpassed all expectations and left their mark on the league immediately, bouncing back from a 4-12 inaugural campaign to reach the playoffs in each of the next four seasons – including an AFC Championship appearance in just their second year – and capped the run with a 1999 record of 14-2. They continued to impress in the postseason, crushing the Miami Dolphins in the Divisional Round with a 62-7 win before falling in the AFC Championship Game to the Tennessee Titans. It was the Jags' second defeat in four years at the final hurdle before the Super Bowl, and they have reached the playoffs just three times since. In 2012, Shahid Khan became the first foreign-born owner of an NFL franchise when he purchased the Jaguars for $770m (a wise investment given the franchise is now valued at $2.8bn) and followed that up by buying Fulham

FC a year later. The stage was set for Khan, who grew up in Pakistan, to focus on the international development of the game; he wanted to stimulate British interest in the NFL by promoting the Jaguars in London.

Naturally, this irked fans in Jacksonville but Khan had a plan. The franchise offered free beer to ticket holders back in Florida, but the promotion didn't exactly work: going into the week eight clash with the 49ers in London, the Jaguars were ranked 29th in attendance across the league. Khan, undeterred by the faltering home attendances, insisted the London market would boost support for the Jaguars. 'Everybody needs to understand that playing games in London is very, very important for Jacksonville and very important for this franchise,' Khan said after announcing the long-term commitment to the International Series. 'We need fans, we need corporate sponsors ... London is the missing piece.' Khan had already used the Fulham connection to promote the Jaguars in the city; the Jags' cheerleaders performed during one of the Cottagers' matches while a British lingerie company even created a calendar for them. Khan was pulling out the stops, and support for his team was growing: the new Union Jax Jaguars fan club in Britain had around 17,000 members ahead of their clash at Wembley.

The players themselves were certainly not against the idea of playing in London. Will Blackmon, a defensive back for the Jags who would become an analyst for Sky Sports' NFL coverage in the UK, explained why players were able to justify the loss of a home game back in the States: 'It was business as usual. I understand the fans were upset because they cannot go unless they plan accordingly. Maybe logistically it was a pain in the butt, but there were a lot of guys on our team who had never been outside the country and very few players can say they actually played in an international American football game.'

Khan proved his long-term commitment to Jacksonville in the summer of 2013. He struck an agreement with the city for $63m worth of renovations to its home stadium, EverBank Field. A small caveat to the deal: Khan would spend just $20m of his own money, while the rest fell on the city of Jacksonville. It appeared that Khan was failing to appease the domestic fans even in committing to the city for the foreseeable future, but international expansion was the true apple of his eye. It was a bold strategy that would only truly pay off if the British audience were not subjected to the football the Jaguars were playing on the other side of the Atlantic. The 49ers did not get the memo.

Even with the worryingly high probability of a blowout San Francisco win and an alarming threat of gale-force winds, 83,559 fans happily went to the match at Wembley – and only one of the 31 NFL stadiums in the US had a larger attendance up to that point in the 2013 season. It proved the International Series' expansion had certainly not diluted the British appetite for American football. The Jags were ready fot the first instalment of a four-year deal to play in Britain, and they had plenty of support even against a famous franchise like the 49ers; large sections of the crowd aggressively waved their giveaway Jags flags throughout the contest. Once again, there was an incredibly diverse representation among fans. From NFL Europe jerseys like the London Monarchs to the standard 32 NFL franchises as well as the variety of accents at the tailgate party, the NFL had certainly succeeded in making the International Series exactly what it is: international. Questions remained over the possibility of a London franchise in the future, but at least the fanbase was proving to be passionate.

The Jaguars came into the game winless at 0-7. An opening day 28-2 defeat to the Kansas City Chiefs set the tone and, after losing to the San Diego Chargers a week before crossing the Atlantic, the Jaguars possessed a depressing points differential of -178. The 49ers, who defeated the Denver Broncos at London's iconic soccer stadium back in 2010, were back for round two. They arrived with a record of 5-2 and since San Francisco's 27-7 defeat to the Indianapolis Colts in week three, they had won four straight games by an aggregate score of 132-51. The franchise brought good-luck charms from the past to inspire further success in London, naming their former quarterback and four-time Super Bowl champion Joe Montana and receiver Dwight Clark as honorary captains – the duo that pulled off 'The Catch' at Candlestick Park to dramatically defeat the Dallas Cowboys in the 1981 NFC Championship Game.

The 49ers predictably got off to a flying start. On the second play of the match, San Francisco quarterback Colin Kaepernick picked out fullback Bruce Miller running down the right sideline for a 43-yard gain. With the team already in Jacksonville territory, Frank Gore rushed 19 yards into the end zone to cap an eight-play, 76-yard drive and give the 49ers a 7-0 lead. A dual-threat quarterback, equally dangerous with his legs as with his arm, Kaepernick had struggled since leading his side to an opening-week win over the Green Bay Packers with 444 all-purpose yards. After Gore's brief moment in the spotlight, the 26-year-old dominated the Jaguars. After a Jags punt, Kaepernick spectacularly scored on a quarterback run as he wheeled left and dived for the pylon to extend the lead to 14-0 with 2:36 left in the first quarter.

A quick three-and-out for the hapless Jags put the ball back in Kaepernick's hands, and the quarterback used his legs to rush 17 yards and set the 49ers up on the 16 before he picked out Anquan Boldin for a 14-yard gain. Kaepernick then found tight end Vernon Davis on a play action pass for the third touchdown of the day to make the score 21-0. Kaepernick wasn't done there; deep passes to Davis for 31 and 19 yards respectively took the 49ers downfield. Two plays later, another fake hand-off allowed Kaepernick to outsprint the Jags defence and power into the end zone himself. Khan may have wanted to inspire a British fanbase, but now they were beginning to understand the plight of Jacksonville fans as they bore witness to a 28-0 shellacking – and the dynamic San

The Tea Bowl saw Pte Frank Dombrowski (left) and Maj Denis Whitaker (right) lead the United States and Canada respectively amid World War Two at White City Stadium in February 1944.

The Fürstenfeldbruck Eagles celebrate scoring the first ever touchdown at Wembley Stadium en route to their win over the Burtonwood Bullets in the 1952 USAFE Football League Final.

Iconic Chicago Bears running back Walter Payton was the star name when the Super Bowl champions arrived in London to contest the 1986 American Bowl.

The London Ravens, donning their famous black and yellow attire, were the first British American football club.

WLAF president Mike Lynn posing with the helmets of the ten teams ahead of the inaugural draft in Orlando, Florida in 1991.

Former Chicago Bear William 'The Refrigerator' Perry signed for the London Monarchs in an attempt to boost ticket sales in 1996.

Scotland's former national rugby captain Gavin Hastings kicks an extra point in the Scottish Claymores' win over the London Monarchs to open the 1996 WLAF season.

Quarterback Eli Manning scores the first touchdown at Wembley Stadium in 2007 as the New York Giants defeated the Miami Dolphins in the first ever regular season game outside of the United States.

New England Patriots quarterback Tom Brady touched down in London against the Tampa Bay Buccaneers – his future team – in 2009.

The 2019 International Series clash between the Chicago Bears and Oakland Raiders marked the debut of the Tottenham Hotspur Stadium, the first purpose-built NFL arena outside of North America.

Atlanta Falcons rookie Kyle Pitts – the highest drafted tight end in NFL history - gets both feet down to score the first touchdown in London since 2019 due to the pandemic.

Bobby Howfield, the first British player in NFL history, went from scoring goals for the likes of Fulham and Watford to kicking field goals for the Denver Broncos and New York Jets.

Osi Umenyiora lifted the Lombardi Trophy for the first time after a 17-14 win for the New York Giants over the New England Patriots in Super Bowl XLII.

Efe Obada was the honorary captain for the Carolina Panthers when he returned to London for the 2019 International Series.

Francisco quarterback was the architect of the Jaguars' culling. His praises were sung by his opponents on that fateful October day, as Jags linebacker Paul Posluszny stated: 'Kaepernick is a stud athlete and he showed it again tonight.' While the quarterback let his gridiron ability do the talking against the Jags under the iconic Wembley arch, it was his actions off the field three years later that made Kaepernick a household name around the world.

Ahead of the 49ers' third preseason game in 2016, Kaepernick sat during the traditional playing of the national anthem, rather than standing as expected. It was not the first time Kaepernick had sat during the anthem, but rather the first time it had truly been noticed. 'I am not going to show pride in a flag for a country that oppresses black people and people of colour,' Kaepernick told reporters after the game as he explained his protest against racial injustice, police brutality and systematic oppression around the country. 'To me, this is bigger than football and it would be selfish on my part to look the other way. There are bodies in the street and people getting paid leave and getting away with murder.' His stance received immense publicity, with the 49ers releasing a statement acknowledging the right of the individual to choose whether to participate in the anthem or not.

Former Seattle Seahawk and Green Beret Nate Boyer penned an open letter to Kaepernick from a military perspective, and the quarterback decided to change his method of protest from sitting to kneeling during the anthem after the two met in person a day earlier. The protests were polarising, with some tremendously praising his stand while others denounced and condemned his actions. Kaepernick ignited a movement, which intensified in September 2017 – over a year since he first kneeled – when President Donald Trump claimed NFL owners should 'fire' players that protest during the anthem. When Kaepernick became a free agent after the 2016 season, he received no offers from other teams, leading analysts and reporters to believe he was being 'blackballed' due to his political statements rather than his on-field performances. Statistics website *FiveThirtyEight* investigated and, in August 2017, concluded the quarterback was a victim of occupational injustice: 'It's obvious Kaepernick is being frozen out for his political opinions … [it is] extraordinary … that a player like him can't find a team … no above-average quarterback [measured by the total quarterback rating] has been unemployed nearly as long as Kaepernick this offseason.'

After Kaepernick withdrew his grievance against the league and its owners, accusing them of colluding to keep him out of the NFL, the support for Kaepernick's cause was still great. Kaepernick's stance was placed back in the public eye after the George Floyd protests against police brutality and racism, with the NFL commissioner offering a statement in its wake: 'We, the National Football League, admit we were wrong for not listening to NFL players earlier, and encourage all to speak out and peacefully protest.' Goodell was criticised for not specifically naming Kaepernick, and the quarterback remains unsigned by any professional team at the time of writing.

Back at Wembley, the Jacksonville Jaguars got points on the board before half-time as Josh Scobee nailed a 38-yard field goal in the closing seconds to make the score 28-3. Ultimately, Khan and his shadow of Jaguars had as much to cheer about in London as they did in Jacksonville.

The Jaguars suffered a turnover on downs on the 49ers' six-yard line after driving 78 yards in 15 plays to open the third quarter, only for San Francisco to make their first error. Gore went to rush to the right but fumbled once he reached the line of scrimmage after defensive end Jason Babin knocked the ball loose, with outside linebacker Russell Allen recovering possession for Jacksonville. This presented the Jaguars with easily their best chance to score a touchdown and mount a sensational comeback – and quarterback Chad Henne obliged on the first order (I am mentioning the name of Jacksonville's quarterback for the first time with three minutes remaining in the third quarter, which should provide an indication of how terrible the Jaguars were). Henne ripped a 29-yard touchdown pass to Mike Brown to make the score 28-10. For domestic Jaguars fans back in the States who had sat through three home games without witnessing a Jacksonville player breach the end zone, seeing the team score 4,259 miles away may have hurt. 'This year hasn't gone the way we wanted it to but at the same time we're going to continue to work,' running back Maurice Jones-Drew declared. 'When it is turned around, it's going to make it that much better because you know how far you've come.' Jones-Drew would get released by the Jags at the end of the season, and he signed for the Oakland Raiders where he played one 3-13 season before retiring.

Kyle Williams returned the kick-off 47 yards to give San Francisco excellent field position. Running back Kendall Hunter burst around the left end and embarked on a 41-yard rush, going out of bounds at the Jacksonville 13. It was Gore's turn to try and reach the end zone, and the legendary back took it a further 11 yards closer to the target on two rushes. Third time proved to be the charm: Gore burst through the frail Jacksonville defensive wall to score his second touchdown of the match. With just over a quarter to go, it was 35-10 in London.

The final nail in the Jacksonville coffin came on the very next drive. Henne completed a six-yard pass to Marcedes Lewis, but the tight end was stripped by San Francisco's hard-hitting defensive star Patrick Willis. The loose ball was scooped up by fellow linebacker Dan Skuta, and the 27-year-old showed off quick feet and evasive running before bundling through Henne to score the defensive touchdown. The game ended in uninspiring circumstances, with the Jaguars embarking on a 17-play drive that lasted over eight minutes before it stalled at the San Francisco four-yard line. The 49ers received possession with five minutes remaining and they held possession to secure the victory.

Kaepernick was the star of the show in London, rushing for a pair of touchdowns and throwing another as the 49ers picked up their fifth straight win of the season. While he wasn't as dominant in the air, he passed for just 164 yards, Kaepernick's performance on the ground – 54 yards rushing – proved to be highly effective when complemented by Gore and Hunter, who finished with 71 and 84 yards respectively. 'He looked like a running back, and that's great courage,' 49ers head coach Jim Harbaugh said of Kaepernick. The 49ers would enjoy a productive season, finishing 12-4 before defeating the Packers and Carolina Panthers in the playoffs. Their campaign would end at the hands of the eventual Super Bowl champion Seattle Seahawks in the NFC Championship Game, falling 23-17 at CenturyLink Field.

The Jaguars took a gamble in signing a four-year deal to play home games in London, and their first trip went about as poorly as the reaction to Khan's original announcement. They were irrelevant offensively and defensively fragmented as the 49ers dominated. The Jaguars were in a deep, deep rut – and their head coach knew it. 'We can take the time to evaluate where we are at with our whole team and recommit to take the next step,' commented Gus Bradley. At 0-8, the Jaguars had a lot to sift through, but they bounced back to top the Titans 29-27 in Tennessee on their next outing. A brief run of four wins in five weeks lifted spirits before three straight losses condemned Jacksonville to a 4-12 record.

The burgeoning relationship between the NFL and the UK was assessed ahead of the 2014 season. The league announced there would be three games at Wembley the following campaign, with the Jaguars welcoming the famous Dallas Cowboys to town. While the result against the 49ers was far from ideal, Jags linebacker Posluszny enjoyed the occasion and spectacle, insisting he was ready to return 12 months later to do it all again: 'It was one of the best NFL atmospheres I've ever been a part of. If Mr [Shahid] Khan says, "Paul, we're playing in London," I'm going to say, "Yes, sir, and I can't wait to get there."'

2014

The Trilogy

NFL REGULAR SEASON WEEK FOUR
28 September 2014
MIAMI DOLPHINS 38
OAKLAND RAIDERS 14
Wembley Stadium

WHEN THE Miami Dolphins and Oakland Raiders landed in London, they brought plenty of baggage with them. The Dolphins had opened the 2014 campaign on the front foot, with third-year quarterback Ryan Tannehill leading his offence to 33 points against Tom Brady and the New England Patriots in Florida, but the Dolphins struggled on the road in week two, falling to the Buffalo Bills 29-10 before returning to Miami for the visit of the Kansas City Chiefs. Tannehill struggled to unlock the Chiefs defence, throwing for 205 yards and a touchdown on a 49 per cent completion rate as the Dolphins suffered a disappointing 34-15 home defeat.

The crushing loss ignited several controversies before the team even boarded their transatlantic flight. Head coach Joe Philbin refused to publicly name Tannehill as the starting quarterback, despite the 24-year-old insisting the coach had privately confirmed he would start. It was a chaotic move by

Philbin, and he publicly apologised: 'One of the functions of the head coach is to create an atmosphere free from distractions. To the degree that I contributed to any of those distractions, intended or not doesn't really matter. That falls on me.' Regardless of the sincerity of his statement, discontent was rife within the Miami camp. There were reports of disharmony on both sides of the ball, as defensive players were reportedly upset with coaching methods. As a sign of solidarity, coaches gave their first-class seats to some players on the flight over – maybe the added comfort could lead to success on the field.

The Raiders arrived in London winless, losing to the New York Jets, Houston Texans and New England Patriots to kick their 2014 season off. Oakland had pieces in place: rookie Khalil Mack – who would go on to be named 2016 NFL Defensive Player of the Year and become a perennial All-Pro – and first-year quarterback Derek Carr had impressed considering the Raiders roster was far from competitive. They finished the 2013 season with a 4-12 record to sit bottom of the AFC West and secure the fifth overall pick used to select Mack. For the Raiders, it appeared their issues lay at the helm as head coach Dennis Allen had won just eight times during his 35 games in charge of the famous franchise. It was not good enough, and the pressure was on to secure a win at Wembley Stadium. Recent history did not bode well for him or the Raiders: Oakland had lost 15 straight games in the Eastern time zone, but perhaps they would fare better in British Summer Time.

The Raiders reached London earlier in the week, allowing players to teach children how to play the sport. Around 150 children gathered to take part at an NFL Play 60 event, learning from 11 Raiders players and the Raiderette cheerleaders. Players were used to taking part in such events back in the States as the NFL had implemented a new initiative to underline the importance of being outside and physically active for an hour each day. 'I was surprised the kids knew who we were,' receiver Andre

Holmes admitted. 'The product here on the field looks more like rugby, but that's alright.' Offensive lineman Kevin Boothe, who came to London with the New York Giants in 2007, was hopeful of the sport's future on these shores: 'These kids are very enthusiastic and most know about the basics of football already.'

The players and fans in attendance, including legendary Dolphins quarterback Dan Marino, were ready for the 2014 slate of International Series games to get underway. This was the first time three regular season games were to be hosted in London, with the NFL gearing up interest to attract British fans. For the match, Manchester-born star Menelik Watson – a British offensive lineman – was announced as the Raiders' honorary captain, and his team flew out the blocks in style.

On the very first play from scrimmage, Carr threw a dime up the right sideline which receiver James Jones hauled in with one hand for a 30-yard gain. After marching downfield, the winless Raiders took the lead when Carr faked the hand-off to Darren McFadden and picked out tight end Brian Leonhardt for the touchdown. Sebastian Janikowski kicked the extra point, so at least the Raiders were getting more use out of the kicker who was extraordinarily selected 17th overall in 2000.

You read that correctly: in the 2000 NFL Draft, the Raiders selected Janikowski – affectionately known as 'Seabass' – with their first-round pick. Born in Poland to a professional soccer player father, kicking was in Janikowski's blood and he even allegedly made an 82-yard field goal while at Seabreeze High School in Daytona Beach. From an organisation's perspective, it required guts to select a kicker in the first round of a draft and the move required the backing of owner Al Davis. David Shaw, who worked as quality control for the Raiders between 1998 and 2000, shed light on the decision: 'As hard as it was at the time, we were making a decision to play field position … there has never been a guy like this. He's 260lbs that likes to hang out on Bourbon Street and just bomb kick-offs and field goals. This is the perfect

Raider ever.' Janikowski played for the Raiders for 18 seasons before spending his final campaign in Seattle, and he holds a number of NFL records, including the most field goals of over 50 yards. Seabass even attempted the longest field goal attempt in league history at a frankly ridiculous 76 yards. Just kick, baby.

It got ugly for Oakland in London after their first-drive score. Tannehill and running back Lamar Miller took the Dolphins downfield, allowing Caleb Sturgis to make a 41-yard field goal to reduce the deficit to just four points. Oakland's Kaluka Maiava – the linebacker who started in place of the absent Sio Moore – picked up an injury on Miami's opening drive, so Tannehill and his receivers took advantage using short inside passes. Tannehill blew through Oakland's defence with six completions on a seven-play drive, including a beautiful 35-yard ball to Brian Hartline. The sixth completion found receiver Mike Wallace, who took it 13 yards for the touchdown.

The combination of Tannehill and a running game carried by Daniel Thomas and Miller took the Dolphins to the Oakland nine-yard line. If the Raiders thought Philbin and the Dolphins would show mercy and kick the points on fourth down they were gravely mistaken, as Tannehill pitched the ball to Miller. With the help of excellent blocking, Miller shook off tackles to score and extend Miami's lead to ten points at 17-7.

Another Raiders drive ended prematurely with a punt before they had even moved the sticks, but they were granted temporary respite when Landry, Miami's rookie return specialist out of LSU, fumbled the punt. Landry's error came after a big hit from Leonhardt, and long snapper Jon Condo recovered the ball. Unfortunately, the Raiders once again failed to pick up a first down as Carr was penalised for intentional grounding, sending his team back 17 yards. Marquette King punted the ball deep into Miami territory, but Tannehill saw starting at his own ten-yard line as a challenge. He picked out Charles Clay, Brandon Gibson and Hartline while also using his legs to drive the Dolphins to the Oakland 18. On second down, Tannehill once again utilised the play action and the Raiders bit on the fake, allowing the quarterback to throw a perfect touchdown strike to Dion Sims and make the score 24-7 at half-time. On this September day, the autumn wind was certainly not a Raider.

'The Autumn Wind' is a sports-themed poem adapted from the 'Pirate Wind' written by Mary Jane Carr, and it defines the Raiders organisation. NFL Films president and co-founder Steve Sabol, son of Ed who founded the company, was charged with the honour of relating it to the NFL. It was quickly adopted by the Raiders who blare the anthem out at home matches, with the stirring ending:

The Autumn Wind is a raider,
Pillaging just for fun.
He'll knock you 'round and upside down,
And laugh when he's conquered and won.

The poem was officially adopted by the team in 1974 when the film of the same title recapped the 1974 season, which ended in defeat to the Pittsburgh Steelers in the AFC Championship Game. Rumour has it that when Raiders owner Davis heard the song for the first time, he sat in silence before uttering to Ed Sabol that it captured everything the iconic Raiders stood for, from a dedicated fanbase and distinctive culture to legendary head coach John Madden.

Unfortunately for British Raider fans, a lot of words could be used to describe the 2014 team and iconic was not one of them. Three plays after Charles Woodson had recovered a fumble for the Raiders, Miami were back in possession deep inside Oakland territory when Carr was picked by Brent Grimes for the Dolphins' first interception of the season. The corner jumped inside McFadden and juked his way past several players to take the ball to the Oakland three-yard line. It took him two attempts, but Miller finally reached the end zone to score his second touchdown of the game to make it 31-3 midway through the third quarter.

Things went from bad to worse when Carr injured both his left ankle and knee on the following drive. Matt McGloin was Oakland's third-string quarterback, only receiving the call to take to the field after backup Matt Schaub didn't fly to London. McGloin completed a short pass to McFadden on his first play, but the second encapsulated the Raiders' miserable adventure to London: a bad snap fired below the bamboozled signal-caller's clutches, and Miami corner Cortland Finnegan was on hand to scoop up the ball and return it 50 yards to the house.

McGloin shortly added an interception to his undesirable box score as he was picked by Jimmy Wilson. Miami did little with possession; offensive penalties sent the Dolphins back before Tannehill was intercepted by TJ Carrie. McGloin would throw a 22-yard touchdown pass to Holmes to reduce the score to 38-14, but it was over. The Dolphins had won to improve their record at Wembley Stadium to 1-1 following their 2007 loss to the Giants.

Tannehill took advantage of a depleted Oakland defence to run riot in London, consistently turning short passes into large gains as he completed 23 of 31 attempts for 278 yards and two touchdowns – a fine riposte to the controversy surrounding him coming into London. Miami head coach Philbin insisted Tannehill had displayed good rhythm and command as the pre-match shenanigans were laid to rest. Tannehill led the Dolphins to victory and Wallace, who hauled in the seventh touchdown in his last ten games, insisted his team were ready to move on from the controversy: 'I don't know if it was coach's intention, but it worked!'

The Dolphins would ultimately end the season 8-8, finishing third in the AFC East behind the 9-7 Buffalo Bills and the New England Patriots, whose 12-4 record would secure the first seed in the AFC. Brady and co. would go on to win Super Bowl XLIX against the Seattle Seahawks thanks to Malcolm Butler's famous last-gasp interception.

As for the Raiders, defeat in London was their tenth straight loss dating back to the previous season. In front of an international crowd that was predominantly filled with silver and black, Oakland struggled on both sides of the ball. 'Obviously, we did not play well,' Allen said. 'We turned the ball over; we did not stop them on defence. We gave up too many explosive plays.' The team slipped to 0-10 – a run of 16 straight defeats – before they picked up their first win of the campaign as they defeated the Kansas City Chiefs 24-20 at home before finishing 3-13. They would use their fourth overall selection in the 2015 NFL Draft on wideout Amari Cooper, who would go on to have greater success at the Dallas Cowboys.

NFL REGULAR SEASON WEEK EIGHT
26 October 2014
DETROIT LIONS 22
ATLANTA FALCONS 21
Wembley Stadium

In the earliest match start in NFL history, the Detroit Lions' win over the Atlanta Falcons was ironically defined by its dramatic late stages. With four seconds to go, Detroit kicker Matt Prater missed a 43-yard field goal as his shot sailed wide right – but a fortunate delay-of-game penalty gave him a second chance. From 48 yards out, Prater nailed the game-winner and secured a road win over Atlanta after the Lions trailed 21-0 at half-time.

The teams came into this clash with contrasting fortunes. With a 5-2 record, the Lions were the leading team in the NFC North, although Jim Caldwell's side suffered an unlikely defeat to the lowly Buffalo Bills three weeks before boarding the flight to London. As for the Falcons, four straight losses left their season hanging by a thread at 2-5 but their playoff hopes were still alive as the NFC South was in dismal shape and no team held a winning record through seven weeks of the season.

On paper, this was hardly a tussle between two historic NFL heavyweights. The franchises had a single Super Bowl appearance between them, when John Elway led the Denver Broncos to victory over the Falcons in Super Bowl XXXIII. Regardless, there was a fun piece of history for the British fans to savour – this was the earliest-ever start for an NFL game. Matches are traditionally played at 1pm EST, which the London games matched by kicking off at 6pm GMT. However, the clash between the Falcons and the Lions kicked off at 1:30pm GMT, meaning fans on America's East Coast tuned in at 9:30am while Pacific coast viewers were forced to set their alarms for a brutal 6:30am start. Fans would simply have to put on a stronger pot of coffee and it was easy like Sunday morning, but the early start did mean the match clashed with church services. They say football is a religion in the state of Georgia; Reverend Bill Britt from Peachtree Road United Methodist Church in Atlanta certainly blurred the lines between the two as he organised to show the match in the church hall between services.

Some 4,197 miles away at Wembley Stadium, the Lions arrived in London with the league's best defence, but Ryan picked it apart with consummate ease as he threw for 160 yards and a pair of touchdowns in the first half alone to the delight of the 83,532 in attendance. On the opening drive, Ryan completed five of six passes to the likes of Julio Jones and Roddy White – a pair of Hall of Fame-calibre receivers – to take the Falcons downfield before he found Devonta Freeman for the opening score, a seven-yard touchdown. Stafford and the Lions tried to respond as the quarterback hit receiver Golden Tate for a pair of completions to move the sticks, but a holding penalty against offensive guard Rob Sims ultimately condemned Detroit to a punt on their opening drive.

Ryan came back in the first quarter, taking the Falcons to the Detroit 21. The veteran signal-caller looked for White in the end zone, but a pass interference call against corner Darius Slay moved the Falcons to the one-yard line. Ryan faked the give to bruising running back Steven Jackson and threw to a wide-open Bear Pascoe, who had employed a form of deception himself as he pretended to block before rushing to the back of the end zone where he collected the pass with both feet in bounds. Suddenly, the Lions found themselves 14-0 down inside the first quarter. Detroit's defence had been so effective in rushing the quarterback through the first seven weeks, but Ryan's quick release ensured the Falcons burst into a two-score lead. Former England captain Andrew Strauss was interviewed on the touchline after the touchdown and essentially admitted that American football was more interesting than cricket, much to the amusement of the boisterous crowd.

While Detroit's offence was struggling, their defence shut the Atlanta run game down, so Ryan took to the air to reach the Detroit 17. On first down, Ryan launched a deep pass towards Julio Jones in the end zone but corner Rashean Mathis was on hand to intercept and return the ball for a 102-yard pick six, only for the play to be brought back due to penalties against Detroit. It was the kind of play that reminded everyone that, no matter the size of the occasion, the Lions are cursed. With the Falcons back in the red zone, Jackson rushed on three successive plays, with the final burst of five yards ensuring the Rams franchise record rusher became the 19th running back to reach 11,000 career rushing yards. Jackson punched it in for the touchdown from a yard out to make the score 21-0 with just 3:45 remaining in the first half. The Lions marched to the Atlanta 35 before Stafford was picked by Robert Alford, meaning Detroit were shut out through the first two quarters in London. 'It felt good in the first half, we were hitting and stopping them,' Falcons cornerback Desmond Trufant said. 'Then the second half, I don't know what happened. We didn't put our foot on the gas.'

The team from Motor City certainly found the juice to fuel them to victory in the second half. Stafford led Detroit to their first points of the game on the opening drive of the third quarter, but the drive stalled at the four-yard line when British defensive end Osi Umenyiora brilliantly broke up a pass to Riddick that was surely set to be a touchdown. Caldwell decided to take the points, and Prater knocked the 22-yard field goal between the sticks to make it 21-3.

The Lions defence began to roar in the third quarter. Defensive end Jason Jones sacked Ryan for a seven-yard loss before Matt Bosher botched his punt just 29 yards, allowing the Lions to begin their drive on the Atlanta 44. In typical Detroit fashion, they made it difficult for themselves: holding and an illegal blindside block were called on guard Garrett Reynolds on successive plays, pushing the Lions back to their own 31. Stafford picked out Riddick on a ten-yard gain before the biggest play of the game truly swung momentum in the way of the nominal visitors.

Operating out of shotgun on an unlikely third-and-25, Stafford evaded the Atlanta pressure on the outside and launched a dime over the helpless defensive backs and into the grateful clutches of Tate in the end zone. The 59-yard score gave the 2009 first overall pick the franchise touchdown record, usurping Hall of Famer Bobby Layne. 'It'll probably mean something when I'm all said and done – I'll look back on [it],' Stafford said before the game. 'During the course of the game, I'm just hoping whoever I throw it to doesn't turn and throw the ball into the stands so I have to fight and go get it.' Tate, who avoided a scrap and kept the ball for his quarterback, starred in London. The former Notre Dame wideout hauled in seven catches for 151 yards including the historic touchdown, and his performance was much needed given superstar receiver Calvin Johnson was absent due to injury.

The Falcons looked to retaliate as Ryan leaned on Jackson to take the ball to the Atlanta 47 before the quarterback inexplicably threw back across his body and was intercepted by corner Cassius

Vaughn, who returned the ball 45 yards to the seven-yard line. While they were in excellent field position and down by 11, the Lions were forced to kick the points on fourth down after two rushes and an incomplete pass.

The Detroit defence continued to dominate their opponents in the fourth quarter; Ezekiel Ansah forced a fumble after he sacked Ryan, only for offensive lineman Jake Matthews to recover the loose ball. When an attempted flea flicker fell incomplete, the Lions went back to basics with a mixture of short passes and effective runs, embarking on a drive spanning ten plays in which no gain was greater than 13 yards. At the Atlanta five-yard line, Stafford faked an end-around hand-off to Tate and threw to Riddick, who danced over the plane to make it 21-19. The Lions went for a two-point conversion to tie the game, but Stafford's pass missed Tate in the end zone.

The Falcons needed to hold the ball and burn the clock. Ryan picked out Jones for a 22-yard gain to move to the Detroit 40, where the Lions held out. Falcons head coach Mike Smith deemed the position too long to attempt a field goal, so Bosher came on to punt the ball to the Detroit seven-yard line. This was the chance for Stafford to deliver; he had previously led the Lions on 13 game-winning drives in his career. It would soon be 14.

Brimming with confidence, Stafford launched a deep pass down the middle of the field to Tate for a 32-yard gain. With no timeouts remaining, the Lions stormed up the pitch with a no huddle offence. He picked out Riddick on a short pass, although the running back deserves a tremendous amount of credit for hauling the ball in with one hand before taking it 20 yards into Atlanta territory. Stafford completed another pass, this time to Jeremy Ross, before he spiked the ball to stop the clock on the Atlanta 31. 'We don't give up. We keep fighting. We believe in what we do. We keep pushing,' Ross said. 'We keep driving, keep fighting, we don't stop.' Bell rushed for a yard with just 24 seconds remaining, only for the Falcons to get called for holding

– a five-yard penalty which stopped the clock. Without the call, the Lions would have faced fourth down with the clock ticking. Detroit would have likely been forced to rush the field goal unit onto the field to kick under pressure, but they were saved by the hands of Paul Soliai.

At the Atlanta 25, the Lions went to kick – a scenario they would rather have avoided. From beyond the 40 and inside the 50, Detroit were 0-7 on the season, and Prater, the team's third kicker of the year, had already missed from this range earlier in the campaign. He stepped up and dragged it wide, only for flags to fly as the Lions had run out the play clock. Prater moved back five yards and nailed the second attempt. 'I knew Prater was going to make it. I played two years with him before,' Vaughn, who picked Ryan off earlier in the game, said. 'When he missed the first one, I was like, "That was just the practice swing." The second one was cake.'

Stafford led Detroit to the win in what can only be described as a game of two halves thanks to his 325 passing yards and two scores – and it was Detroit's second comeback win in as many weeks after they triumphed at home against the New Orleans Saints on 19 October. Atlanta had thrown the game from a 21-point half-time lead due to a catalogue of individual errors. It was tied for the biggest blown half-time lead in Atlanta history – and it perhaps laid the groundwork for their ultimate choke job on the biggest stage at Super Bowl LI, where the franchise lost a 25-point lead to the New England Patriots in just over a quarter.

Against the Lions and in their previous five games, the Falcons had been outscored 70-7 in the final period. 'This is as tough a loss to take as any that I've been a part of,' said Ryan, who threw for 228 yards on 74 per cent completion. Ultimately, clock management issues and indiscipline condemned the Falcons to the loss and a 2-6 record.

The Lions carried the momentum to finish 11-5 in 2014, claiming a wildcard spot in the playoffs while the 12-4 Green

Bay Packers clinched the division. Unfortunately, Detroit could not secure their first postseason win since 1991 as they fell to the Cowboys 24-20. The Falcons improved in the second half of the campaign, but their 6-10 record was only good enough for third place in the NFC South.

This was a game that the International Series needed. With fans in awe at the spectacle they had just witnessed, NFL UK managing director Alistair Kirkwood was understandably thrilled and he confirmed there would be another slate of three matches at the home of football in 2015: 'There are logistic reasons around the Rugby World Cup that means we won't be going to four or five. The twist is we are looking at staging two games back to back in successive weeks to test this support base.' London's next step to NFL significance would be to host two matches in two weeks, but 2015 was a year away. The final international match of 2014, between the Dallas Cowboys and the Jacksonville-London Jaguars, would arrive just 14 days later.

NFL REGULAR SEASON WEEK TEN
9 November 2014
DALLAS COWBOYS 31
JACKSONVILLE JAGUARS 17
Wembley Stadium

While the Falcons suffered a rough defeat to the Lions on the other side of the Atlantic Ocean, Dallas's Tony Romo went down injured during the Cowboys' home loss to Washington when linebacker Keenan Robinson inadvertently planted his knee into the quarterback's back. The 20-17 loss hurt America's Team, sure, but they were more concerned about the health of their veteran signal-caller. Romo, who had led the Cowboys to six straight wins following an opening-day loss to the San Francisco 49ers, suffered two fractured vertebrae in his lower back, and he missed Dallas's next game – a 28-17 loss to the Arizona Cardinals, with Brandon

Weeden starting in his absence. It appeared unlikely Romo would suit up in London, but he passed a late fitness test. 'Anybody who's had anything broken before knows it's uncomfortable at times,' Romo said ahead of the clash with the Jaguars. 'At the end of the day, no one actually cares once you step out onto the field.'

The Cowboys were seeking their first meaningful international win after making ten appearances abroad, but this was the first time their regular season record was on the line. It was another step in the right direction for both the British and the wider international fanbase, but there was still more to achieve. With a Brit on the inside of the NFL, it felt like the sky was the limit.

Mark Waller – a Tottenham Hotspur fan, the club that would partner with the league to construct a purpose-built stadium in London – joined the NFL in February 2006 to lead the development of the game on an international level. He had overseen the success of the International Series. It was reported that nine of ten tickets sold were purchased by people who live within three hours' travel of London, while 2.8 million people considered themselves 'very interested' in the NFL. Naturally, questions were asked whether a franchise could permanently reside on these shores. 'To permanently relocate an NFL team to the UK is massive,' Waller said. 'There is a lot still to be done, because any team we put here has to be competitive. It's not just about putting a team in the marketplace, that team has to be able to win the Super Bowl.' Therein lies the issue.

Waller's insistence that a team would have to be competitive suggested that, while support in the UK for football was growing, it was not strong enough to sustain a losing franchise. Waller was optimistic for the future, and he acknowledged that the presence of NFL owners within the British sporting sphere – Rams owner Stan Kroenke at Arsenal, the Glazers at the Buccaneers and Manchester United, and Jacksonville's Shahid Khan at Fulham – was undoubtedly a positive.

Even at the Cowboys–Jaguars clash, the shadow of association football loomed over the NFL's International Series. The game was played at Wembley with the likes of Chelsea manager Jose Mourinho and Manchester City striker Sergio Aguero in attendance. Soccer will always be dominant in the UK, but Fox colour commentator Darryl Johnston declared there were over 35,000 members of the Union Jax in the United Kingdom, up from 22,500 just 12 months prior. Union Jax were the Jaguars' official fan club in the UK, and in the last two years had risen from 30th to ninth in terms of franchise popularity; the deal to play four London home games in four years was paying off.

Romo, despite his fragile back, was ready to ensure the Cowboys remained more popular than the lowly Jags with an impressive showing in the Big Smoke. But he hardly started well. On the opening drive, he leaned on stud running back DeMarco Murray – whose record streak of eight straight 100-yard games to start the season was ended by Arizona the week before – to move to the Jacksonville 36 before Romo overthrew a wide-open Jason Witten on third down with the end zone begging. There was no defensive player within a five-yard radius of the tight end and Dallas fans undoubtedly feared the back injury was affecting their quarterback. Kicker Dan Bailey subsequently trotted onto the field to kick a 54-yard field goal to give the Cowboys the lead, but the Jags hit back immediately.

Led by rookie quarterback Blake Bortles, the Jaguars moved downfield with relative ease. Bortles frequently utilised receiver Allen Robinson but running back Denard Robinson took the plaudits when he capped the nine-play drive by rushing in a touchdown from 32 yards out to give Jacksonville a 7-3 lead – and then things went downhill. 'We kind of shot ourselves in the foot for two or three drives after that and never really got it rolling again,' Bortles said. While Dallas and Romo struggled to get going, they received an immense shot in the arm when Jacksonville punt returner Ace Sanders let the ball slip through his clutches for a fumble which was ultimately recovered by Dallas safety CJ Spillman on the six-yard line. 'That was the play early on that really swung the tide,' Dallas head coach Jason Garrett said of the fumble after the game. 'We played pretty solid football after that.'

Three plays later, the Cowboys reclaimed a lead they would not relinquish. Romo showed off his elusiveness to avoid the pressure of Tyson Alualu, rolling right before throwing a two-yard touchdown dart to Witten to make the score 10-7 to Dallas.

Bryant – the star receiver for the Cowboys who held the franchise record for most receiving touchdowns when he left the team – turned 26 earlier in the week, and he celebrated the occasion in the second quarter against the Jags. After Murray and Witten had taken the Cowboys to the Jacksonville 35, Romo found Bryant on a short pass which the receiver collected at the line of scrimmage and showed off his bulldozing strength to shrug off five Jacksonville defenders to score. It was a sensational play from Bryant, but he was not done there.

If Bryant's first score was about strength, his second showcased speed. Romo, operating out of shotgun with just 31 seconds remaining, rifled a deep pass to the right sideline where Bryant had burned past corner Dwayne Gratz. The receiver stiff-armed safety Johnathan Cyprien to score the 68-yard touchdown, granting the Cowboys a commanding 24-7 half-time lead.

The second half was uglier than the first. Jacksonville punted the ball on their opening drive and the Cowboys made them pay. Starting from their 13, Romo and Murray took Dallas into Jacksonville territory before backup running back Joseph Randle broke through two particularly shoddy tackle attempts to the dismay of the Union Jax. His 40-yard touchdown rush saw the Cowboys move to a 31-7 lead.

With little to lose, the Jaguars went for a fourth down conversion on their own 29 and predictably came up short when

Toby Gerhart was engulfed by a stampede of Cowboys, although there was an element of respite for the poor AFC outfit when Bailey missed his field goal.

The British crowd finally had something to truly cheer about on Jacksonville's next drive. Jack Crawford – who grew up in Kilburn, just four stops from Wembley on the Underground – sacked Bortles and forced a fumble recovered by offensive lineman Luke Bowanko. The British defensive end had left his mark on the International Series, and Jacksonville's recovery meant little in the end as they once again turned the ball over on downs.

The catalogue of errors that defined this match continued deep into the fourth quarter when, after Romo was sacked back at his own five-yard line, Dallas punted, only for special teams to concede a safety as Kyle Wilber was called for offensive holding in his own end zone. Bortles then completed two passes to move downfield, but the rookie quarterback showed his inexperience by staring down receiver Cecil Shorts and throwing an interception to linebacker Bruce Carter. With the game won at 31-9, Dallas pulled Romo from the game. The precautionary move meant Weeden was in charge of the offence, although the Cowboys were simply looking to secure the win without injury.

Bortles and the Jaguars took over with approximately three minutes remaining and Robinson later strolled in for a one-yard touchdown, his second of the game. The team made the two-point conversion but it was too little, too late for Khan's franchise. Jacksonville had suffered a 31-17 defeat, and their record in London worsened to 0-2.

While much of the pre-match chatter surrounded Romo, he completed 20 of 27 attempts for 246 yards and three touchdowns while compiling a season-high rating of 138.8. '[He] didn't seem like he had any physical restrictions, moved around in the pocket, some subtle pocket movements to allow things to develop,' Cowboys coach Garrett said of Romo after the game. His performance should have been expected, as Romo extended his record in November to 25-5 while the Cowboys moved to 7-3 on the season.

Dallas went on to finish atop the NFC East with a 12-4 record, and they beat the Lions – who had played in London too – before facing the Green Bay Packers in the NFC Divisional Round. The game will be forever remembered for Bryant's controversial catch that wasn't. On fourth down, with the Cowboys camped on the Packers' 32, Romo launched a deep ball towards Bryant, who caught the ball with both feet in bounds but seemed to lose control as he stretched to score. Referees initially ruled the receiver down at the one-yard line, but the call was reversed and marked incomplete after Packers coach Mike McCarthy challenged the decision. Referee Gene Steratore explained that while Bryant reclaimed possession, the move was irrelevant as the loose ball had contacted the ground, marking the pass incomplete. The controversy led to Dean Blandino, NFL vice president of officiating, tweeting and even visiting the Cowboys to explain the decision during the following offseason.

As for the Jaguars, the London loss – their ninth in ten matches – was simply more of the same. 'We wanted to do something special but we didn't play as well as we wanted to,' head coach Gus Bradley admitted. 'We have great enthusiasm and toughness but we also had some self-inflicted wounds and sloppiness.' It was a tough season for Jacksonville as they compiled a 3-13 record in 2014. It was not enough to finish bottom of the AFC South as the Tennessee Titans recorded a 2-14 campaign.

The 2015 International Series was set to be another year of firsts, headlined by the clash between the New York Jets and Miami Dolphins – the first divisional match to be played abroad.

2015

A Year of Firsts

NFL REGULAR SEASON WEEK FOUR
4 October 2015
NEW YORK JETS 27
MIAMI DOLPHINS 14
Wembley Stadium

THE 2015 International Series games were set to be played in the early afternoon for the first time, a move aimed at enhancing the prestige of the games. 'The early kick-offs make it a national game in the States, so the visibility of London and the UK is higher,' said Alastair Kirkwood. 'It also opens up other markets, because it is more time zone friendly in Asia than other games that kick off at normal times. And the fact that Sunday's game will be shown on BBC2 gives us a really good platform for further growth.' The seeds sown during the first International Series game in London back in 2007 were growing – and it was time for the next stage of the series' development. A new time slot was great, but so was having the country's first divisional matchup.

This was the Miami Dolphins' third appearance at Wembley, and they were set to receive the full backing of the 83,986 in attendance as the nominal home team thanks to the legacy of Channel 4's coverage of the 1980s – but Miami were certainly not the same team that reached Super Bowl XIX with legendary quarterback Dan Marino at the helm. They had lost two of their opening three matches, including a 41-14 thumping by the Buffalo Bills the week before flying across the Atlantic. Miami heavily invested in their defensive line during the offseason, making Ndamukong Suh the highest paid defensive player in football with a six-year deal worth over $114m, approximately $60m of which was fully guaranteed. Suh, a 6ft 4in phenom, had struggled in the opening games, and the fierce partnership he hoped to strike with Cameron Wake had reaped just one sack through three hours of football. As a result, Joe Philbin was the favourite to become the first coach to lose his job in the new campaign.

The New York Jets arrived in slightly better form than their AFC East rivals. New head coach Todd Bowles, who took over after Rex Ryan's mildly successful six seasons, had overseen two wins in his first two games: a 31-10 triumph over the Cleveland Browns and a 20-7 victory at Indianapolis. However, the Philadelphia Eagles left the Big Apple with the win after exploding out the gates to a 24-0 lead in the second quarter as New York quarterback Ryan Fitzpatrick threw three interceptions and the visitors held on despite the Jets scoring 17 unanswered points.

The Jets took to the Wembley pitch amid a chorus of jeers, while the Dolphins must have felt like they were back in Miami when accompanied by flagbearers, cheerleaders and pyrotechnics. With viewers on the East Coast keen to tune in at 9:30am EST, the American and British national anthems played, before 'London Calling' by The Clash blared out around the iconic, sun-laden venue.

After an uninspiring opening drive by the Dolphins, Fitzpatrick lived up to his 'FitzMagic' nickname as he launched a spectacular 58-yard bomb to former Dolphin Brandon Marshall on the team's first play from scrimmage. The Jets soon led 7-0 as Chris Ivory stormed past Suh for the touchdown, with replays confirming the running back had broken the plane to score before he lost control of the ball as he fell to the ground.

Jets kicker Nick Folk added field goals before Miami finally woke up on offence in the second quarter. Jarvis Landry breathed life into the unit with a 14-yard run before back-to-back pass interference penalties took Miami to the New York eight-yard line. Ryan Tannehill, who inked a $96m contract extension in May, showed immense composure as he stood his ground and picked out Jake Stoneburger to reduce the deficit to six points, but the Jets returned to the end zone before half-time.

Fitzpatrick and Ivory did the damage, with the quarterback showing a surprising turn of pace to pick up 19 yards on third down before he threw an 11-yard touchdown dart to Eric Decker. Suddenly, the Jets were back with a comfortable lead of 20-7 and they were threatening to call game on the Dolphins in London. By the break, New York had tallied 282 net yards compared to Miami's 65. For all the money and big names on the Dolphins defensive line, it was the Jets defence that impressed and gave Tannehill no time to operate behind his porous offensive line.

The Jets finished off their rivals on the opening drive of the second half. Fitzpatrick and Ivory carved the hapless Miami defence apart, but it was backup back Zac Stacy who took the Wembley applause when he rushed in from two yards. The Jets had a chance to extend their lead six minutes later, but Folk fluffed his lines in what was really the only smear on his team's fun day out. Fitzpatrick was intercepted by Zack Bowman, but Miami couldn't take advantage and punted on the resulting drive. Miami scored on their next possession, aided by a 28-yard return by Landry which set them up on the Jets 37. Tannehill hit Kenny Stills with two passes, the second of which found the end zone for a ten-yard touchdown, making the score 27-14.

It was ultimately a career high for Ivory, as his 166 yards – the most by a Jet since Thomas Jones ran for 210 in 2009 – helped the Jets tally 425 total offensive yards under the Wembley arch. Defensively, it was a different story as Bowles's team gave up a frustrating 163 yards on 14 plays, although both Darrelle Revis and Marcus Williams snatched interceptions late. 'We play aggressive, so some of that's going to happen,' linebacker Calvin Pace said, 'but we know we've got to clean up our play.'

While Fitzpatrick led New York to the win with 218 yards and a touchdown, it was the shackling of big-money signing Suh that ultimately secured the victory. He had no sacks and only three tackles, and his first didn't come until the third quarter. The craziest part? Suh, the most expensive defensive player in football history, was manhandled by a backup. Brian Winters, a third-year guard, was called in to start and assigned to Suh following an injury to Willie Colon. It was the type of underdog performance that belonged in England's FA Cup. 'He came up with some plays today. I was proud of him,' said Bowles of Winters after the win.

Three straight defeats left Miami with a 1-3 record, and there were plenty of suggestions that both coach Philbin and defensive coordinator Kevin Coyle were set to be replaced. The *Palm Beach Post* even quoted an unnamed player as saying the team was ready to 'throw in the towel' if they lost in London – which they duly did. Miami failed to make big plays in key situations, including no third down conversions. 'We've got to find a way to make plays. As ugly as it may have seemed, at the end of the day we had opportunities to win that game,' an optimistic Philbin insisted. 'We can't panic. It can seem like the walls are closing in on you.' Unfortunately for Philbin, the walls engulfed him. He was fired after the game, and the premature ending of his tenure was met with a favourable reaction from fans and critics alike. Miami would go on to suffer a frustrating year as they went 6-10 and finished rock bottom of the AFC East.

The Jets fared a lot better, finishing with a 10-6 record – just two games behind the New England Patriots – but they agonisingly missed out on a playoff berth despite matching the record of the Pittsburgh Steelers, who snuck in instead.

NFL REGULAR SEASON WEEK SEVEN
25 October 2015
BUFFALO BILLS 31
JACKSONVILLE JAGUARS 34
Wembley Stadium

An old adage indicates third time is the charm, and after two years of threatening to alienate their developing fanbase, the Jacksonville Jaguars finally won on British soil. The result was frankly surprising given the Jags had come into the clash with only ten wins since the beginning of the 2012 season, and for a worrying moment it looked as though they had let a 24-point lead slip. Thanks to Blake Bortles's late touchdown pass to Allen Hurns, the Jags clawed back the win.

The Buffalo Bills should not have been favourites given their own abysmal record in international games. The Bills were actually the first team to venture into and commit to a new market through the ill-fated Bills Toronto Series from 2008 to 2013 as Buffalo played six home regular season matches at the Rogers Centre in The Six.

The reaction from their fans back in upstate New York changed from anger to a resentful acceptance so long as the generated revenue was invested back into the team, but even team CEO Russ Brandon suggested the move was poor and their performances showed, losing five of the six matches in Canada. Brandon claimed there were positives: attendance from Canadian fans in Buffalo increased from 11 per cent to 20 per cent at the time of the series' renewal. They renewed the agreement for five additional years in January 2013 but, in December 2014, the franchise saw the light and terminated the remainder of the contract. The experiment was over.

Unfortunately for Bills fans, a new trial began in 2015. Starting quarterback Tyrod Taylor sprained a ligament in his left knee during a 14-13 win over Tennessee, so EJ Manuel was in. Rex Ryan, the former Jets coach, was at the helm and he led them to a solid 3-3 record in which they were competitive in a defeat to the all-conquering New England Patriots. There was a renewed hope in Buffalo, but Taylor's injury damaged such hopes – particularly with Manuel throwing an interception in the previous week's defeat to Cincinnati.

The 2015 Jaguars were still very much looking like the 2014 team. They travelled across the Atlantic with a 1-5 record following a 31-20 loss to the Houston Texans before their clash at Wembley. Regardless, they attracted the second-highest NFL crowd to the iconic stadium – behind only the Patriots' win over the Tampa Bay Buccaneers – with 84,021 turning up to finally see Jacksonville win in London.

The Bills took the lead when Dan Carpenter thumped a 31-yard field goal through the sticks, but the Jags hit back when they took over five minutes later. Bortles used his second-year smarts to rely on his two best offensive weapons in Hurns and star wideout Allen Robinson, hitting them for 22 and 23 yards respectively to march to the Buffalo ten. From there, the sophomore threw a touchdown to Robinson to take the lead – and then Manuel became the unlikely star of the Jaguars' show.

Facing third down, the Buffalo quarterback took a long look at the play sheet on his left wrist. He certainly didn't plan what happened next. Aaron Colvin ate Manuel with a huge sack, forcing a fumble that was scooped up by defensive end Chris Clemons to charge into the end zone. On the next play from scrimmage, Jacksonville had scored again after Manuel stared down receiver Robert Woods, making it clear to almost each and every individual in the HA9 0FA postcode who he was going to throw to while he was in triple coverage. Telvin Smith made the interception and returned it to the house. Jacksonville had not scored a single defensive touchdown in the 2015 season, but suddenly found two in seven seconds to take a stunning 21-3 lead.

Buffalo looked to try and steady the ship on the following possession as Manuel, not particularly trusting of his arm, used his legs to pick up 12 yards. LeSean McCoy had two rushes that went nowhere, and on third down once again, Manuel issued a turnover as he threw towards Chris Hogan only for Paul Posluszny to make a stellar diving pick. The Jaguars offence expressed their gratitude for the impressive field position when TJ Yeldon somehow beat the defenders to burst into the end zone from 28 yards out, giving the Jags a 27-3 lead after kicker Jason Myers missed the extra point. Across the NFL, there had been 141 rushing touchdowns in the first six weeks of the 2015 season – finally Jacksonville had scored one themselves.

Manuel's errors gave Jacksonville the chance to claim a 24-point lead early, but the backup quarterback settled and led the rally that saw Buffalo, against all odds, reclaim the lead. The Bills' resurgence began on the next possession, with Manuel driving downfield on a 12-play drive capped off with a fine 16-yard touchdown pass to Woods, who brilliantly hauled in the pass and got his feet down to score. Another Carpenter field goal soon after made it 27-13 at half-time.

On the first possession of the third quarter, the Jaguars methodically drove to the Buffalo one-yard line after nearly ten minutes of possession, but it was all for naught when running back Toby Gerhart was denied at the goal line by a terrific Bills defensive stand. Buffalo kicked another field goal in the third quarter to make it an 11-point game with a quarter of action remaining, but the Bills looked as if they had blown their chance when McCoy fumbled with the end zone after he was hit hard by Johnathan Cyprien.

Buffalo got the touchdown they craved in the fourth quarter when Manuel hit Marcus Easley on a spectacular 58-yard pass – magic from the third-year signal-caller. The play was Buffalo's longest of the season, although it came close to losing that title just 82 seconds later as safety Corey Graham intercepted Bortles's horrendous looping throw and returned it 44 yards for the pick six. In an instant, the Bills possessed a 31-27 lead that seemed impossible in the second quarter.

In the end, though, this was Jacksonville's day. Bortles, aided by a ropey defensive pass interference call against Nickell Robey, picked out Hurns for the go-ahead score with 2:26 remaining. Bortles faked the hand-off to Yeldon and scrambled left before throwing a perfect ball hauled in exceptionally by Hurns, who clattered into the pylon for six. 'What we're seeing in Blake is that he does keep his eyes downfield,' Jaguars head coach Gus Bradley said of the game-winning play.

The Jaguars got over the line, securing their second win of the season. The players were ecstatic, with linebacker Smith – who scored the second defensive touchdown – referring to the locker room as 'electric', saying, 'You can't even see Gus's eyes because he is smiling so much.' He was right – Bradley was thrilled and hoped it would signal a turning point in Jacksonville's season. 'We have been in this situation before but on the sidelines our players were saying, "We're not going to give this one up." Our players will take this and grow from it.' The Jaguars did build on the triumph, winning two of their next three games before collapsing and finishing 5-11, sealing third place in the AFC South and a playoff-less season once again.

After slipping to 3-4, Ryan and the Bills felt the jet lag of another frustrating start to the season. With a bye week imminent as was tradition for London games, the head coach was hopeful his starting quarterback Taylor would return before the divisional clash with the Dolphins on 8 November. 'I've never known a team that needed a bye week so badly,' Ryan said. Taylor returned and torched Miami with 92 per cent completion as the Bills won 33-17, but the quarterback could not inspire the inconsistent Bills to a greater record than 8-8. The mediocre season left them in third place in the AFC East, behind Ryan's former team, the Jets.

NFL REGULAR SEASON WEEK EIGHT
1 November 2015
DETROIT LIONS 10
KANSAS CITY CHIEFS 45
Wembley Stadium

If the British American football faithful were introduced to the Detroit Lions 372 days ago when Matt Prater's kick sealed a last-gasp win over the Atlanta Falcons, they met the real Lions on this winter day at Wembley. It was a decent introduction to the Kansas City Chiefs, too.

Kansas City triumphed by 35 points to seal the second-largest margin of victory since the NFL began their regular season experiment in London back in 2007, with only the Patriots' 45-7 spanking of the St Louis Rams three years earlier a wider gap. It was a much-needed result for the Chiefs, who arrived in London with a 2-5 record after suffering five straight losses bookended by wins over Houston and Pittsburgh. The Chiefs scored 38 unanswered points to record their biggest win of the season – and it would kickstart a fine turnaround that saw them qualify for the postseason against all odds.

The Chiefs didn't exactly dominate from the off as Prater kicked a 35-yard field goal on the Lions' opening drive, which appeared to vindicate not only Detroit's decision to arrive in London before Kansas City, but also their decision to switch offensive coordinators. Detroit had lost their opening five games before they defeated the Chicago Bears in overtime two weeks prior. However, Detroit suffered a 28-19 loss at the hands of the Minnesota Vikings in Motor City: Joe Lombardi was out and Jim Bob Cooter was handed the play-calling reins.

The swift 3-0 lead was as good as it got for Detroit in the Big Smoke – and it unravelled rather quickly. Lions coach Jim Caldwell said afterwards that the trip to London was 'obviously' not a good outing, an early contender for understatement of the year as the Chiefs responded immediately to take the lead. Knile Davis returned Prater's kick-off 50 yards to the Kansas City 44, and Smith leaned on Travis Kelce and running back Charcandrick West to progress downfield before De'Anthony Thomas ran in for a ten-yard score.

The game very quickly became a battle won on the ground rather than the air, and Chiefs quarterback Smith got in on the action. Following a Detroit punt to open the second quarter, the quarterback took off on a career-best 49-yard rush. He read the play beautifully, breaking through the middle of the line before bursting to the left and running out of bounds at the Detroit 24. Moments later on third down, Smith ran into the end zone for a 12-yard score to give the Chiefs a 14-3 lead. 'It was a lot of fun but you are not going to make a living as an NFL quarterback by running,' Smith said after the game, clearly not anticipating the emergence of Lamar Jackson a few years later. The veteran quarterback would hardly influence the next generation with his ability to make plays on the ground – but certainly inspired many thanks to his mentality that produced one of sport's great comebacks.

In week five of the 2020 NFL season, the Washington Football Team lost to the Los Angeles Rams in a tough 30-10 beating. In normal circumstances, people wouldn't take any notice of such a result, but the events at FedExField will live long in the memory. Smith, now the quarterback in the capitol after a young superstar named Patrick Mahomes usurped him in Kansas City, completed a seemingly impossible return to NFL action after the traumatic events of 18 November 2018. Smith was sacked by Houston defenders Kareem Jackson and JJ Watt, and the quarterback suffered a horrific spiral and compound fracture to his tibia and fibula in his right leg. The injury drew haunting parallels to former Washington quarterback Joe Theismann, who was also 34 years of age when he too broke his leg 33 years to the day before Smith – and Theismann subsequently retired without ever being able to return. Smith spent a month in hospital before contracting life-threatening necrotising fasciitis, which caused a sepsis that required 17 surgeries across four separate hospital stays over a nine-month period. Amputation from above the knee was believed to be his only option before a crucial operation transferring muscle from his left quadriceps saved his right leg. Never letting go of his dream to return to the league, Smith slowly regained his strength and was activated to the main roster on 16 August 2020.

As the third-string quarterback behind Dwayne Haskins and free agency signing Kyle Allen, it was unlikely that Smith would take to the field. Against the Rams, Haskins was benched due to erratic play and Allen was hit hard before half-time, knocking him out of the game. After a brutal 693 days, this was Smith's chance – and the fans, including his family, cheered as he completed a pass to JD McKissic on his first play. Even his opposition was full of praise; LA quarterback Jared Goff said, 'I will be able to tell people forever that I watched that.' Smith might not have lit it up that season, but he was named NFL Comeback Player of the Year after overcoming such adversity.

Back in London, Stafford was trying to get things going for the Lions to no avail with interceptions on successive drives. The first, picked by Sean Smith, led to a 33-yard field goal from Cairo Santos and Justin Houston's deflected interception allowed West to run in a touchdown from eight yards out. The Lions went into half-time 24-3 down, but they had some hope – they had trailed by 21 points at Wembley before, and they erased that deficit to defeat the Falcons.

Unfortunately for the Lions, this was a new year. An unsportsmanlike conduct penalty set the tone on a drive that culminated in Kelce collecting a two-yard pass from Smith and bundling his way into the end zone to make it 31-3. With the game essentially over, especially after Stafford was sacked by Houston and Tamba Hali on fourth down to open the final quarter, Jeremy

Maclin caught a 17-yard touchdown pass to extend the lead. The receiver had missed the win over Pittsburgh the week before due to concussion, but his presence certainly added another layer to this burgeoning Chiefs offence.

Stafford picked out Lance Moore for a rare Detroit highlight – a 21-yard touchdown which was the receiver's third of the season – but Kansas City weren't satisfied yet and Spencer Ware forced his way in from four yards to score his first NFL touchdown and cap off a fine team performance. It meant Smith, Thomas, West and Ware had all scored, the first time the Chiefs had four different players score a rushing touchdown in the same game since 1960.

The Lions were now 1-7 after making the playoffs last year and Stafford struggled to get going, but it was hardly his fault. He suffered six sacks and barely had time to breathe as he threw two interceptions to boot, totalling 11 on the year – the most in the NFL. While he defended his team-mates after the game, the writing was on the wall for the Lions and coach Caldwell. The bye week proved to be instrumental in saving their season; Detroit won six of their final eight matches to finish a respectable 8-8, and Caldwell retained his job.

The Chiefs literally ran riot in London as Smith rushed for a career-high 78 yards from five attempts and made the Lions pay for utilising man coverage. Like Detroit, Andy Reid's side had a brilliant second half of the season in which they became the league's form team. After sitting at 1-5, they won all ten of their remaining matches to finish one game shy of the Denver Broncos' AFC West-winning record of 12-4. While the Broncos went on to win the Super Bowl, the Chiefs defeated the Texans 30-0 in Houston on Wildcard Weekend before falling to Tom Brady and the Patriots in Foxborough.

It didn't end in confetti, but the Chiefs had shown the potential of an elite team during their astonishing run to close out the 2015 campaign. In Kelce, they had arguably the game's greatest receiving tight end and they added speedster Tyreek Hill to their armoury in the fifth round of the 2016 draft. The Chiefs were assembling the furniture of an offensive juggernaut, and they added the centrepiece on 27 April 2017. With the tenth overall selection, Kansas City took a chance on a young quarterback from Texas A&M. The rest, as they say, is history: the Mahomes era had begun.

2016

Twickenham Debut

NFL REGULAR SEASON WEEK FOUR
2 October 2016
INDIANAPOLIS COLTS 27
JACKSONVILLE JAGUARS 30
Wembley Stadium

ANOTHER YEAR, another win for the Jacksonville Jaguars in London. For the second successive season, Jacksonville threatened to throw away a dominant lead only to secure victory late, ensuring the growing British fandom got their money's worth at Wembley.

The game was a monumental one in the grand scheme of the NFL's International Series. In the series' tenth year, the Indianapolis Colts' trip to London to face the Jaguars was the 15th match played at Wembley. The iconic stadium appeared to be nearing the end of its NFL tenancy, as Twickenham – the home of English rugby – was to host the clash between the New York Giants and Los Angeles Rams. With Tottenham Hotspur confirmed as a partner of the NFL, Wembley was only ever going to be a temporary home for a sport seeking to permanently settle on these shores.

It seemed right, then, that the Colts were making their British bow with Andrew Luck as their main man. The quarterback was a highly touted prospect out of Stanford when Indianapolis took him first overall in the 2012 draft, and he certainly hadn't disappointed as a three-time Pro Bowl selection as well as the NFL's leader in passing touchdowns in 2014 with 40. Despite being so far from home, Luck – whose father Oliver oversaw the rebranding of the WLAF to NFL Europe – was in a familiar setting as he spent three years of his youth living in London just off Finchley Road, a mere 25-minute drive from Wembley Stadium.

The Colts had missed the playoffs in 2015 with an 8-8 record, and they brought their frustrating form into 2016 as they slipped to an 0-2 start following losses to the Detroit Lions and the reigning Super Bowl champions, the Denver Broncos. However, a 26-22 win over the San Diego Chargers, in which Luck passed for 331 yards and a touchdown, looked to put them back on track. The Jaguars came into the game winless, losing twice at home to the Green Bay Packers and Baltimore Ravens either side of a road loss in San Diego. They were not only looking to secure their first 'home' win of the season in the Big Smoke, but the Jags were also hoping to take their record on British soil to a respectable 2-2.

Wembley announced a sold-out attendance of 83,764 which appeared to be evenly divided between the two sides, although it felt like a home game for Jacksonville when the Colts took to the field to a muted reception. Gus Bradley's team emerged out of the mouth of a giant inflatable jaguar to big cheers, but there was one thing on the mind of many in the stadium. Many fans were seen donning Colin Kaepernick jerseys after the anthem controversy took hold, with the league failing to properly act. 'The Star-Spangled Banner' rung out around the stadium, and one player took a knee as a sign of solidarity with the quarterback. Colts cornerback Antonio Cromartie, who had promised to maintain his peaceful protest throughout the campaign, knelt with his right fist raised, and stood for the British anthem 'God

Save the Queen'. Many issues are bigger than football, but you wouldn't know it once the anthems finished.

The Jaguars defence made the first notable play of the game. On second down on his own 42, Luck tried to hit Chester Rogers on a slant route but Dante Fowler – the Jags' third overall pick in the 2015 draft – deflected the ball into the arms of rookie defensive end Yannick Ngakoue. With excellent field position, Bortles drove 24 yards and capped it off with a three-yard touchdown pass to Allen Robinson after the wideout escaped Cromartie. The Colts responded with 43-year-old legend Adam Vinatieri kicking field goals either side of a Jacksonville point to make it a one-point game at 7-6 midway through the second quarter.

Jacksonville got their offence going on the next drive, with TJ Yeldon and Bortles working their magic. From the Indianapolis one-yard line following a pass interference call, Bortles looked for Robinson yet again but the receiver spilled the ball incomplete, so the quarterback took matters quite literally into his own hands. He utilised the pass-run option and ducked inside the defensive line to run in the score himself. Once more, Jacksonville sacked Luck to force a punt with 1:06 remaining in the half, and Jacksonville got another lucky break when safety TJ Green was called for unnecessary roughness. Kicker Jason Myers clipped a 22-yard field goal through the sticks as time expired to give the Jags a 17-6 lead.

Jacksonville were equally as efficient to open the second half, driving downfield with no play longer than 13 yards before Myers kicked a 46-yard attempt to extend the lead to 20-6 and added another, nine minutes later. With the game slipping away from the Colts, they needed Luck to step up to the plate and mount the comeback. It was reported prior to the match that Bradley's position as head coach of the Jaguars was reportedly safe barring a 'total debacle' against Indy – and for the first nine minutes of the fourth quarter, his seat appeared particularly hot.

Luck leaned on legendary running back Frank Gore in both the ground game and a safety blanket in the air before he hit Rogers for a 19-yard spectacular diving catch. Once again, this was a drive riddled with defensive penalties: Dante Fowler Jr was called offside while Johnathan Cyprien flagged for pass interference. On the Jacksonville one-yard line, Gore punched it in on the second play of the fourth quarter to make the score read 20-13. The back, who would retire third on the NFL all-time rushing list with 16,000 yards, took his chance in London to add to his odd status as the league's greatest rusher on foreign soil. The Jags match was his fourth regular season clash abroad since his rookie year of 2005, when he played in Mexico City. Gore also played in London for the 49ers, tallying 66 total carries for 264 yards and four touchdowns across four trips.

After a Jacksonville punt, Luck drove 78 yards in 12 plays to hit TY Hilton for the touchdown when the receiver ran a perfect stutter route, planting his foot and standing stationary between the Jags linebackers before bursting into the space in the back corner of the end zone.

The Jaguars were leaking points, and it was time for Bortles to respond to Luck's impressive period – who doubted him? He hit Yeldon on successive plays for a combined gain of 31 yards and on the Indianapolis 42, Bortles picked out Allen Hurns on a short out-route. The play looked innocent enough, but Hurns excellently spun away from backup corner Rashaan Melvin before cutting inside through the middle of the field for a 42-yard touchdown. At 30-20 with 5:31 remaining, it appeared the Jacksonville – and Bradley's job – were safe.

They weren't out the woods just yet. After Luck was sacked for a fifth time to take Indy to third-and-long on their own 36, the generational superstar launched a 64-yard touchdown bomb to Phillip Dorsett, who had left Jags rookie corner Jalen Ramsey trailing in his wake. Suddenly, a game that was a slow burner had become a fast-paced shootout. The Colts defence held firm and earned a shot for Luck to win the game, and it all came down to the final play on the Jacksonville 49. On fourth down – needing just a single yard to keep their hopes of a British win alive – Luck danced around the pocket and threw a pop pass towards Dwayne Allen but safety Peyton Thompson made a sensational diving play at the last second to knock the ball loose from the tight end's hands. The pass fell incomplete and the Jags were victors in London once again.

The Colts were the masters of their own demise as their offensive weapons dropped catchable balls and their defence gifted the Jags penalties like it was the holiday season, with pass interference and unnecessary roughness calls needlessly extending three of Jacksonville's scoring drives. While the Colts would finish the season 8-8, Luck himself would decide he couldn't – or rather, didn't want to – continue in the NFL. The superstar quarterback was stuck behind a penetrable offensive line and suffered multiple injuries as a result, with the constant rehabilitation taking its toll. After seven seasons and at just 29 years of age, Luck announced his retirement on 24 August 2019: 'I've been stuck in this process. I haven't been able to live the life I want to live. It's taken the joy out of this game. The only way forward for me is to remove myself from football. This is not an easy decision. It's the hardest decision of my life, but it is the right decision for me.'

Unfortunately, Colts fans didn't take too kindly to the news that Luck, one of the best professional athletes to prematurely walk away from his sport, was to retire and booed him following a preseason loss immediately after the news broke.

The win for the Jaguars was needed, but their fans hopefully savoured the feeling as they would only experience it a couple more times in 2016. Their 3-13 record was bad enough for the fourth overall selection in the 2017 draft, and Jacksonville used it to bring in LSU running back Leonard Fournette with the likes of future superstars Christian McCaffrey, TJ Watt and Patrick Mahomes on the board. Nonetheless, Fournette was a solid pick and he would be a key cog in the Jacksonville machine that would finally reap the reward of consistently high picks.

NFL REGULAR SEASON WEEK EIGHT
23 October 2016
NEW YORK GIANTS 17
LOS ANGELES RAMS 10
Twickenham Stadium

For six weeks of the 2016 NFL season, the New York Giants defence struggled to get their hands on the ball. The change of scenery did the franchise wonders as they collected four interceptions in London, and the new setting also breathed new life into the International Series. American football matches at the home of English rugby seemed particularly far-fetched just a few years prior – but after ten years and 15 matches at Wembley, the move to Twickenham felt like a natural evolution.

Both teams arrived in patchy form. After flying out the gates at 2-0, the Giants suffered three straight defeats against Washington, Minnesota and Green Bay before a win over Baltimore steadied the ship at 3-3. In Odell Beckham Jr – who caught two touchdowns in the victory over the Ravens – Victor Cruz and rookie Sterling Shepard, two-time Super Bowl-winning quarterback Eli Manning had weapons at his disposal, but the same could not really be said about the Los Angeles Rams offence piloted by Case Keenum. The veteran was given the reins by head coach Jeff Fisher instead of 2016 first overall pick Jared Goff, and the Rams had actually been fairly competitive to open the season.

They bounced back from a 28-0 defeat in San Francisco with three straight wins before crashing back to earth with losses to Buffalo and Detroit. They had an identical record to the Giants and both teams hoped to leave London on a positive note. The two teams opted for different strategies to deal with jet lag, with Los Angeles deciding to fly overnight from Detroit after their

31-28 while the Giants prepared in the Big Apple before jetting to London on Friday. Fisher's choice to arrive early paid dividends in the first quarter.

The Giants touched down in London with the worst turnover differential in the NFC at -10 and they continued the poor form on the opening drive. Seemingly influenced by the fact he was in a rugby stadium, tight end Larry Donnell released the ball after being hit by Lamarcus Joyner and Rams corner EJ Gaines recovered possession on the Giants 35. On third down from the ten-yard line, Keenum hit Tavon Austin through the middle on a touchdown strike to give Los Angeles the early lead.

The Giants were struggling against an aggressive Rams defence as they registered a single first down in the opening quarter – an 11-yard completion to Shepard. The Rams collected the New York punt and scored on their second drive, albeit from a Greg Zuerlein 36-yard field goal to make it 10-0 with under ten minutes played. They dictated the early stages of the game, controlling possession for 11 and a half minutes of the 15-minute period with seven first downs. The Rams weren't going to get ahead of themselves, though. Fisher had travelled with the team to London in 2012, where they opened the scoring before the Patriots inevitably came back to win 45-7, but that was a different time, a different team, from a different city.

The Rams' tenure in St Louis had come to an end barely 11 months prior. Negotiations to keep the franchise in the city failed even after St Louis offered a viable stadium plan, with franchise management of the opinion that too much of the cost fell on the team. Naturally, fans in St Louis were furious with owner Stan Kroenke – dubbed 'Silent Stan' due to his refusal to speak about the team and a potential move – and COO Kevin Demoff as locals believed the duo had lied about their intentions to keep the franchise in Missouri. The day after the 2015 season concluded, the Rams – joined by the Oakland Raiders and San Diego Chargers – each applied to relocate to

Los Angeles. Undeterred by a $550m relocation fee, the Rams returned to the West Coast after NFL team owners voted 30-2 in favour of their move to LA, with the team becoming the first major league sports franchise to move since 2011 when NHL's Atlanta Thrashers became the Winnipeg Jets. The Los Angeles Memorial Stadium was to be their home, but it was only ever going to be temporary.

On 5 January 2015, the *Los Angeles Times* reported Kroenke was partnering with investment company Stockbridge Capital Group to develop a new, state-o-the-art NFL stadium on an Inglewood property. Inglewood City Council approved the stadium the following month, and construction on the 70,000-seater arena – which could be expanded to 100,000 plus for major events – began in December 2015. Sharing the incredible stadium with the Chargers, the Rams moved into SoFi Stadium for the 2020 season.

The move to Los Angeles meant the players were certainly feeling groggier than four years earlier. The combination of an eight-hour time difference and the early kick-off time – 6:30am in LA when the Giants received the opening kick – was an added complication. After New York kicker Robbie Gould – replacing John Brown after he was placed on the commissioner exemption list due to domestic abuse – nailed a 29-yard field goal, the first instance of fatigue from the Rams came to light.

Keenum's dart to Austin deflected off the receiver's hands and into the air before landing in the clutches of star safety Landon Collins. Collins returned the pick 44 yards for a sensational touchdown, evading tackles as he weaved his way into the end zone with his defensive team-mates acting as blockers to will him over the line. The exceptional play from Collins – just the second interception of his career – was so incredible that fans in the stadium surely didn't mind the barren run of offensive play either side of half-time, in which the Giants and Rams combined for 11 straight punts.

With 12:20 remaining in the game, those in attendance were finally treated to some action – and it was Collins in the thick of it once more. After Keenum missed a wide-open Brian Quick, the quarterback was punished as his throw towards Austin deflected again to Collins, who returned the ball 18 yards to the New York 35. On third down, Manning found Beckham Jr to advance 22 yards downfield and Rashad Jennings eventually powered into the end zone to crucially give his team a 17-10 lead.

Los Angeles, the nominal home team, were certainly not the team the British fans wanted to see win. The screens around Twickenham stated 'Quiet please, offence at work' but the capacity crowd roared their support for the Giants. The Rams drove to the New York 37 before Keenum was picked by Dominique Rodgers-Cromartie, and it was déjà vu on the doomed final drive. Following a nice gain of 23 yards to Quick, Keenum added the final nail to his own coffin with 50 seconds remaining on the New York 15. Quick didn't hear the quarterback's audible, and Keenum floated a fade into the end zone which was easily picked off by Rodgers-Cromartie to send the Giants home happy. After the game, Jennings spoke of how the defence won the game for Big Blue – and he wasn't wrong. Both Collins and Rodgers-Cromartie collected two interceptions each in the win while the Giants allowed just ten points at Twickenham.

Keenum, who finished with 291 yards and a touchdown, had thrown an interception on the Rams' final offensive play in each of their last three games, fuelling further debate surrounding the starting role with Goff waiting in the wings. After the Rams came out of their bye week with a loss to Carolina, a 9-6 win over the Jets in New York led Fisher to change his quarterback. Goff came in, and the Rams didn't win another game as they slipped to 4-12.

The Giants finished the season with an impressive 11-5 record before losing 38-13 to Green Bay at Lambeau Field in the Wildcard Round. While it was not the way they wanted the season to end, 2016 was a good year for the Giants; as of the

2021 season, they are yet to achieve more than six wins in a single campaign. New York may look back on this trip to London in the same way Twickenham officials do – a successful business trip for all involved, except Keenum and the Rams.

NFL REGULAR SEASON WEEK NINE
30 October 2016
WASHINGTON REDSKINS 27
CINCINNATI BENGALS 27
Wembley Stadium

The NFL's International Series concluded its 2016 slate with a familiar result for British soccer fans: a draw befitting of Wembley Stadium, the home of the England national football team. It was the second tied game of the NFL season – the first time multiple games had ended in stalemate since 1997 – and it proved to be an exhilarating finale for the London games in front of a record attendance of 84,448 satisfied customers. With the Tottenham Hotspur Stadium confirmed and under construction, professional American football appeared destined to remain on British shores.

The clash with Washington, whose record stood at 4-3 compared to Cincinnati's 3-4, was technically a home game for the Bengals despite the fact they travelled nearly 4,000 miles to do battle, and head coach Marvin Lewis was oddly philosophical about the prospect: 'We're not going to London, we're playing the Redskins and it happens to be in London.' While Lewis clearly didn't intend on playing tourist and seeing sights, neither did Washington.

Quarterback Kirk Cousins led the Redskins from their own 20 to the end zone on a 15-play drive that controlled the clock, using almost seven and a half minutes before Robert Kelley juked inside to score a four-yard rush. It was the first NFL rushing touchdown for Kelly in his career after the undrafted rookie from Tulane started ahead of the injured Matt Jones. The Bengals responded immediately as Alex Erickson carried a kick return 66 yards up the right sideline before Bashaud Breeland tackled him out of bounds. Cincinnati were back on level terms at 7-7 soon after; Giovani Bernard rushed eight yards to score following sensational blocking from his offensive line.

Washington took a 10-7 lead into half-time after a red zone defensive stand from Cincinnati, with Dustin Hopkins chipping in from 20 yards. Bengals kicker Mike Nugent, who struggled from distance across his 12-year career, had a chance to tie the game but his low-trajectory effort from 51 yards out went wide left. It was no less than the Redskins deserved as Cousins started well and threw for 183 yards, the bulk of which went to tight end duo Jordan Reed and Vernon Davis. At half-time, Washington had compiled 220 yards to Cincinnati's 82 and had spent nearly nine more minutes with the ball in their hands, but they led by just three points. A missed field goal from Hopkins – whose effort was astonishingly underhit – and three potential interceptions dropped by star corner Josh Norman kept the Bengals in the game, and it felt like a matter of time before Andy Dalton and his offence hit back. They did just that in the second half.

Dalton led the Bengals downfield, and they again benefitted from the poor hands of Norman as the corner – who had signed a five-year, $75m deal with the Redskins in the offseason to surpass Darrelle Revis as the highest-paid cornerback in NFL history – was flagged for illegal use of the hands. Dalton hit Tyler Eifert for a 15-yard touchdown, although Nugent shanked the extra point wide in what was quickly becoming a painful theme. After a quick Washington three-and-out, the Bengals found the end zone again as quarterback Dalton faked a give to Jeremy Hill before running in himself from a yard out to give the Bengals a 20-10 lead in the third quarter.

It was a lead that would last little over two minutes. Starting on their own nine-yard line, Dalton hit Desean Jackson on a deep pass for 38 yards before Kelley drew an unnecessary roughness penalty to move to the Cincinnati 26. Kelley rushed for three yards before Cousins found Reed on an out-route, and the tight end took it to the house for a 23-yard touchdown reception, diving over the plane to score. Dalton was then intercepted by linebacker Will Compton on an awry pass intended for Eifert, and Cousins hit Davis for a 26-yard gain before he picked out Jamison Crowder for a 33-yard touchdown. It was a historic moment: the 100th touchdown scored in the 17th game played in London. The momentous score gave Washington a 24-20 lead with 9:30 remaining in the fourth quarter – but the to-and-fro nature of the match continued as Cincinnati retaliated.

Several short plays later, Dalton found Eifert in midfield before another Norman pass interference on AJ Green was declined after the two-time All-Pro receiver somehow pulled off a terrific diving catch with the corner all over him. The play set up Hill's touchdown, with the running back rushing in from a yard out to give the Bengals a three-point lead. With just over a minute remaining in regulation time, Hopkins shrugged off his earlier miss and made a 40-yard field goal to tie the game at 27-27 – and just like that, London was treated to its first overtime experience.

Offences struggled in the additional period as both teams punted, before Washington drove to the Cincinnati 16 and the game came down to one swing of Hopkins's boot. The kicker nailed his first attempt from 34 yards, but Bengals head coach Lewis managed to sneak a timeout in just before the ball was snapped. It is a standard play in the NFL, an attempt at 'icing the kicker'; essentially, trying to force the kicker to allow the pressure of the moment to get to him. It worked. Hopkins scooped his second effort wide left and into the stands to the delight of the British fans. His team-mate Norman, who had not exactly experienced a banner day himself, was quick to defend Hopkins on Twitter: 'If you're putting this game on [Hopkins] for missing the field goal, you suck, know nothing about football. It's a team game.' Hopkins himself was surprisingly calm afterwards, suggesting it was slick on the pitch but that the conditions didn't affect him.

The game wasn't quite over yet. Chris Baker and Will Compton stripped the ball loose from Dalton's clutches, allowing Anthony Lanier to recover. Washington had one more chance to win the game with a minute remaining, but Cousins could not connect and he threw his final pass out of bounds to secure the draw.

It was a crazy game littered with penalties, particularly by the Redskins. Washington was flagged 15 times for 106 yards, leading to eight Bengals first downs and damaging Washington's overtime drives into Bengals territory. The Redskins went on to finish 8-7-1, good enough for third in the NFC East. Cincinnati had seven penalties for 85 yards, leaving with a 3-4-1 record before finishing 6-9-1. Unsurprisingly, both teams missed the playoffs.

During the game, Washington safety Will Blackmon fractured and dislocated his left thumb and while he returned to action when his replacement, Duke Ihenacho, suffered a concussion, Blackmon left Wembley in a cast – but it did not dampen his London experience. 'It was really fun. The biggest game in terms of the stage I played on was obviously the Super Bowl [with the Giants at Super Bowl XLVI] but my experience playing here at Wembley was similar. We were here all week for the festivities – it was more about that than trying to actually get ready and prepare!' While he enjoyed his second game in London, Blackmon commented on the difficulties of playing at the home of soccer. 'Wembley is not the best place for football in terms of the pitch! The grass is slick so it is designed for a soccer ball to fly down the field, not so much stopping and starting – but other than that I had a blast. I'm really happy my family got to experience it.'

Blackmon became an NFL analyst at Sky Sports for the 2019 and 2021 seasons and is a big advocate of expanding the sport on British shores. He admitted he loves the direction American football is headed on an international scale, but Blackmon understands the name of the game for the league's powers-that-be: 'It is very financially beneficial for the NFL to [hold the International Series], so let's not kid ourselves about that!'

Professional American football in the United Kingdom had certainly come a long way from the days of NFL Europe, where teams folded on an annual basis and the league reportedly lost $30m a year.

2017

Fantastic Four

NFL REGULAR SEASON WEEK THREE
24 September 2017
BALTIMORE RAVENS 7
JACKSONVILLE JAGUARS 44
Wembley Stadium

FINALLY, THE Jacksonville Jaguars started to feel at home in London. Their clash with the Baltimore Ravens was their fifth match and third successive victory on British soil. Armed with a winning record at Wembley Stadium, disgruntled rumblings in Florida regarding their 'home' team were quieter than ever. Winning truly does cure everything, after all.

It was the Ravens' first trip across the Atlantic – and this was a chastening loss after the Ravens had started 2-0 with wins over AFC North rivals Cincinnati and Cleveland. The Ravens were humbled and crushed at the hands of the Jaguars, who came into the contest with a record of 1-1 after following up their win at Houston with a loss at home to Tennessee. Yet again, the Jags picked up their first home win of the season in the Big Smoke.

As the teams took to the field, the home crowd – clearly in favour of the black, gold and teal-clad Jaguars – had a reason to cheer for Baltimore. Ravens rookie right guard Jermaine

Eluemunor, a London-born fifth-round pick out of Texas A&M, made his debut after being inactive for the first two games. Eluemunor was what the International Series was all about – he became interested in American football by stumbling across the first match between the New York Giants and Miami Dolphins in 2007. The process was working.

The 2016 social injustice protest led by Colin Kaepernick remained ongoing and had been ignited further following controversial comments by President Trump. During a rally in Huntsville, Alabama on 22 September 2017, Trump took aim at the NFL and insisted any owner with a protesting player should 'get that son of a bitch off the field' – and his comments beautifully backfired not only across the league, but the Atlantic Ocean. Players throughout the league spoke out against Trump and the protest started by Kaepernick was given new life. In total, 27 Jaguars and Ravens knelt on the sideline – the most ever in a single NFL game – while players, coaches and even Jags owner Shahid Khan linked arms. This was a stance of unity and brotherhood that not even the leader of a global superpower could break.

While the players showed their solidarity off the field, the two teams were going in different directions on it. The Ravens managed just 186 yards of total offence as they were swarmed by the Jaguars defence. The Jags, sensing their opportunity to impress, put points on the board on their first three drives with Jason Myers kicking field goals either side of a touchdown scored by Marcedes Lewis, who quickly became the star of the show. This was not a Jaguars performance the British faithful had become accustomed to. Against the Bills in 2015 and the Colts in 2016, the Jags had a 17-point lead only to win by three – but this team was different. Six plays took the Jaguars from their own 20 to the Baltimore 17 with Blake Bortles and Leonard Fournette leading the charge. Bortles faked a hand-off to his running back and Marquise Lee before he floated a perfect throw into the hands of Lewis to dive over the line. With Myers's second kick – a 45-yard field goal – the Jags were sitting pretty at 13-0 with just under 11 minutes remaining in the second quarter.

After almost 22 minutes of regulation time, Flacco finally threw a pass that was caught – but it wasn't what he or the Ravens wanted. The quarterback and Super Bowl XLVII MVP threw a lofted ball down the left-hand sideline only for Jeremy Maclin to juggle the ball into the arms of AJ Bouye, and the corner – who would be named a Second-Team All-Pro in 2017 – took the ball 19 yards to the Baltimore 28. The Jags took advantage of the field position: both Fournette and Bortles used their legs to get to the five-yard line before the quarterback picked out Allen Hurns for the touchdown. The receiver extended Jacksonville's lead to 20-0, holding onto the ball despite being cleaned up by CJ Mosley as he made the catch. With the touchdown, Hurns – who had scored in each of the Jags' last three London games – matched Brandon Lloyd as the only players to score three touchdowns at Wembley Stadium after Lloyd scored once for the Broncos in 2010 and twice for the Patriots in 2012. 'It's been three years straight with a touchdown,' said Hurns, nicknamed 'Mr London' by his team-mates. 'It's kind of like a second home here. It's always great having the game here with the atmosphere.' Another Baltimore punt led to another Jacksonville field goal, sending the 'home' team into half-time with a crushing 23-0 lead.

Jacksonville dominated the Ravens in every possible way during the first half. The Jags defence forced a three-and-out on the Ravens' first four possessions en route to their commanding lead, and they picked up where they left off in the third quarter.

Baltimore's first drive of the second half ended in predictable fashion. Flacco, aiming for Mike Wallace on a deep pass down the middle of the turf, was intercepted by the Jags sophomore corner and budding superstar Jalen Ramsey. Ramsey became renowned for his trash talk, but the corner walked the walk as much as he talked the talk in London, cutting inside his man to dive and snatch possession for Jacksonville. Two plays later, and the Jags had scored again when Lewis was found by Bortles on a 30-yard touchdown dagger.

The Ravens, still alive but barely breathing at 30-0 down, crossed midfield three times in total but they didn't break into Jacksonville territory until the third quarter when Terrance West rushed to the Jags 45. The rare Baltimore optimism was extinguished on the very next play, with West fumbling after a spectacular tackle from Calais Campbell as he dived and punched the ball free, with linebacker Telvin Smith scooping up for a 52-yard gain to set the Jags up at the Baltimore two-yard line. The Ravens were struggling and Flacco, who joked at practice on Friday that he thought the players would be 'zombies', insisted the travel was not to blame for their shoddy performance. After all, the Jags had made the same journey.

If the Jaguars were suffering in the same way as the Ravens, they did not show it. Fournette was pushed back to the Baltimore four-yard line, but Bortles simply threw it up for Lewis to claim his third touchdown of the day, completing a hat-trick at Wembley Stadium. Lewis had zero receptions through the first two games and three touchdowns in the last two seasons combined – but on this day, he was the mayor of London. It was the first three-touchdown game of his career, and the tight end became the third Jags player to collect three touchdowns in a single game after Jimmy Smith in 2000 and Allen Robinson in 2015.

The Jaguars were in an uncompromising mood, tallying 410 yards of total offence – easily their best output of the season – and delivered the Ravens their worst defeat since 9 November 1997, when they were crushed 37-0 by the Steelers in Pittsburgh. The Jags punctuated their victory by running a fake punt to close the fourth quarter for a 58-yard gain. Fournette then rushed in from three yards out to become the first Jaguars player to run for a touchdown in each of his first three games. His score made it

44-0 in favour of Jacksonville. Forget knocking – these Jaguars were smashing down the Ravens' chamber door.

Bortles left the game at 44-0, deciding his work was done. To open the fourth quarter, Bortles was replaced by Chad Henne after completing 20 of 31 passes for 244 yards – and the 125.5 passer rating was the second best of his NFL career.

Finally, Baltimore got on the board. The Ravens drove 76 yards in nine plays with backup quarterback Ryan Mallett, who relieved Flacco of his nightmare, picking out tight end Benjamin Watson for a six-yard touchdown. At least there would be no shutout for the sorry Ravens fans who went to Wembley to cheer their team. Flacco finished the game with a total of 28 yards, no touchdowns and two interceptions, while his 12.0 passer rating was the worst of his career. The Ravens recovered from their British bashing to finish 9-7, narrowly missing out on the playoffs due to a late defeat to the Cincinnati Bengals. Games like the International Series crushing led to rumblings of fan discontent with Flacco, but Baltimore would soon have a reason to be excited at the quarterback position. The Ravens traded back into the first round of the 2018 NFL Draft to select Heisman Trophy winner Lamar Jackson out of Louisville, and his dynamic running ability was unlike anything the NFL had ever seen. Jackson became the second unanimous MVP in league history after a stellar 2019 campaign, and only time will tell if he can replicate Flacco and lead the Ravens to a Lombardi Trophy.

The Jaguars' crushing win over the Ravens gave their fans plenty of reasons to be hopeful and they carried that momentum throughout their 2017 campaign until they were within touching distance of the Super Bowl. The Jaguars finish the year 10-6, the franchise's best record since 2007, where they were dumped out of the playoffs by the undefeated New England Patriots at the Divisional Round. Jacksonville defeated the Buffalo Bills on Wildcard Weekend, with Ramsey making an incredible interception to secure a 10-3 win at EverBank

Field. The Jags rolled into Pittsburgh where they contested an unbelievable shootout against the Steelers, one of the most successful NFL franchises in history with six Super Bowl championships. Rookie star Fournette rushed for 109 yards and three touchdowns while Bortles contributed 214 yards and a score to lead the Jags to an unlikely 45-42 victory – setting up a trip to the AFC Championship Game, just one win away from the Super Bowl. The team standing in their way? The New England Patriots.

The 2018 AFC Championship Game is one of the great 'what if' moments in recent NFL history. The Jags led 17-10 heading into the fourth quarter and Myles Jack made a truly unbelievable fumble recovery on Dion Lewis only for the referees to rule that the linebacker was down, denying him and the Jags a sure-fire touchdown. While the Jags claimed possession, their offence began to stagnate and New England retaliated. With 2:50 remaining, Danny Amendola made a brilliant toe-tap touchdown for his second score to give the Patriots the lead. The Jags drove to win, but corner Stephon Gilmore denied Bortles's attempted pass to rookie Dede Westbrook, and Foxborough erupted while Jacksonville were eliminated.

The 2017 team was filled with immense potential, but it blew up just as quickly as it burst onto the scene. A toxic atmosphere took hold of the franchise and led to the departures of Bouye, Ngakoue, Campbell, Ramsey and Fournette, among others.

NFL REGULAR SEASON WEEK FOUR
1 October 2017
NEW ORLEANS SAINTS 20
MIAMI DOLPHINS 0
Wembley Stadium

The New Orleans Saints landed in the United Kingdom with a losing record at 1-2, but the 1-1 Miami Dolphins proved to be the perfect opponent to kickstart a season that would take them to within seconds of the NFC Championship Game.

They say you have to appreciate a goalless draw in order to be a true soccer fan and, under the Wembley arch, British fans were treated to the gridiron equivalent – a proper penalty-laden, error-filled, lacklustre clash between the Saints and Dolphins. At least fans could say they witnessed history: it was the first NFL shutout in London as well as the city's lowest-scoring game, which clearly makes the entry fee worth it.

On a rainy British afternoon, there was a discouraging suggestion that the NFL wanted to move on from the social justice movement led by Colin Kaepernick. After seeing record numbers protest the previous week, just three Miami players – receiver Kenny Stills, safety Michael Thomas and tight end Julius Thomas – took a knee compared to ten players in their last outing at MetLife Stadium, a 20-6 loss to the New York Jets. The Saints opted for a different route, kneeling before the anthem after collectively deciding to stand during it.

When Miami took to the field for the game's opening drive, they were met by an expectant roar from the 84,423 in attendance. Jay Cutler appeared to feed off the energy and drove the Dolphins into the opposition red zone – and then the quarterback seemed to remember who he was. Cutler, described as a 'terrible leader' by former team-mates from his time in Chicago, was prone to errors and it was to nobody's immense surprise that the veteran quarterback completely overthrew Thomas, placing the ball in a spot where only Ken Crawley could make a play on it – and the corner duly made the interception in the end zone.

The opening drive, capped off by a rushed Cutler throwing off-balance, set the tone for the entire match. The Saints looked to take advantage, with legendary quarterback Drew Brees leaning on offensive weapons in Michael Thomas and rookie star Alvin Kamara to take New Orleans to the Miami 23-yard line. Not wanting Cutler to take the spotlight, kicker Will Lutz shanked a 41-yard effort wide right on the second play of the second quarter. The miss meant the two teams threatened to play the first scoreless opening half since week 14 of the 2011 season, but Lutz regained his composure to thump a 43-yard field goal and make it 3-0 as time expired in the second quarter.

This was an ugly game of few big plays and the sport's innate stop-start nature was particularly painful as the teams combined for 19 penalties in the game. It was a tough watch and Saints head coach Sean Payton refused to get carried away even after securing the win to take his team to 2-2. 'It doesn't have to be aesthetically pleasing to be effective,' Payton declared. 'The first half was fairly sloppy and there are a number of things we are going to have to clean up, but we won.' After arriving in London on Monday, it took New Orleans six days and 30 minutes of gridiron action before they finally appeared to shake off the jet lag.

The Saints travelled 77 yards in 11 plays to open the third quarter, with Brees expertly pump faking a defender before hitting Brandon Coleman for a 31-yard gain on a deep pass down the left-hand sideline. The Saints meticulously got nearer and nearer to the end zone, with Kamara pushed out of bounds at the three-yard line following a gain of 12. Brees rolled right and found Thomas, who withstood a huge hit from Cordrea Tankersley to score the first touchdown of the game and make it 10-0 with just over nine minutes remaining in the third quarter.

Three straight punts followed, before Lutz converted a 45-yard field goal, extending the Saints' lead to 13. The match was ultimately summarised by an excellent passage on the following Miami drive. On second down from the Miami 39, Cutler was sacked by Cameron Jordan, who brilliantly knocked the ball loose. Five Saints players, including Jordan, made a move to collect the ball with only Cutler and British running back Jay Ajayi as conceivable threats to the recovery. They all missed the ball, somehow allowing tackle Ja'Wuan James to retain possession for the Dolphins. It was a catalogue of errors that was hardly the most compelling advert for any British fan on the fence about the sport. The recovery came to nothing – Miami punted back to the Saints, who then put the game out of reach.

Brees hit Thomas for a 30-yard gain to get their fourth quarter drive going, and followed that up with a throw to Ted Ginn Jr. The former Dolphin made a terrific catch after confusing Bobby McCain to the point that the corner fell over, unsure of where Ginn was. On third-and-goal from the 12, Brees nailed a shovel pass to the onrushing Kamara, who burst inside the Miami defence to score and seal victory at 20-0 with just under four minutes remaining.

The Dolphins' desperate attempt to score any points ended in vain with a turnover on downs. Brees insisted the shutout win was significant, with the offence doing all they needed to win the game. It was a generous assessment of the Saints, but they had picked up their second win of the 2017 season thanks to Brees's 268 yards and pair of touchdown passes.

The victory was the second on an eight-match streak that took the Saints to the top of the NFC South, and they ended the season 11-5 – good enough to win the division and book a playoff match against the Carolina Panthers. The Saints were too strong for their rivals, winning 31-26 at the Mercedes-Benz Superdome, but it was their match – and the fateful final play – against Minnesota that will live long in the memory.

The Saints came back from a 17–0 first-half deficit and established a 24–23 lead over the Vikings with just 25 seconds remaining. It seemed as though, with the Philadelphia Eagles missing starting quarterback Carson Wentz due to injury, the Saints and Brees could finally return to the Super Bowl since their emotional Super Bowl XLIV win in 2010. On the last play of the game, Vikings quarterback Case Keenum threw a 27-yard pass to Stefon Diggs and it appeared Saints safety Marcus Williams would easily stop the receiver. Instead, Williams missed the straightforward tackle and Diggs ran to the end zone to score and win the game for Minnesota on a 61-yard touchdown pass. It was the first game in playoff history to end in a touchdown as time expired, with radio announcer Paul Allen's cementing the play in NFL lore under an iconic guise: the Minneapolis Miracle.

Back in London, the loss was not the grand homecoming Ajayi wanted as he finished with 46 yards on 12 carries. 'We didn't put any points on the board so it is extremely frustrating,' he admitted. 'It doesn't make sense because we have the talent.' Ajayi's talent was certainly spotted, with Philadelphia trading for the running back to help them win the championship – which is exactly what Ajayi did as the Eagles surprisingly defeated the Patriots to win Super Bowl LII. Miami head coach Adam Gase called on his team not to panic despite dropping to a losing record, as they had recovered from 1-4 a year ago to make the playoffs. Lightning didn't strike twice though, as the Dolphins limped home to finish 6-10.

Over 80,000 fans sat in the rain to watch a game of football that was genuinely difficult to watch, which was perhaps British stubbornness shining through. It was either that, or the United Kingdom truly liked American football.

NFL REGULAR SEASON WEEK SEVEN
22 October 2017
ARIZONA CARDINALS 0
LOS ANGELES RAMS 33
Twickenham Stadium

Fans would be forgiven for thinking that if a team scored 33 points in a shutout win at Twickenham Stadium in late October, it was either England or New Zealand's All Blacks going to town in rugby union's autumn internationals. Instead, it was simply the Los Angeles Rams' turn to lay down the gauntlet as they overwhelmed their NFC West rivals, the Arizona Cardinals, at the home of rugby.

It was Arizona's first taste of International Series action after president Michael Bidwill had enjoyed his time in the Big Smoke three years earlier. 'In 2014, I attended the Raiders–Dolphins game at Wembley Stadium and experienced first-hand the incredible enthusiasm UK fans have for the NFL,' Bidwill said in a statement announcing Arizona's participation in the International Series. 'I also encountered a huge number of Cardinals fans asking when our team would be playing there. I know this is great news for them as well as the US members of the Red Sea who couldn't have a cooler destination to see a road game.'

The match was the second time the Cardinals played a regular season game outside the United States, as the team took a 31-14 victory over the San Francisco 49ers in Mexico City back in 2005 in front of a then-NFL record attendance of 103,467. It wasn't the first time the franchise had played in England either, as the Cardinals faced the Minnesota Vikings at Wembley in 1983 when they resided in St Louis. They lost that match, and head coach Bruce Arians was hoping the team could find some momentum on British soil after defeating the Buccaneers the previous week to go 3-3.

The Rams had impressed so far under new head coach Sean McVay, defeating the new-look Jaguars in Jacksonville to move to 4-2 ahead of the clash with Arizona. Both of their defeats had come at home, demonstrating how poor attendances at the Los Angeles Memorial Coliseum meant homefield advantage was not something the franchise were enjoying. In fact, losing a home game was not necessarily the worst thing for the Rams, who wanted to avenge their 17-10 defeat to the Giants at Twickenham almost 12 months to the day earlier.

Adrian Peterson was gearing up to play his second match for the Cardinals since being acquired via trade with the New Orleans Saints, after rushing for 134 yards and two touchdowns in his debut a week ago. For any of the 73,736 fans packed into Twickenham who thought they would witness a fired-up Cardinals and rejuvenated Peterson, it wasn't to be.

On the opening drive, Phil Dawson missed a 32-yard field goal to condemn Arizona to a point-less start, and it was a miss that the Cardinals would never recover from. The Rams took the lead through the leg of Greg Zuerlein who made no mistake from 23 yards after a potential Cooper Kupp touchdown fell incomplete, and the kicker added another from 33 on the first drive of the second quarter. Both efforts came either side of an incredibly touching moment when those inside the stadium paid tribute midway through the first quarter to late American broadcaster Kevin Cadle, a true legend within British circles, credited with growing the game immensely in the UK.

At 6-0 with six minutes remaining of the first half, the game spiralled away from the Cardinals. Carson Palmer was hit by Alec Ogletree and intercepted by Lamarcus Joyner, who returned it to the Arizona 18-yard line. The veteran quarterback exited the game after suffering the blow to his arm, and the Rams added insult to genuine injury when running back Todd Gurley rushed in on the very next play for an 18-yard touchdown. It was a fine run from the third-year back, who would be named a First-Team All-Pro and NFL Offensive Player of the Year as he scored 19 total touchdowns.

The Rams forced an Arizona punt and took the ball 88 yards in just eight plays, with Gurley showing off his unique combination of pace, power and evasiveness to break for a 35-yard gain. Goff hit Kupp for 16 yards and found himself in the end zone when he turned a zone-read keeper into a nine-yard touchdown. With 41 seconds remaining in the first half, the Rams were somehow still not done as backup quarterback Drew Stanton was immediately intercepted by linebacker Mark Barron, setting up Zuerlein's third field goal – the longest of the day at 53 yards out.

The Rams led 23-0 at half-time after outscoring Arizona 17-0 in the last six minutes of the first half. With a commanding lead in place, the Rams cruised to victory but added to their 23-point lead with another field goal from the boot of Zuerlein. The kicker had set a franchise record by making seven field goals in their win over the Dallas Cowboys three weeks earlier, and his fine form continued in London as he made the kick from 34 yards.

Goff threw a poor interception to Deone Buchannon, but Kupp finished the scoring by taking a screen pass and cutting inside for an 18-yard touchdown with just under four minutes remaining. It was a fine outing for Goff, who completed 22 of 37 passes for 235 yards and two total scores, while Gurley firmly put his disappointing 2016 season behind him by carrying the ball 22 times for 106 yards and a touchdown.

While the Rams offence deserves praise for scoring 33 points, their defence dominated to secure the franchise's first shutout since a 24-0 road win against Washington on 7 December 2014. On the flipside, it was the first time the Cardinals had failed to score since a crushing 58-0 defeat at the hands of the Seattle Seahawks on 9 December 2012. History was made in London, which hosted its second successive shutout after both teams had scored in each of the previous 19 International Series matches.

Peterson was held to just 21 yards on 11 carries on a disappointing day for the Cardinals. 'That was like one of them tapes you burn,' offensive coordinator Harold Goodwin said. 'And then you burn it again and then you burn it again. It was a nightmare, and it was a long ride home, brother. Long ride home.' The talented-but-ageing Cardinals roster went on to finish 8-8, and Arians – who was named the 2014 Coach of the Year and took Arizona to the NFC Championship Game the following year – announced his retirement. Arians would return to football to take the Tampa Bay job in 2019, picking up free agent Tom Brady in 2020 before leading the franchise to Super Bowl glory.

As for the Rams, the win continued their fine start to life under McVay. The team's record stood at 5-2, winning five of their first seven matches for the first time since 2003 – the last time the Rams finished with a winning record. Under their rookie head coach's tutelage and mind for an intricate offensive playbook, the Rams breezed to an 11-5 record to secure the third seed in the NFC. Four of their five losses came at home, which was a warning for their playoff meeting with the Atlanta Falcons in Los Angeles.

The Rams lost 26-13 to Atlanta, but the future was bright with McVay at the helm and a roster filled with stars, including 2017 Defensive Player of the Year Aaron Donald. As London prepared to host its unprecedented fourth NFL game in a single season, the future of gridiron football on these shores had never been brighter.

NFL REGULAR SEASON WEEK EIGHT
29 October 2017
MINNESOTA VIKINGS 33
CLEVELAND BROWNS 16
Twickenham Stadium

Last time Vikings invaded England, they conquered Pittsburgh. The time before that, the warriors claimed the entire country. On this autumnal afternoon, London – and Cleveland – sufficed for Minnesota's Norsemen.

The two teams charged with closing the largest slate of NFL regular season games in London were left with the age-old (or rather, since 2007) question: when is the optimal time to travel? The Vikings opted for Wednesday night, landing at 10am GMT with head coach Mike Zimmer instructing his players to sleep on the nine-hour flight as they had their first practice five hours after landing – and Zimmer was aware of the record of teams landing first. 'We've had sleep people come talk to us, you know we're getting the whole gamut. I was looking into all the scientific things for this; I'll either look smart or I'll look dumb.' He would certainly look better than opposite number Hue Jackson.

Jackson was a staff member for the London Monarchs as they sensationally won the inaugural World Bowl in 1991, but he was on a significantly worse team relative to their competition when he returned to the capital with the 0-7 Cleveland Browns. Dubbed the 'quarterback whisperer' – a classic football cliché awarded to coaches with a record of developing players in the game's most crucial position – Jackson needed to raise his voice in London. His handling of rookie quarterback DeShone Kizer was perplexing: after originally naming the second-round pick the starter out of training camp, Kizer started the first five games of the 2017 season before getting benched halfway through the home loss to the New York Jets. He sat out the sixth game but returned for the defeat to the Tennessee Titans only to be benched again – and then Kizer was named the starter for the London trip. It's important to remember Cleveland were hardly the model franchise of the NFL during this time, holding the number one pick for successive years in 2017 and 2018.

Even without 2017 first overall selection Myles Garrett, the Browns made the first significant play in London. Minnesota quarterback Case Keenum, returning to London after he threw four picks against the Giants as a Ram, was picked off on his fourth attempt of the opening drive by linebacker Joe Schobert after Carl Nassib deflected the ball into the air. Cleveland's offence, missing tackle Joe Thomas for the first time since 2006 after he suffered a torn triceps muscle, took their opportunity and found the end zone. Isaiah Crowell somehow snuck through the Minnesota defence and showed off his pace to burn away from Harrison Smith for his first touchdown of the year. Kicker Zane Gonzalez missed the extra point, much to the displeasure of the 74,237 packed into Twickenham.

The Browns defence forced a punt on Minnesota's second drive, only for special teams to do something particularly ordinary when returner Bryce Treggs muffed the catch, allowing Minnesota to recover at the Cleveland 20. Keenum couldn't take full advantage, but kicker Kai Forbath obliged to kick the first of his four field goals in the game from 35 yards out.

Both teams were struggling offensively, with five punts shared between them before Minnesota scored their opening touchdown. Keenum found his groove with a pair of passes to David Morgan and Jerrick McKinnon to get to the 18, before utilising a play action to hit Adam Thielen all alone in the back of the end zone. Thielen, forgetting the venue was Twickenham and not Wembley, celebrated giving the Vikings the 9-6 lead with a soccer-style knee slide. Forbath's extra point attempt was blocked.

The Cleveland offence, to the surprise of everyone on both sides of the Atlantic, responded immediately. With two minutes remaining and facing a troublesome third-and-12 from their own 16-yard line, Kizer flashed the quality that Jackson saw in him as he completed a 37-yard pass to Ricardo Louis and a shovel pass to Crowell, who took it 38 yards. Kizer capped the eight-play, 82-yard drive with a sneak to break the plane and regain the lead for the Browns. It was a lead they would take into half-time, although another Forbath kick made it a slender one-point advantage at 13-12.

It was the first time Cleveland were in front at the halfway stage in a match since a 7-0 lead over the Pittsburgh Steelers in the final week of the 2016 season, a game they would lose in overtime to seal a 1-15 record. The Browns had optimistic designs of securing a rare win in London, but their hopes began to fade on the second half's opening play from scrimmage. Danielle Hunter ripped the ball from Crowell, and Anthony Harris recovered it to set up Forbath's hat-trick. The kicker nailed it from 43 yards to give the Vikings a narrow 15-13 lead.

Forbath's opposite number did not have such a productive day. Gonzalez, a rookie, was 11 for 11 on extra points in his NFL career until this match, missing the added attempt as well as a 35-yard field goal as the Browns looked to retaliate in the third quarter. The GrassMaster hybrid turf-grass field at Twickenham may have had an impact; the rare system is common on soccer pitches but only a handful of NFL stadiums had installed it, including Lambeau Field and Lincoln Financial Field. It was hardly an excuse given Forbath's performance, and Gonzalez did hit on a 23-yard attempt to reclaim the lead – but the Vikings dominated from there, scoring 18 unanswered points.

Keenum was feeling himself under the Twickenham twilight, completing passes to Thielen and McKinnon for 25 and 11 yards respectively to advance to the Cleveland 15-yard line before cornerback Briean Boddy-Calhoun was called for pass interference in the end zone. From one yard out, McKinnon punched it in for the touchdown before rushing in the two-point conversion to make it a one-score game. The Browns went three-and-out on their next possession and the Vikings could smell blood. Cleveland didn't help themselves: penalties on Jamar Taylor and Boddy-Calhoun cost them a combined 33 yards. Minnesota drove 84 yards to score, with Keenum picking out Kyle Rudolph to toe-tap in the end zone from four yards out. At 33-16, it was game over.

Fans began to leave the stadium, and who could blame them late in a 17-point game. Those that left prematurely didn't miss much, with six drives – three from each team – combining for 38 yards and a 51-yard field goal as Forbath benefitted from a turnover on downs.

Keenum, who became the first player to appear in two NFL games at Twickenham, led Minnesota to their sixth win of the season with 288 yards and two touchdowns. Kizer struggled after a productive first half and was in danger of finishing the match below 50 per cent completion rate, but a run of passes against a disinterested Minnesota defence in garbage time allowed him to finish with 179 yards without a score.

The Twickenham fans were seeing a historic team in the making – just perhaps not the type of history they or the franchise wanted. Cleveland left London at 0-8 and would become the second team in NFL history to finish a season winless, losing each of their 16 matches. The 2007 Detroit Lions were the other team to suffer such an indignity, but these Browns were worse. Their record of 4-36 in the past three seasons was exceptionally poor, and it remains to be seen if such a disheartening run will be replicated. You're welcome, London.

The Vikings enjoyed a tremendous season, finishing 13-3 to win the NFC North and embark on a playoff run that saw the birth of the Minneapolis Miracle. However, it turned into a nightmare when Minnesota were handed an embarrassing 38-7 defeat at the hands of Nick Foles and the Philadelphia Eagles in the NFC Championship Game.

With the Vikings' comfortable win over the Browns at Twickenham, the 2017 London games drew to a close. The unprecedented slate of four matches was a resounding success both on and off the pitch, as four of the eight teams that played and won in London went on to win their respective divisions: New Orleans Saints, Los Angeles Rams, Jacksonville Jaguars and the Vikings.

With three games set to be held at Wembley Stadium in 2018, six teams hoped to use an international win to catapult them into the postseason in a bid to reach Super Bowl LIII.

2018

Super Bowl Champions Headline London

NFL REGULAR SEASON WEEK SIX
14 October 2018
SEATTLE SEAHAWKS 27
OAKLAND RAIDERS 3
Wembley Stadium

SINCE THE International Series began in 2007, the popularity of American football and the NFL has increased annually. After several years of quiet murmurs, the genuine hope of a London-based NFL team reached fever pitch in 2018 following Jacksonville Jaguars owner Shahid Khan's remarkable bid to purchase Wembley Stadium.

Khan held 'healthy' talks with the Football Association and wrote to the governing body outlining assurances that Wembley would remain England's national football stadium. There were certainly no plans to move Fulham from Craven Cottage, which suggested the move would be to accommodate the NFL – despite the Tottenham Hotspur Stadium, set to be the first specifically designed football stadium outside of North America, already under construction.

The bid fizzled out in mid-October when Khan withdrew from talks.

The match between the Seattle Seahawks and Oakland Raiders was also shrouded in mystery, although a dose of rain ensured at least some familiarity. The 2-3 Seahawks had recovered from their poor start to the season but were coming off a tight 33-31 loss at home to the Los Angeles Rams, while the Raiders – without defensive superstar Khalil Mack after he was traded to Chicago – were 1-4, under new head coach Jon Gruden. Gruden had swapped the booth for the sideline after the Raiders signed him to a ten-year, $100m contract in what was an unprecedented and unforeseen move. Three years later, the Raiders would certainly regret the deal as Gruden resigned in disgrace amid the release of controversial racist, homophobic and misogynistic emails between 2011 and 2018. Another great football mind lost to abhorrent personal actions.

With both the Seahawks and Raiders struggling to get going in 2018, a ten-hour flight to Europe from the West Coast was always going to be a welcome change for a fortunate team and a nightmare for the other.

Gruden, who picked Roger Moore as his favourite James Bond, tried to inject some humour when discussing the flight before a match between the two NFL teams furthest away from London: 'It was a great flight, I have these great flat beds, I got to sleep next to Daryl Worley and Emmanuel Lamur!' Raiders linebacker Tahir Whitehead was making his third trip to London after two appearances for the Detroit Lions, and he was a keen advocate of the NFL playing abroad. 'It's a good feeling to know the sport in and of itself is growing and I enjoy it,' Whitehead said of British fans wearing their favourite jerseys regardless of whether their team is playing. 'It's grown a great deal. The more we continue to travel and play in different places like here, the bigger the game is going to get.'

The game was certainly growing. The attendance of 84,922 was the largest for an NFL game at Wembley Stadium, so the novelty of the sport was certainly not wearing off as the International Series entered its 12th campaign.

In front of the record crowd, Seahawks quarterback Russell Wilson ensured there were no growing pains with his new offensive coordinator Brian Schottenheimer on the opening drive. Outside of a 23-yard pass to tight end Tyrone Swoopes, Wilson orchestrated a series that lasted 82 yards over seven minutes, with no gains of more than eight yards, as the Seahawks opted for death by a thousand cuts in London. Jaron Brown delivered the first killer blow, with Wilson taking his time to survey the field before throwing the five-yard touchdown strike as the receiver cut inside the end zone.

Oakland responded by attempting to establish former Seahawk great Marshawn Lynch in the run game. Lynch, affectionately known as 'Beast Mode' due to his powerful running style and ability to consistently bully defenders, struggled on the Raiders' first drive, gaining a single yard over three rushes before his team punted. It got worse for Oakland on their next drive, with Frank Clark breaching the protection to sack quarterback Derek Carr and force a fumble, recovered by Seattle defensive tackle Jarran Reed.

On third-and-five, a low snap appeared to ruin Seattle's touchdown hopes but Wilson worked the magic that is almost expected of him. He collected the ball off the floor, faked a throw, before stepping forward and floating a perfect lobbed pass over Daryl Worley to David Moore at the back of the end zone. Moore punctuated his third touchdown in Seattle's past two games by accidentally crashing into and flipping over the advertising board. Moore saw the board late and didn't realise how hard it would be until colliding into it, although the receiver didn't seem to care – the Seahawks were 14-0 up.

The Raiders tried to retaliate and reached the Seattle 23 before Carr was sacked. Out came rookie kicker Matt McCrane, signed as injury cover just three weeks before the match, who pulled his 48-yard attempt left. Kicking is a cut-throat business: McCrane was waived by the Raiders just nine days later.

The kicking conundrum in Oakland began when they opted not to re-sign long-term kicker Sebastian Janikowski, their first-round pick back in 2000. Raiders quarterback Carr labelled the kicker as one of his favourite team-mates when Seabass was in Oakland. How quickly friends become enemies on the field; Janikowski made the Raiders pay by kicking a 44-yard attempt just inside the posts to extend Seattle's lead to 17-0 at half-time.

The Raiders started the third quarter with another Carr fumble after yet another sack by Clark. An offensive holding penalty would kill the Oakland drive before it got going, and Janikowski chipped a 26-yard attempt to make it 20-0 to Seattle soon after. Aside from an interception made by Worley on a pass intended for partner in crime Doug Baldwin, Wilson was excellent and registered a passer rating of 125.4 for his efforts. He added a third touchdown to his box score on the first play of the fourth quarter, hitting Tyler Lockett for a ten-yard score. It was classic play from the dynamic quarterback as he showed off electric athleticism to juke away from defenders before floating the pass to the speedy Lockett.

Oakland avoided their first shutout since 2014 – and the third at Wembley in the past four games – when McCrane kicked a 43-yard field goal, but the Raiders had little to celebrate as the barrage of sacks took its toll on their quarterback. Carr left the game with a left arm injury and the Seahawks ran out the clock, holding possession of the ball for over eight minutes to secure the 27-3 win.

The Raiders left London frustrated. Lynch, playing in his first game against his old team, was held to just 45 yards on 13 carries while Carr was under constant duress all game. After trading Mack and suffering another defeat to slip to 1-5, heat was rising on Gruden and his nine-figure deal. The Raiders finished 4-12, securing the fourth overall pick in the 2019 NFL Draft. They spent the pick on Clelin Ferrell, a serviceable player who never reached the heights expected of him after his surprise selection.

Thanks to a terrific defence which sacked Carr six times, the Seahawks departed London with a comfortable road win. Pete Carroll's team continued their form to finish 10-6 and seal a spot in the Wildcard Round with the Rams atop the NFC West. However, their journey to the Super Bowl would end in Arlington, Texas as the Dallas Cowboys edged them 24-22.

While the Seahawks didn't win the Super Bowl, their appearance in the playoffs continued London's streak of victorious teams reaching the postseason. With the Los Angeles Chargers and Tennessee Titans ready to do battle at Wembley seven days later, history suggested the winner will have something to look forward to once they returned home.

NFL REGULAR SEASON WEEK SEVEN
21 October 2018
TENNESSEE TITANS 19
LOS ANGELES CHARGERS 20
Wembley Stadium

Unlike many European countries, gambling was illegal in the United Kingdom until 1960 with the first casino opening in 1961. Fifty-seven years later on a sun-soaked October day in London, Tennessee head coach Mike Vrabel was guilty of betting on Marcus Mariota and his offence.

The Titans had driven 89 yards over the final five minutes before their quarterback hit tight end Luke Stocker for a one-yard touchdown, just moments after diving short of the end zone himself. Instead of kicking the point that would have taken the game to overtime, Vrabel – perhaps knowing many of the 84,301 in attendance including myself had trains to catch – pinned it all on a single play. All or nothing. Mariota scrambled and evaded tackles before throwing an incompletion intended for Tajae Sharp, but it was negated by defensive holding against Los Angeles corner Casey Hayward. Handed a second opportunity to win, the game fell on Mariota's shoulders with 25 seconds left.

The Titans arrived in London atop the AFC South despite possessing a 3-3 record, not good enough for second place in any of the other divisions in their conference. They built momentum by defeating the Super Bowl champions, the Philadelphia Eagles, as well as AFC Championship runner-up Jacksonville, but lost their mojo with a narrow defeat at Buffalo before suffering a 21-0 shutout at home to the Baltimore Ravens last time out. Mariota, in his fourth season, was sacked a franchise record 11 times, but the Hawaiian was taking nothing for granted when he arrived at Syon House, the 1769 residence hosting the team in London: 'The thing about where I'm from, an island in the middle of the Pacific, you're talking about growing up there, [now] playing in London … it's pretty surreal.'

The Chargers had only recently entered new surroundings themselves, making their first trip to London since moving from San Diego to Los Angeles in 2017. The team, coached by Anthony Lynn and quarterbacked by Philip Rivers, were sitting at 4-2 behind the 5-1 Chiefs in the AFC West, but they arrived in the UK in good spirits after a three-game win streak. The Chargers were the home team for this clash, as the NFL requires a franchise that moves cities to host an international game – which is why the Las Vegas-bound Raiders 'welcomed' the Seahawks to London. The Chargers were hoping to be less gracious hosts than their division rivals.

If the Chargers were the home team, it was difficult to tell. The traditional cauldron of all 32 NFL teams being represented around Wembley Park was in effect, but the powder blue was the dominant colour. Unfortunately, both the Chargers and the Titans don that colour – but support did seem evenly split with plenty of fans from both sides crossing the Atlantic to support their team.

The Titans received the kick-off and drove downfield, converting twice on third down but failing on the third scenario to settle for a 28-yard field goal from Ryan Succop. The calculated approach of the Tennessee offence contrasted the Chargers' game plan, and that was evident on the first play from scrimmage. Rivers dropped back and threw a deep pass down the left sideline for receiver Tyrell Williams, who had burned away from Logan Ryan to catch and score untouched. A breathtaking start sent Wembley into raptures with the 84,301 in attendance on their feet as the Chargers burst into a 7-3 lead. 'I remember [the atmosphere] being good ten years ago but not this good,' Rivers said of the 'home' crowd.

The Chargers would give their fans more to cheer about late in the first quarter, with a 10-play drive – including a deep pass to a wide-open Keenan Allen for 24 yards – ending in a 29-yard field goal from kicker Mike Badgley. Tennessee would immediately respond, driving from their own 35 to the Chargers 15 only to settle for a Succop field goal.

At 10-6, the Titans defence forced a punt to set up the chance to take the lead into half-time. Mariota's offence was threatening to score as the quarterback hit Sharp for a 19-yard gain while also rushing himself to pick up a first down. On first-and-goal with 29 seconds remaining, Mariota's pass was deflected by Melvin Ingram and fellow linebacker Denzel Perryman made the interception to ensure the Chargers went into the break with a slender lead.

The Chargers clearly did not make offensive adjustments as they opened the second half much like the first. Rivers completed passes to Travis Benjamin and Austin Ekeler before firing a 55-yard looping touchdown strike to receiver Mike Williams to stroll into the end zone. With a Badgley extra point, the Chargers led 17-6. Tennessee had not scored in ten quarters of action and they needed to respond. A 37-yard kick return from Darius Jennings, coupled with an unnecessary roughness call against the Chargers, was the perfect antidote to conceding big-play touchdowns. Seven plays later, the Titans were in the end zone through the exceptional Derrick Henry, who punched it in from one yard out.

The remainder of the third quarter was particularly cagey, with the teams vying for a standout play to give them a field position advantage. Rivers and receiver Allen were seen shouting at one another and had to be held apart after the veteran quarterback threw an incompletion towards Williams in the end zone on third down in the fourth quarter, setting up a Badgley field goal to increase their lead to 20-13. Allen had beaten Titans corner Ryan and was wide open, with the wideout kicking a pylon in frustration. 'He ran a route so good he felt like he needed the ball – and he should,' Rivers clarified after the match. 'It's a passionate, emotional game. That won't be the last argument that any of us have on the sideline and I won't worry about it after two seconds.'

Tennessee looked to respond, but they couldn't as receiver Corey Davis dropped a seemingly simple catch on third down. The squandered opportunity was compounded when Succop missed a 51-yard attempt wide left, but the Titans would get one more chance after their defence forced a Los Angeles punt.

Mariota took a deep breath. With 31 seconds left and his team facing a 20-19 deficit, they were going for two for the second time. On the one-yard line, the Titans entrusted their quarterback instead of their bruising back Henry. Mariota's pass to Taywan Taylor deflected off safety Adrian Phillips's fingertips and fell incomplete. Vrabel showed his cards, but Lynn had the better hand. The gamble had not paid off, and the Titans left London with a losing record of 3-4.

The fans packed inside Wembley loved the gutsy call, and Vrabel himself was philosophical about the decision: 'When that drive started I thought in my mind if we scored – when we scored – if there was less than 40 seconds we were going for two and we were going to win the game. If there was a minute and 30, we were going to kick the extra point and go play defence. I'm not going to second-guess the call. Just didn't work out.' The Titans would finish the season 9-7, missing the playoffs following a defeat in London. They were the latest victims of the curse.

The crucial play went in Los Angeles' favour, and the players could board the ten-and-a-half hour flight with smiles on their faces. The Chargers won their next two games to finish the regular season at 12-4, but the team was forced to settle for a wildcard berth as the Kansas City Chiefs – who had compiled the same record – nicked the AFC West title. The Chargers defeated the Lamar Jackson-led Ravens 23-17 in Baltimore to set up a clash with the New England Patriots in Foxborough. Unfortunately, Tom Brady is Rivers' kryptonite: the Pats won 41-28 with Sony Michel scoring three touchdowns as Brady moved to 8-0 against Rivers in his career. Brady and the Patriots would add their final ring together, defeating the Rams in Super Bowl LIII.

The stodgy 13-3 win earned the Patriots some sort of revenge after they fell to the Eagles at the final hurdle last season. Before New England could reclaim their crown, Philadelphia would travel to London to face the Jacksonville Jaguars at Wembley in the final International Series clash of the year.

NFL REGULAR SEASON WEEK EIGHT
28 October 2018
PHILADELPHIA EAGLES 24
JACKSONVILLE JAGUARS 18
Wembley Stadium

Before the Super Bowl champion Philadelphia Eagles took to the hallowed Wembley pitch, 28 of the NFL's 32 teams had played a game in London. This late-October clash was Philadelphia's first transatlantic battle, and they were facing the International Series veterans: the Jacksonville Jaguars.

With three victories, no team had won or played more in London than the Jags. Their fate against Philadelphia promised to be successful, as first-time teams often leave London without picking up the win. Of the 16 teams who had played a single game in the Big Smoke, nine lost and two had tied.

However, these Eagles were different. They were history-makers. On 4 February 2018 – 58 years after their last title and 79 years after Tommy Thompson led Philadelphia to their second successive title – Nick Foles, the backup quarterback starting in place of the injured starter and MVP candidate Carson Wentz, outduelled Tom Brady. Brady arguably put up his finest postseason performance of his career as he threw for 505 yards and three touchdowns without a turnover, but Foles threw for 373 yards and three scores himself – and even caught the 'Philly Special' for a touchdown in what is surely one of the great play calls in NFL history. The Eagles put on a show to win 41-33 and secure their maiden Super Bowl championship.

Wentz was back, but Foles was still lingering around and had led the team to a 1-1 record before the starter was medically cleared to return. The Eagles had struggled immensely to open their campaign, suffering three losses in the four matches leading up to London, including a 21-17 home loss to the Carolina Panthers in which Philly led 17-0 in the fourth quarter. This was a must-win game for the Eagles – but they were still keen to enjoy their trip.

Head coach Doug Pederson referred to the NFL as becoming 'exciting', global and international as he settled into his London camp, while defensive end Michael Bennett admitted he has travelled to the city a number of times. 'I like going to Harrods. They've got all the good food downstairs. I've been to the London Eye. I like the parks, I like London,' Bennett revealed. 'It's just super expensive though.' I don't believe any of the record 85,870 in attendance would disagree.

Jacksonville owner Shahid Khan wanted to use the International Series matches in London to broaden interest in the Jaguars on a global scale, as well as stimulate economic support and awareness of the city. Unfortunately, the team were in the headlines for all the wrong reasons prior to the match after it emerged four players – Barry Church, Ronnie Harrison, DJ Hayden and Jarrod Wilson – allegedly attempted to leave a London nightclub without paying a £50,000 bar bill. 'There was definitely a misunderstanding, but as far as my actions are concerned, I take full responsibility,' Church said after the game. 'I don't want to be a distraction or anything like that to my team and my team-mates, but we handled it as a private matter within the team and we'll just go from there.' It was hardly the best preparation for Doug Marrone's team, but they got off to a good start come Sunday.

Wentz magically completed the first pass of the game to himself, with Calais Campbell batting the ball into the air for the quarterback to collect and dive for a first down to the amazement of the record attendance. He then brilliantly hit Jordan Matthews for 31 yards on third-and-14 on his own 32, but disaster struck on the following play when Marcell Dareus sacked Wentz and forced a fumble recovered by Jacksonville. The Jags turned the turnover into a lead, getting as far as the Philadelphia 33 before Josh Lambo thumped a 50-yard field goal through the sticks.

Unfortunately for Eagles fans, the next drive was more of the same. Wentz showed off his athleticism and scrambled for a first down, then found Nelson Agholor for a 39-yard completion to move to the Jacksonville 24. After a Josh Adams rush was swallowed for a one-yard gain, Wentz looked for tight end Josh Perkins in the end zone but star corner Jalen Ramsey had read the play and easily picked off the 2016 second overall pick.

The Jaguars could not take advantage of the turnover, and the Eagles tied the game through Jake Elliot after a 13-play drive stalled following a Campbell sack. The Jaguars instantly hit back as Bortles linked up with TJ Yeldon to shorten a third-and-21 to a fourth-and-six and move into Lambo's range as he kicked a 57-yard effort to give the Jags a 6-3 lead. After a Philadelphia punt, the Jags looked to extend their advantage but rookie corner Avonte Maddox popped the ball from receiver Keelan Cole, and Malcolm Jenkins – who clearly enjoyed his time in the United Kingdom as he would later become a minority investor in Burnley FC – scooped it up to give the Eagles excellent field position. Wentz needed just two plays: he rushed 13 yards on third down before launching a pass to tight end Dallas Goedert. Goedert evaded rookie defensive back Quenton Meeks with a nasty juke inside to burst into the end zone for a 32-yard touchdown with just 29 seconds remaining. At half-time, Philadelphia led 10-6 in London.

The Eagles pressed home their advantage in the second half. Wentz hit Wendell Smallwood on a screen pass, and the back found space down the left sideline following a crucial Shelton Gibson block to run into the end zone for a 36-yard touchdown. The score followed a 95-yard drive to give the Eagles a 17-6 lead with 8:39 remaining in the third quarter. The Jaguars, desperate not to be upstaged in front of their burgeoning fandom, retaliated instantly, driving to the Philadelphia 11 before Bortles floated a pass to receiver Westbrook, who brilliantly got his feet in bounds at the back of the end zone. The Jags went for the two-point conversion that burned the Tennessee Titans a week earlier and suffered a similar fate, maintaining the Eagles' lead at five points.

Westbrook was feeling himself and returned a Philadelphia punt 23 yards after a quick three-and-out for Wentz. A long, 13-play Jaguars drive ran out of steam at the Philadelphia 15, and Lambo hit the short field goal to narrow the lead once more. Fearing a collapse akin to their disastrous showing at home to Carolina the week before, the Eagles offence had to respond. They did so in style; Wentz hit Matthews for a 36-yard gain on the first play of the drive, before runs from the quarterback and Josh Adams – who finished with a team-high 61 yards rushing – set up a five-yard touchdown pass to Zach Ertz. At 24-15, a repeat of the Panthers debacle appeared unlikely.

The Jags' response was less of a roar and more of a gentle growl, with Bortles leading them to within touching distance of a crucial touchdown but his third-and-goal pass was juggled and inexplicably dropped by DJ Chark. Lambo made his kick, reducing the deficit to six points at 24-18. Jacksonville regained possession with just over five minutes to play, and Bortles brilliantly kept their hopes alive with a four-yard rush on fourth down. On fourth-and-two at their own 48, Bortles – under immense pressure from Fletcher Cox and an Eagles defence that tallied four sacks in London – fired off an incomplete pass. A 13-yard completion to Matthews and runs from Smallwood secured the win, and the Eagles returned to their Philadelphia nest with a 4-4 record.

The win gave the Eagles momentum heading into their bye week, as well as the opportunity to recover as tackle Lane Johnson and defensive back Jalen Mills both left the game due to injury. Defensive end Chris Long was pleased to secure the victory on foreign soil – and he was under no illusions regarding the weight of the result: 'It did feel like a must-win, there is no use lying about it. When you get on a slide, people start wondering what is going to go wrong. But not today, we had to get up just one more time and we will see what happens after the bye.' The Eagles lost their next two games but recovered to finish 9-7, enough to clinch a wildcard berth. They defeated the Chicago Bears after the NFC North champions suffered the infamous 'Double Doink' as kicker Cody Parker – formerly an Eagle – hit the upright and crossbar as his attempt fell short, gifting Philadelphia their first road playoff win since 2008. Their season ended with a 20-14 defeat in New Orleans, ensuring a new Super Bowl champion would be crowned for the 14th straight season.

It was not a good season for Jacksonville. They slipped to 3-5 after defeat at Wembley, and they limped home to finish with a familiar losing record at 5-11. The Jaguars undoubtedly wanted to put their season behind them and look ahead to 2019, set to be a monumental year for the International Series in London.

For the first time, the purpose-built Tottenham Hotspur Stadium was to be used for its purpose. The NFL was headed to north London.

2019:

A New Home in North London

NFL REGULAR SEASON WEEK FIVE
6 October 2019
CHICAGO BEARS 21
OAKLAND RAIDERS 24
Tottenham Hotspur Stadium

ON TUESDAY, 1 October 2019, just five days before the NFL christened its new north London home, Tottenham Hotspur were battered 7-2 in a humiliating UEFA Champions League clash with Bayern Munich. While the Premier League side could take little pride in their performance, their stadium was a modern marvel.

The groundwork began soon after full time: the centre circle replaced by an NFL crest, penalty boxes exchanged for end zones and grass swapped out for turf. The pitch retracts in a similar way to the Arizona Cardinals' home arena, the State Farm Stadium, but the Tottenham Hotspur Stadium is the first in the world to divide into three sections before the process begins. The pitch splits to accommodate the two columns supporting the South Stand while retracting, and each of the three sections weigh more than 3,000 tonnes. The retracting pitch slides into the car park beneath the South Stand and south podium, allowing the surface to be switched in under an hour. When fitted, the NFL field is 1.6 metres beneath the natural turf surface in order to allow ideal sightlines for front-row fans, since NFL personnel stand on the sidelines which could block views from the front row.

The purpose-built stadium was ready for its first test of purpose. 'We want our teams to have best-in-class experiences,' said Christopher Halpin, the NFL's executive vice-president and chief strategy and growth officer. 'It is customised with the field and facilities all up to NFL standard. In terms of overall fan experience, we can do all of the angles – that south-end ramp is like nothing else – or the two NFL-only locker rooms, or the field. The finished product is like nothing else in the world.' Spurs' stadium, which cost £1bn to complete with £10m contributed from the NFL itself, was built in a unique shape to create an atmosphere designed to accommodate the short bursts of intensity seen on the pitch.

The match between the Raiders and Bears, dubbed the Khalil Mack revenge game, felt monumental; it was a real landmark moment for the league. It was the apex of the NFL's rise in the United Kingdom following over 12 years of investment from commissioner Roger Goodell and Mark Waller, as well as the 32 owners. It was time for attention to go from the stands of Spurs' amphitheatre to the pitch that it surrounds – and the gladiators were ready to do battle.

Following his team's disappointing loss to the Seattle Seahawks in London a year ago, head coach Jon Gruden insisted he had learned his lesson: jet lag existed. The Raiders arrived in London on Monday, just in time to watch Bayern's Serge Gnabry steal the show at Tottenham's coliseum. Gruden hoped the Bears – who arrived on Thursday – and Mack would be too tired to imitate the German winger's performance on Sunday. He was right.

The Raiders arrived in London with an even 2-2 record following a 31-24 win in Indianapolis, while the Bears had recovered from a 10-3 opening-day defeat to the Green Bay Packers to kick off the NFL's 100th season. Since then, Chicago had won three in a row to sit at 3-1 with their fierce defence dominating opponents. Mack was ready to get revenge on the team that traded him over a year ago, but the Bears would be without starting quarterback Mitch Trubisky as the 2017 second overall pick was nursing a shoulder issue. Trubisky's absence meant career backup Chase Daniel would start in front of the 60,463 fans packed inside the brand-new stadium.

The Bears were hit by another injury early into proceedings, with talismanic defensive stalwart Akiem Hicks suffering a sickening elbow issue with his team-mates immediately summoning medical assistance. The Raiders took advantage of the weakened defence, driving 90 yards and converting twice on crucial third downs, including a 21-yard gain from rookie star running back Josh Jacobs on third-and-one while Derek Carr hit Derek Carrier on third-and-six for 20 yards. After a scoreless first quarter, Jacobs burst into the end zone for a 12-yard touchdown on the first play in the second quarter. 'They were talking a bunch of trash that first drive,' guard Richie Incognito said. 'We came out that first drive, then punched them in the mouth and all that talk stopped.' Oakland led in London.

The Raiders began to ransack their opponents as they scored their second touchdown in five minutes to lead 14-0. Daniel was intercepted by linebacker Nicholas Morrow on a pass intended for Trey Burton, and Oakland began their drive on the Chicago 24. After dicing the Bears defence, a defensive holding penalty against Kyle Fuller derailed Chicago's goal-line stance and DeAndre Washington powered into the end zone on a three-yard touchdown run.

With 1:56 remaining in the first half, Daniel Carlson nailed a 41-yard field goal to give the Raiders a 17-point lead. The Raiders had outgained the Bears 208 yards to 44 and had picked up 12 more first downs, with Gruden's team neutralising Mack.

Ironically, the Raiders came into the game with a league-low 18 sacks since the beginning of 2018, but they tallied three in the first half in London after Maxx Crosby, Benson Mayowa and Maurice Hurst made key plays. They would get a fourth on the final play of the match as Daniel struggled throughout.

Mack made his mark to open the third quarter. The Bears defence recorded their first takeaway of the game, although it was more of a giveaway by the Raiders offence. Carr tossed a ball towards Jacobs only for the rookie to miss the pass completely, allowing the former Raider to claim possession at the Oakland 14. Three plays later, Chicago were in the end zone as David Montgomery charged in from a yard out. The Bears defence forced a punt and the offence turned that into another score as Daniel hit former Jags star Allen Robinson for a diving four-yard touchdown. Chicago had driven downfield in style, capturing the imagination of the British fans with a sensational third-down grab by Anthony Miller for 32 yards over defensive back Lamarcus Joyner.

This was very much a game of two halves, and Chicago continued to fight back in the third quarter. Tarik Cohen returned a punt 71 yards to the Oakland 16, and Daniel found Robinson in the end zone again, with the receiver beating Gareon Conley to the jump ball. An incredible turnaround left the Bears leading 21-17 with a quarter remaining, and the crowd sensed a grandstand finish in Tottenham Hotspur's new stadium.

It truly felt like it was going to be Chicago's day when Sherrick McManis forced a fumble from Oakland receiver Trevor Davis and corner Prince Amukamara recovered possession at his own one-yard line. An insane toe-tapping catch on the sideline by Robinson paired with a roughing the passer call on Hurst – crucially overturning an interception – allowed the Bears to move the ball off their own goal line, granting them some much-needed breathing room. They pinned Oakland back to their own three with a punt as the Bears dared the Raiders to complete their longest fourth quarter game-winning drive in over 20 years.

The Raiders covered 97 yards in 13 plays, including a fourth down conversion deep inside their own territory. The Raiders originally punted, only for the Bears to suffer a penalty for running into the returner, and Chicago head coach Matt Nagy cut a frustrated figure as Erik Harris converted on fourth down. Drama reigned as Harris fumbled but was ruled down by contact, and Carr took advantage. He drove and set up Jacobs's second touchdown of the game as the rookie leaped over the defence to score and reclaim the lead. 'We were up for the challenge,' the running back out of Alabama said. 'All week that's all we heard was how good their defence was and they are a great defence – but we wanted to prove we're a great offence.' Jacobs, acquired with one of the first-round picks Oakland received in the Mack deal, rushed for 123 yards and a pair of scores against a defence that had not allowed 100 yards rushing to a single team all season. The Raiders had certainly proved themselves.

Their defence made a final play, with Conley intercepting Daniel on the Oakland 23 to seal the win and bring one of London's greatest games to an end. It was a fitting opening act for the Tottenham Hotspur Stadium.

The Mack trade was heavily scrutinised after the linebacker starred for Chicago as they reached the playoffs the prior season, but Gruden and Oakland felt vindicated after this win. 'I'm so proud of you, you don't know,' Gruden bellowed to his team in the brand-new locker rooms. 'You just showed that you can beat anyone, anywhere on any fucking time zone. Now have the whole week off.' The Raiders would struggle to replicate the impressive performance across the season, ending the franchise's 60th anniversary campaign at 7-9 as they missed the playoffs for the third straight year and 16th time in the previous 17 seasons.

Nagy was more philosophical about his team than Gruden, noting that they still had a 3-2 record ahead of their bye week.

Chicago were hoping to have a campaign to remember as they marked their 100th season as a franchise, dating back to the NFL's inaugural season in 1920 – but it wasn't to be. The team finished 8-8 and missed the postseason.

Nagy was clearly devastated at the podium in London's new arena, but he did save some positive words for the first purpose-built NFL stadium outside the United States, describing it as 'phenomenal'. The victorious Raiders were more direct in their praise, with Carr insisting it was perhaps the best stadium he had played at in his career. Incognito gave some insight into the improvement against Wembley: 'It's first class. Wembley does feel like a soccer stadium; this feels like an NFL locker room.'

There was only a week before the Carolina Panthers and Tampa Bay Buccaneers rolled into town to play at the new stadium, but the future of American football in the UK felt limitless. 'This is one of the league's biggest growth areas,' Halpin added. 'The opportunities are significant. It's exciting to be in the growth part of one of the world's biggest sports.' The new stadium was a permanent marker of the sport's impact on the capital and beyond – and this was just the first of four games as gridiron fever swarmed London in 2019.

NFL REGULAR SEASON WEEK SIX
13 October 2019
CAROLINA PANTHERS 37
TAMPA BAY BUCCANEERS 26
Tottenham Hotspur Stadium

The new turf of the Tottenham Hotspur Stadium had been christened just one week earlier and British fans were excited to cheer for the Carolina Panthers and the 'home' team Tampa Bay Buccaneers. The crowd was especially passionate to see one man in particular: not Carolina's MVP candidate Christian McCaffrey, nor star Bucs receiver Chris Godwin, but Efe Obada.

Born in Nigeria, Obada grew up in London and started playing American football at 22. He became the first international player to go straight from a European American football league to the NFL, transitioning from starring in the BAFA National Leagues with the London Warriors to the pinnacle of the sport with the Panthers. Head coach Ron Rivera made the defensive end an honorary captain for the game, undoubtedly adding to the emotion within the stadium as a pro-Panthers crowd of 60,087 gave the Brit – and face of the NFL's International Player Pathway – a round of applause at the coin toss.

Obada's defensive unit made an instant impact. On the first play from scrimmage, Bucs quarterback Jameis Winston was intercepted by James Bradberry, who brilliantly wrestled the ball away from Mike Evans to set the Panthers up on the Tampa Bay 29. The match was ultimately bookended by two Bradberry picks, as the corner snatched another on the Bucs' final play of the match to secure a miserable day for Winston. The Panthers offence could not imitate the play of their defence out the gate and kicker Joey Slye – who missed three times in their win over the Jacksonville Jaguars the previous week – gave Carolina the lead from 49 yards.

The Bucs pinned a punt on the Carolina one-yard line, clearly thinking that would stop a Panthers offence that was yet to get going. The Panthers offence moved the chains, capping the impressive drive with a McCaffrey touchdown – his fifth in the last two weeks – from a yard out. Rivera and offensive coordinator Norv Turner made the decision to go for it on fourth-and-goal, and it paid off as the Buccaneers surrendered just the second 99-yard drive since 1999.

The Bucs punted and found some level of success on special teams once again as returner Ray McCloud fumbled after a hard hit from Ryan Smith, setting the offence up in Carolina territory. Winston completed a 30-yard pass to towering tight end OJ Howard before Ronald Jones burst into the end zone with a five-yard touchdown. At 10-7 with 12:43 remaining in the second quarter, it was game on between these two NFC South rivals in north London.

Winston is a solid quarterback, but his decision-making has never been a strong point. The first overall pick in the 2015 draft, it was always a strange case of 'Dr Jekyll and Mr Hyde' with Winston, never knowing which version of him will turn up on any given play, let alone day. Sure enough, just as momentum appeared to be swinging to the Bucs, Carolina linebacker Bruce Irvin forced an awful throw that sailed over the head of Howard and was picked by Javien Elliott. It led to the play of the game: quarterback Kyle Allen hit McCaffrey on a checkdown pass and the running back juked Vernon Hargreaves III to the floor before cutting inside to stiff-arm Devin White and score. It was a sensational 25-yard touchdown from one of the NFL's brightest offensive stars, and it sent the British crowd wild.

Tampa looked to recover and reached the red zone before fumbles on successive plays were forced on Winston from Vernon Butler – the second of which was recovered by Irvin. 'When one guy makes a play, guys feel like, "Man, I have to make a play, too,"' the former Seahawk said. Carolina head coach Rivera clearly thought he had to make a special play too, and he flexed his football knowledge as he opted for a rare play at the end of the first half. The Panthers called for a fair catch at the 50 with one second remaining in the second quarter. Rivera, perhaps influenced by the British atmosphere, elected to attempt a free kick. It gave Slye the opportunity to kick for points from the 50 with no rush from the Buccaneers defence, who could only watch as they were forced to stand ten yards back. Slye claimed he was comfortable from 70 yards on a free kick, but he thought a slight breeze would help swing the ball left. 'I played the ball where I wanted it,' the kicker said. 'Had it on the right post but it didn't move. I was waiting for it to come back.' Leaving an expectant crowd somewhat disappointed, Slye could not quite bend it like David Beckham.

Slye made amends early in the third quarter, clipping a 46-yard field goal between the sticks after a 30-yard gain from Curtis Samuel. Hoping to respond after slipping to a 20-7 deficit, what was quickly becoming a bad day for the Bucs got worse when Winston was easily intercepted by Luke Kuechly deep inside Tampa territory. 'I felt like every single time they were on offence, our defence had a chance to get a turnover or a sack,' McCaffrey said of his 'unbelievable' defence. The offence took advantage of the excellent field position, needing one play to score as Samuel sped into the end zone on an end-around from eight yards out.

The Bucs finally added some points through Matt Gay's curling 54-yard field goal – which far more resembled Beckham in his prime than Slye's earlier effort – with just over five minutes remaining in the third quarter. The Panthers hit back soon after; Samuel scored his second touchdown of the game as he made an incredible falling catch, beating Carlton Davis's defensive efforts. The receiver celebrated by planting his hands on his helmet in disbelief at his own heroic play. Perhaps the more improbable moment came on the next drive, as big plays from Godwin and Dare Ogunbowale allowed Winston to pick out tight end Cameron Brate for a ten-yard touchdown. Evans caught a deflected pass on the two-point conversion to make it 34-18 with just over 12 minutes remaining. The Bucs couldn't, could they?

No, they couldn't. Bucs returner Bobo Wilson thought he had gotten away with an error as he scooped up his own muffed punt, only to again fumble on the following attempt which the Panthers recovered at the Tampa 12. Slye kicked a field goal to make it a three-score game with just eight minutes to play, sending Tampa Bay head coach Bruce Arians into a frenzy. 'The punt drops were huge in the game,' Arians admitted. 'We were fighting back, down two scores in the game at that point in time and had it going pretty good. Just catch the damn ball. It's not that hard.'

The Buccaneers, perhaps spurred on through sheer fear of Arians's wrath, refused to go down without at least some sort of fight. Winston shook off a sack from former team-mate Gerald McCoy to pick out Brate for a 37-yard gain, ultimately setting up Ogunbowale to run in a touchdown from four yards out. Another two-point conversion was successful as Winston showed off his wheels to make it 37-26. The Bucs showed grit and fight as they found themselves in midfield with 2:31 remaining but Winston was picked yet again, this time by future Buccaneer Ross Cockrell.

Carolina's Slye couldn't take the Panthers to 40 points on the day as he pushed his final effort narrowly wide right from 41 yards out. It gave Winston the opportunity to secure one last interception, with Bradberry snatching his second of the evening to earn Carolina a franchise record-tying seventh takeaway to pair nicely with seven sacks on the day.

The turnovers were a frustrating pattern for Winston throughout his career. After this game, the quarterback had endured five games with at least four turnovers, and no other player had recorded more than two such games since Winston came into the league in 2015. His record of 86 turnovers was also the worst in the NFL since his debut. 'Throw the damn ball away,' Arians said of Winston's tough outing in London. 'You ain't throwing it anywhere – throw it away. He has a habit of trying to be Superman and that's been a problem in the past.' The enigma of Winston was hammered home in 2019: he became just the eighth quarterback in NFL history to throw for 5,000 yards in a single season – the first Buccaneer to do so – as well as the first quarterback in league history to throw at least 30 touchdowns and 30 interceptions, seven of which were returned for scores, in a single campaign. The Bucs, who fell to 2-4 with the loss and 0-3 in NFL International Series games, finished 7-9 – but success was on the horizon. The team opted against re-signing Winston in favour of securing the signature of Tom Brady, and they would storm to a 31-9 victory over the Kansas City Chiefs in Super LV.

The Panthers moved to 4-2 with the win, as Allen – who threw for 227 yards and two touchdowns – improved to 5-0 as a starter in his young career while McCaffrey, the 2019 NFL leader in touchdowns, rushing yards and total yards from scrimmage, starred. Carolina suffered an eight-game losing streak – their worst since 2001, where they finished 1-15 – to end the season with a 5-11 record. It was a period of transition for the franchise, with the likes of Kuechly retiring while coach Rivera and quarterback Cam Newton, injured and unavailable for the London game, left the team at the end of the campaign.

Carolina's London bow was a success, and it was a tremendous finale for the Tottenham portion of the NFL's London slate. Whispers of a permanent franchise were subsiding despite the new infrastructure, as league owners reportedly favoured rotating NFL teams on an annual basis. Regardless, the Tottenham Hotspur Stadium had impressed. Now it was time for Wembley's NFL swansong, at least for the next couple of years.

NFL REGULAR SEASON WEEK EIGHT
27 October 2019
CINCINNATI BENGALS 10
LOS ANGELES RAMS 24
Wembley Stadium

The Cincinnati Bengals and Los Angeles Rams arrived in London for their regular season clash and while they were technically in the same location, the teams were in very different places.

The Bengals were winless at 0-7 with rookie head coach Zac Taylor yet to register a career victory since leaving the Rams to take the reins at Cincinnati. While in Los Angeles, Taylor was an assistant wide receiver coach in 2017 and quarterbacks coach in 2018, helping Rams head coach Sean McVay develop Jared Goff into a winning quarterback that reached and lost Super Bowl LIII. He may have been a quarterback guru, but Taylor was focused on getting the run game going through star back Joe Mixon, who had tallied 1,168 yards and eight touchdowns in 2018. 'It's frustrating for everybody when the run game isn't going,' Taylor said ahead of the trip to London. 'Joe is easy to deal with. Joe understands. Joe wants to win.' History was on the side of Taylor heading into the clash: the Bengals had won their last three matches against the Rams, holding an 8-5 all-time series lead.

The Rams were having similar problems. Their two-time First-Team All-Pro running back Todd Gurley had seen limited touches since injuring his left knee late last season, which was determined to be arthritis in March 2019. The 2017 NFL Offensive Player of the Year had not rushed for over 100 yards in a game since an NFC playoff victory over the Dallas Cowboys back in January 2019. McVay rotated Gurley and rookie Darrell Henderson in the Rams' 37-10 win over the Atlanta Falcons the previous week, taking the team to 4-3 on the season. While a fan of London and the international games, Gurley was not particularly keen on the adjustments made to player routines – like staying in Jacksonville two years ago to train before coming to London. 'I like London, but during the season, I wish we could've been there all week,' Gurley said before boarding the flight from Atlanta. 'At least we're not in Jacksonville.'

Gurley had played in two International Series games before: the 17-10 loss to the New York Giants in 2016 in which he rushed for 57 yards and the 33-0 win over the Arizona Cardinals in 2017, where he registered 106 yards and a touchdown. The Rams' offensive star hoped the fans would push him to new heights in 2019, saying: 'Those fans are a little different over there – pretty much get excited for everything. A good opportunity for a lot of guys to get a little stamp on their passport and go over there and experience everything.'

The anthems blared as 83,270 fans prepared for the return of gridiron action to the home of English football for the 13th successive year. After Mixon earned a first down on the second play from scrimmage, the Rams quickly forced a punt before Goff hit Robert Woods on a rollout that the receiver took 31 yards.

Los Angeles opened the scoring as Greg Zuerlein chipped in from 23 yards out to much applause. The Bengals impressively responded; quarterback Andy Dalton twice found Tyler Eifert to move the sticks before he picked out Tyler Boyd on fourth down. Cincinnati's drive stalled at the Rams 10, and Randy Bullock levelled proceedings at 3-3 with the opening play of the second quarter.

Goff led the Rams on an impressive 92-yard drive culminating in the first score of the game, with the former first overall pick throwing a perfect touch pass over the fingertips of linebacker Germaine Pratt for a 31-yard touchdown to Josh Reynolds. The Bengals looked to answer aggressively, converting a fourth down thanks to Mixon. Their run game had certainly improved as Giovani Bernard rushed 25 yards to take the Bengals deep inside Rams territory before Dalton, with Cincinnati on the one-yard line, hit a wide-open Mixon for the score.

If Los Angeles were learning to respect Cincinnati's ground game, the Bengals would soon learn to do the same to the Rams' passing offence. On first down from their own 35, Woods ran a reverse and threw the ball back to Goff. The quarterback briefly surveyed his options before he launched the ball to Kupp, who benefitted from cornerback BW Webb's slip on the pitch as he went to hit the receiver. The 26-year-old burned away from the defence and dived over the plane to score a touchdown on the 65-yard flea flicker. It received a tremendous roar from the British crowd as they were treated to a blockbuster moment that gave the Rams a lead they wouldn't lose. 'I joke about it, we don't run any trick plays,' Goff said after the game, clearly thrilled with the play call. 'That was the first and best one we've ever had. Maybe we can talk Sean into doing a few more now.' McVay admitted they had the play drawn up and ready to go since running a double reverse against the Browns on 23 September, and it was timed to perfection to give the Rams a 17-10 lead.

After the break, the Rams landed the killer blow. On successive third downs, Goff found Kupp for 15 and 40 yards to open the third quarter, with the latter being the receiver's final play as he failed to make another catch in the remaining 27 minutes. It didn't matter: Kupp had already registered a career high of 165 yards by half-time, and Gurley scored a three-yard touchdown on a halfback toss to put the Rams 24-10 up. The Rams were heading to their first win over the Bengals since 2003.

Truth be told, the game became fairly ugly after Gurley's score. Six straight punts followed the touchdown, with Cincinnati dropping three sure-fire interceptions but still holding strong to keep LA out of the end zone. The Rams stopped the Bengals on fourth-and-goal from the six-yard line with just five minutes remaining in the fourth, swallowing Stanley Morgan's rush to wrap up the game. The Bengals came back on the final drive, with Dalton hitting Auden Tate for what appeared to be a touchdown before it was ruled incomplete with just four seconds remaining on the clock.

The Bengals' first win of the season remained as elusive at Wembley as it was on American soil. The franchise slipped to 0-8 for the first time since 2008, with Taylor failing to defeat his former mentor in McVay. His team finished with 104 yards rushing – Mixon with 66 alone – from 22 carries, without a touchdown. It was the halfway point of a difficult season for the Bengals, who would pick up their first win in week 13 against the New York Jets as they ambled to a 2-14 record. They would at least receive compensation for their poor season: the number one pick in the 2020 NFL Draft, used to select Ohio native Joe Burrow. He would prove to be the saviour of the franchise, bouncing back from an ACL tear to lead the Bengals to a Super Bowl LVI clash against the Rams in Los Angeles in just his second season.

The Rams received a worrying glimpse of what was to come as Goff struggled immensely in the second half – 273 of his 372 passing yards came in the opening two quarters – while Gurley was once again underwhelming with 44 yards and a score on limited touches. The Rams left London with their second successive win in the city but went on to finish 9-7 and miss the playoffs, just a year removed from a Super Bowl appearance. A team that had looked destined to be a mainstay at the top of the league while armed with the likes of Aaron Donald and Jalen Ramsey – who was traded from the Jacksonville Jaguars a fortnight before the Bengals clash – suddenly had lost their offensive razzmatazz as Goff and Gurley struggled for different reasons. The Rams got their mojo back on 30 January 2021 when they sent Goff and two first-round picks to the Detroit Lions in exchange for Matthew Stafford.

NFL REGULAR SEASON WEEK NINE
3 November 2019
HOUSTON TEXANS 26
JACKSONVILLE JAGUARS 3
Wembley Stadium

As the sun rose on Sunday morning in London, tens of thousands of keen American football fans were ready to head to Wembley Park – but one man was particularly excited. Safety Justin Reid of the Houston Texans took to social media to speak of his hype for the Texans' first trip to the home of football as he tweeted: 'Dreamed of playing in Wembley Stadium when I was a young kid. I was playing fútbol at the time so not exactly the same way I pictured it but hey … dreams still do come true.' It was another piece of evidence that players do truly enjoy coming to London, despite the difficult logistics.

Was this Wembley's final American football match? Time will tell, but after being christened by the Burtonwood Bullets in the USAFE Football League Final back in 1952, a storied chapter of gridiron football history in the United Kingdom was set to close. The potential finale drew 84,771 spectators willing to watch Houston's first visit to London, leaving the Green Bay

Packers as the only team yet to come to the English capital since the NFL started the matches on an annual basis in 2007.

The Texans arrived on the back of a 27-24 win over Oakland to take them to 5-3, challenging the Tennessee Titans at the top of the AFC South and the Jacksonville Jaguars – who, to their credit, had now earned a foothold as the presumptive team of London and the United Kingdom – were still in the fight for the division, too. The distraction of Jalen Ramsey's contract stand-off was behind them following his trade to the Rams, and the Jags had fought back to defeat the Bengals and Jets – arguably the two worst teams in football – to climb back to 4-4. The Wembley finale was primed to be a season-defining clash for both teams, and so it proved.

The Texans wasted no time in opening the scoring, taking the first possession of the game to the Jacksonville 34 before Ka'imi Fairbairn kicked a 52-yard field goal despite his team racking up 30 yards in penalties. It was the first time this season the Texans had scored on their opening drive, and it kicked off a miserable afternoon for the Jags.

Early in the second quarter, the Texans made it a two-score lead following a 14-play drive that covered 80 yards and spanned an impressive eight minutes. It also included arguably the play of the game from star quarterback Deshaun Watson. With Jags linemen Taven Bryan and Yannick Ngakoue dragging him to the floor, Watson somehow eluded them and flipped a lateral to running back Carlos Hyde, who took it seven yards for a first down inside Jacksonville territory. 'It's great to play with a quarterback like Deshaun Watson,' said superstar wideout DeAndre Hopkins. 'You see what he can do. It was amazing, right?' The incredible play didn't even count as a pass completion for Watson as it went backwards, adding to Hyde's rushing total instead – not that the quarterback or those watching cared. Three plays later, Watson found Darren Fells from a yard out to extend the score to 9-0, with Fairbairn's extra point attempt blocked.

The Jaguars finally got on the board inside the two-minute warning prior to half-time. Ryquell Armstead made a tremendous 38-yard catch and run to breathe life into the Jags offence, before two incompletions from rookie quarterback Gardner Minshew either side of a stuffed rush from Leonard Fournette forced Josh Lambo to kick a 30-yard field goal. On the ensuing possession, Watson picked out Duke Johnson for a 17-yard gain that needed a review as the scrambling quarterback somehow found the running back as he fell to the ground, with officials checking if it was a sack or a Texans gain. It didn't matter in the end; Fairbairn missed from 58 yards to keep the score at 9-3 entering the break.

It was a dominant first half from the Texans, who held the ball for 19 minutes and 39 seconds compared to just over ten minutes for the Jags. The de facto British team wanted to start the third quarter on the front foot, but on third-and-14 from the Houston 31, receiver DJ Chark had a catch at the Houston four-yard line nullified by a tough interference call. Jacksonville settled for the points that never came as a botched fake field goal forced a turnover on downs. What should have become a three-point deficit turned into a two-score game after defensive end Calais Campbell was perhaps harshly penalised for diving at Watson head first only to completely miss him. The personal foul allowed Houston to kick for a 12-3 lead – and then the floodgates opened.

The Texans followed a Jags punt by driving 79 yards in five plays to score. Johnson ripped through the defence on a 48-yard gain before Watson hit Hopkins for a 21-yard completion to take Houston to the Jacksonville one-yard line, and Johnson bowled over cornerback Tre Herndon to score and make it 19-3. Texans defensive back Gareon Conley – traded to Houston from Oakland the previous month – then ripped the ball from the clutches of Jags receiver Chris Conley, who appeared certain to convert a fourth down pass into a new set of downs. Jacksonville challenged the ruling but the officials stuck to their guns: it was another turnover on downs.

The final quarter was a smorgasbord of errors. First, Minshew was picked by corner Jahleel Addae after blatantly overthrowing Keelan Cole. Then, Hyde broke through a gap in the Jacksonville defensive line and was surely going to score before a Herculean effort from Jarrod Wilson saw the safety punch the ball free, and the Jags recovered. On the very next play, Minshew sent a pass towards Josh Oliver but the attempt floated over the rookie tight end's head and into the arms of Reid. Reid, desperate to score on the hallowed Wembley turf, weaved his way through a sea of Jacksonville players before he was tackled at the three. He might not have scored his goal, but Reid had certainly earned a celebration under the Wembley arch. His dream had come true.

Two plays later, the Texans were back in the end zone as Watson and Hopkins linked up for a one-yard touchdown to make it 26-3 with over four minutes remaining. Those four minutes saw Minshew fumble twice, with the Texans taking over on both occasions. If this was Jacksonville's last match at Wembley, it was a sad way to go.

Watson was undoubtedly the star of the show. He finished with 22 completions from 28 attempts for 201 yards and two touchdowns. Watson was hit seven times but sacked just once, highlighting his exceptional evasive ability that was summarised by his lateral to Hyde, who had a fine day himself with 19 carries for 160 yards. For Jacksonville, Minshew barely completed 50 per cent of his passes as he threw two interceptions and no touchdowns while also losing a pair of fumbles. The rookie threw for 309 yards, but almost all of that came when the Texans had mentally checked out. The defence may have been out on the grass, but their focus was already on the flight back to Texas.

The AFC South now appeared to be Houston's for the taking as they sat at 6-3, and they would indeed claim the crown as the Texans finished 10-6, one game ahead of the Titans. Houston sensationally defeated the Buffalo Bills in the playoffs, overturning a 16-0 second-half deficit to win 22-19 in overtime.

They continued their hot form for a single quarter in Kansas City as they rushed into a 24-0 lead before Patrick Mahomes and the Chiefs blew them away. The Super Bowl champions-to-be scored 28 points in the second quarter en route to a crushing 51-31 win.

As for the Jaguars, they still had hope at 4-5 but that feeling quickly dissipated after the bye week. The Texans loss started a run of five straight defeats by 17 points or more, becoming the first team since the 1986 Tampa Bay Buccaneers to suffer such a run as they plummeted to finish 6-10.

This was the 28th NFL match played in London, with question marks looming over the NFL's future at Wembley given the Tottenham Hotspur Stadium had just opened. The new stadium had a deal with the NFL to stage at least two games annually across a 10-year period, suggesting it was set to usurp the national stadium as the British home of American football.

Regardless, fans left Wembley excited for the 2020 games at the new multipurpose home, which was ready to assume full hosting responsibilities. Unfortunately, the 2020 International Series never came.

2021

The Triumphant Return

NFL REGULAR SEASON WEEK FIVE
10 October 2021
NEW YORK JETS 20
ATLANTA FALCONS 27
Tottenham Hotspur Stadium

Football did not come to the United Kingdom in 2020 as attention turned from the turf to the stands. The coronavirus was not bound to a team nor restricted by borders as the pandemic struck the British Isles, the United States and the rest of the world. It devastated nations; in the 708 days between the last NFL game in London back in 2019 and its return, 728,303 people had lost their lives in America while 136,953 British men and women had died as a result of Covid-19. In total, it was enough to sell out the new Tottenham Hotspur Stadium almost 14 times over. Before avid gridiron fans could celebrate the return of their sporting gladiators back to London, they needed to first appreciate those who selflessly worked on the frontlines of healthcare during the ongoing pandemic. When the Jets and Falcons took to the field, fans were back in stadiums, a direct result of the exceptional work of the healthcare sector. If football players are gladiators, it is difficult to find the right word to summarise the tireless sacrifice each doctor, nurse and medical worker endured. One term stands above all others, though – they were heroes. The 60,589 in attendance at the Tottenham Hotspur Stadium owed the privilege of watching the NFL's London return to such selfless people.

It was as if the weather understood its assignment. Overcast clouds with light morning rain made way for sunny spells throughout the contest in north London. The temporary home team, the Atlanta Falcons, touched down on Friday morning and went straight to their base, The Grove hotel in Watford. Matt Ryan, Atlanta's long-time quarterback and the 2016 NFL MVP, was hoping to make amends after agonisingly losing his previous transatlantic trip, a 22-21 defeat to the Detroit Lions seven years earlier. 'The routine is different from the last time I came over here in 2014, where we spent the whole week here trying to get ready for that game,' the 36-year-old declared. Ryan played down the vintage issue of jet lag, insisting that the change in venue and scenery would give his team the required buzz to perform on Sunday. Rookie head coach Arthur Smith was perhaps more honest, admitting he was going to 'guzzle' coffee to get up to speed. The Falcons certainly needed the extra boost as they arrived in London with a 1-3 record following a tough 34-30 loss at home to Washington, but their opponents appeared to be there for the taking.

The New York Jets came to London with a 1-3 record themselves after they had defeated the Tennessee Titans 27-24 in overtime the previous week. Their first win of the season came at a welcome time for the Jets, as the hopeful optimism of preseason – buoyed by second overall draft pick Zach Wilson's insertion at quarterback and new head coach Robert Saleh – was extinguished after three weeks. An opening-day loss to Carolina was followed by a 25-6 home defeat to the Patriots, their 11th straight loss to New England, in which Wilson threw four interceptions, and then the Jets were shut out 26-0 in Denver. The win over the Titans inspired renewed hope – could the team from the Big Apple find success in the Big Smoke?

As thousands of fans joyfully took to the Tottenham Hotspur Stadium amidst a sea of colour, a beautiful sense of normality was all they wanted – but organisers had other plans for the NFL's glorious return. Broadway singer and actor Marisha Wallace nailed 'The Star-Spangled Banner' from atop the purpose-built arena as a jet plane flyover combined with red, white and blue fireworks. After a two-year break, the NFL was most definitely back.

Despite the absence of star receiver Calvin Ridley, Ryan utilised the likes of Cordarrelle Patterson, Mike Davis and rookie Kyle Pitts – the highest drafted tight end in NFL history when the Falcons took him fourth overall – to move to the Jets 13. Younghoe Koo kicked the 31-yard field goal, imitating fellow South Korean Son Heung-Min by scoring at Spurs' ground to give the Falcons the lead. Pitts had struggled to find momentum through the first four games of his career, but he excelled on his team's second drive as the rookie hauled in a fine grab to take the Falcons into Jets territory. Four plays later, Ryan and Pitts linked up for the first touchdown of his career, a two-yard pass after the former Florida Gator beat his defender on a fade route to make it 10-0.

It took 14 minutes of gridiron action before Wilson completed his first pass, an 11-yard gain on third-and-13. The Jets subsequently punted and the Falcons torched downfield to score again. Ryan hit Pitts for a spectacular one-handed catch that went for 22 yards before the quarterback slung a 17-yard touchdown pass to Hayden Hurst, who found some space inside before bursting into the end zone.

As the Jets tried to respond, things turned sour for Wilson as his deep ball to Keelan Cole was intercepted by a diving Jaylinn Hawkins. It was an NFL-worst ninth interception as the rookie desperately struggled to make the simple plays. 'Falling back in a hole early in the first half, it's just hard to do that in this league no matter who you're playing,' linebacker CJ Mosley said. 'When you get down that early that fast, it's always hard to come back.'

Mosley made the Jets' biggest play of the first half as he stripped the ball from Hurst, with cornerback Michael Carter coming out on top of a struggle to recover possession. It allowed Wilson to find some rhythm, picking out Corey Davis and Jamison Crowder to reach the red zone before the Jets drive stalled out. Rookie kicker Matt Ammendola converted the 31-yard field goal to put New York on the board with just over two minutes remaining, and it proved to be too much time for Atlanta. Ryan used Pitts again to get into Koo's range, and the Korean converted from 52 yards to make the score 20-3 at the halfway point.

The half-time entertainment was provided by Aitch, and perhaps the Jets seemed to enjoy the rapper's show more than the Falcons as New York started the third quarter on fire. Tevin Coleman returned the ball 65 yards to set the Jets offence up on the Atlanta 29, and Wilson used the run game led by Michael Carter and Ty Johnson to drive to the one-yard line before Johnson punched it in to reduce the deficit, although Ammendola missed the extra point.

The Falcons soon found their way into the Jets' red zone before the New York defence made another crucial play. As Falcons back Davis burst through a gap, he was met by two titanic Jets in Quincy Williams and Jamien Sherwood, popping the ball loose for Shaq Lawson to recover. The Jets offence unfortunately could not deliver as they were sent packing with a three-and-out, but they found form on their next drive following another defensive stop. Wilson completed passes to Crowder and Cole before launching a deep bomb towards Elijah Moore only for stud young cornerback AJ Terrell to commit pass interference. The 41-yard penalty allowed Carter to leap into the end zone and it was game on at 20-17.

Ryan ensured the result was never in doubt on the following drive. On the very first play from scrimmage, he hit Pitts once again for a 39-yard gain to kick off a drive and brutally deflate the crowd, desperate to see some late drama. All hopes for a crazy finish were ended by Davis's three-yard touchdown run with 2:19 left to play. Ammendola added a field goal with seconds remaining, but the Falcons were set to jet off from London with a 27-20 win.

Falcons coach Smith, who worked his way up the ranks at the Titans before accepting his first head coaching job ahead of the 2021 season, found a way to get Pitts involved as the rookie offensive stud shone in north London. 'Kyle stepped up today,' the 39-year-old offensive guru said of his first-round pick. 'We'll continue to involve him and he won his one-on-one matchups. Everybody wants the hot takes after week one, but that's why he's here and he'll continue to improve.' Pitts, a 6ft 6in-tall speedster who is essentially a receiver–tight end hybrid, stole the show ahead of Wilson, the other rookie that fans excitedly came to see. The 22-year-old completed 19 of 32 attempts on his London bow for no scores and an interception. Coach Saleh spoke of the work Wilson would put in over the upcoming bye week: 'Study the tape. Look at all the decisions and execution and figure out what the answer is over this next week and come up with something because it's got to be better.'

The Falcons would go on to finish 7-10 following the addition of the 17th game, missing the playoffs for the fourth successive year. The New York Jets continued their particularly barren run of missing the postseason, falling to a 4-13 record in the first year of the Saleh–Wilson era. The Jets' last playoff game was the 2010 AFC Championship, and their current postseason drought is tied for the longest in team history.

During the NFL's triumphant return to London, rumours of an International Series expansion to new territory in Germany suggested the NFL was ready to grow across the continent. Regardless, the Falcons' win over the Jets highlighted one thing: the league had a home at Tottenham – and it was here to stay.

NFL REGULAR SEASON WEEK SIX
17 October 2021
MIAMI DOLPHINS 20
JACKSONVILLE JAGUARS 23
Tottenham Hotspur Stadium

The fixture chosen to close the 2021 slate of London games was a rematch between the quarterbacks who contested the 2018 College National Championship game between Alabama and Clemson. On that day, Trevor Lawrence and Clemson defeated Tua Tagovailoa's Alabama 44-16, and the two were set to meet again. On this occasion, their battle would take place at the Tottenham Hotspur Stadium in the NFL. Lawrence, selected first overall by the Jacksonville Jaguars in the 2021 draft, had been tipped to become an NFL star since he was 14. It felt appropriate, then, that the first win of his professional career was secured by a software engineer-turned-NFL kicker as time expired in front of 60,784 captivated fans.

The Jaguars arrived in London without a win in 2021. The franchise hadn't won a game since a 27-20 victory over the Indianapolis Colts to open the 2020 season, and the 20-game losing streak was the second-longest in the Super Bowl era behind only the 1976–77 Tampa Bay Buccaneers, who suffered 26 straight defeats. While the Jags didn't yet have that record, they were appearing in England for a record eighth time, taking on the Miami Dolphins – who had played the second-most matches in the Big Smoke.

Lawrence was lauded with pre-draft hype, and the 22-year-old was struggling to deliver. His opposite number Tagovailoa needed a win himself. Miami were unfortunate to miss the playoffs in 2020 after going 10-6 thanks to their immaculate defence while their quarterback experienced an underwhelming introduction to the NFL. He rushed back from a rib injury to return to the turf in London, with durability among the many concerns surrounding the Hawaiian. The concerns appeared to be unfounded on the first drive. After the anthems played and mascot Jaxson de Ville spectacularly somersaulted from the stadium's roof, Tagovailoa began to take control. He converted three third downs, including a 20-yard pass to tight end Mike Gesicki and a quarterback scramble to the six-yard line, to lead the Dolphins 75 yards to score. The drive culminated with a six-yard slant to rookie Jaylen Waddle, highlighting the Alabama connection Miami had hoped would translate to the field when they drafted the receiver sixth overall just six months earlier. Waddle came into the game as the second-most targeted rookie receiver in the league, and he continued to deliver across the Atlantic.

Clearly inspired by watching his former adversary shine, Lawrence wasted no time in showcasing his talent with a 24-yard throw to Jamal Agnew. He then converted a third down of his own, launching a 19-yard pass to tight end Dan Arnold, who had only recently arrived via trade from the Carolina Panthers. Matthew Wright, a 25-year-old kicker who had only had four field goal attempts in the NFL before being signed to Jacksonville's practice squad on 27 September, nailed the 40-yard attempt. It was the Jags' very first field goal in 2021 after being the only team in the NFL not to have made a single kick entering week six.

It was Tua's time to respond, and the sophomore appeared to be in confident mood as he immediately picked out Waddle for an 18-yard gain and Gesicki for a 22-yard play. The Dolphins subbed in backup quarterback Jacoby Brissett on third-and-one, and a fine play action allowed Brissett to find tight end Durham Smythe for 25 yards, but the drive stalled out. Jason Sanders extended the Miami lead to 10-3 with his 33-yard field goal.

After a quick three-and-out from the Jags, Tagovailoa let a golden opportunity go begging. On third-and-two, the quarterback avoided pressure with a fine scramble before overthrowing Waddle after opting not to simply rush for the first down, despite the open field. Tagovailoa linked up with Mack

Hollins for a 20-yard gain to move the sticks on fourth down, but the Jags red zone defence held firm. Out came Sanders, and he converted his second field goal, this time from 24 yards.

Trailing 13-3 with under two minutes remaining in the first half, Lawrence found some momentum as he twice picked out Laviska Shenault before firing a perfect 28-yard touchdown bomb to Marvin Jones Jr. With starting cornerbacks Xavien Howard and Byron Jones missing due to injury, the former Lions receiver beat backup corner Noah Igbinoghene for the jump ball and made the thrilling play to make the score read 13-10.

With 40 seconds remaining in the first half, Tagovailoa almost threw a horrible interception before hitting tight ends Smythe and Gesicki – who went for a game-high 115 yards – near the sideline. It set up a chance for Sanders, but he was denied a hat-trick from distance when his 58-yard field goal deflected off a defensive hand and fell short.

The Dolphins struggled as they came out for the second half, and the Jaguars sensed an opportunity. Lawrence hit Agnew for 29 yards before an unnecessary roughness call on safety Jevon Holland gave the Jags another 15 yards. Elusive power runner James Robinson then burned down the middle on a 24-yard rush. The sophomore, signed as an undrafted rookie before exploding for 1,070 yards in 2020, punched it in from a yard out to give the Jags a rare lead at 17-13.

Ugly sequences soon began to seep into the game. Miami had a fumble recovery after Christian Wilkins – Lawrence's former team-mate at Clemson – sacked the Jags signal-caller and knocked the ball loose, allowing defensive tackle Zach Sieler to claim possession for Miami. It wouldn't be a particularly lengthy drive as one turnover quickly became two in north London: Tagovailoa faked the hand-off to Malcolm Brown before horribly overthrowing his open back, with the pass collected by Nevin Lawson for the first interception of the corner's career. The Jaguars wanted to quickly take advantage of the swinging momentum, and Lawrence drove his team to the Miami 18 following a 21-yard completion to rookie tight end Luke Farrell on what was the final play of the third quarter. On third down, Lawrence failed to find Laquon Treadwell in the back of the end zone with a pass placed agonisingly in front of the receiver before Robinson was denied on fourth down, granting Miami a turnover on downs.

Tagovailoa, perhaps inspired by his defence, then piloted a seven-play drive to take the Dolphins 91 yards to score a two-yard touchdown pass to Waddle and reclaim the lead with 10:22 to play. The two teams exchanged punts before Jacksonville advanced to set up Wright's second field goal of the day with a clutch, swerving 54-yard conversion that would have been more appropriate in the Premier League. The game was tied at 20-20, perfectly poised for a hero to emerge before the British fanbase.

Taking over with 3:40 remaining, Tagovailoa leaned on short passes and the run game to reach their own 46. Facing a fourth-and-one inside their own territory, Brown was stuffed by the Jags defence for no gain. The gamble had not paid off, and the Jaguars were given an unlikely chance to perhaps snatch the win. The Jags took over and suffered immediate adversity as a false start penalty and an Emmanuel Ogbah sack saw them slip out of field goal range, which meant the capacity crowd in north London appeared set to be treated to overtime with the Jaguars facing fourth-and-eight with five seconds to go. Lawrence then connected on a nine-yard slant pass to Shenault and head coach Urban Meyer dramatically called a timeout with a single second remaining on the clock. Jacksonville would get an opportunity to snap their historic losing streak from the Miami 44.

The chance to win the Jags' first game of the season fell on the right leg of Wright. The Jags reportedly had planned to launch it into the end zone in a Hail Mary-style play, but the Dolphins called a timeout and, after assessing the situation, the Jaguars opted to kick for the win instead. Wright's 53-yard field goal attempt appeared to be flying wide left before it incredibly swerved back inside and narrowly went over, sending the Tottenham Hotspur crowd berserk. 'I don't think anybody on our team ever heard him speak until about ten minutes ago,' Jags head coach Meyer said of Wright. 'Just not a huge talker, just here to do my job,' the kicker retorted. It appears that London was the right place, and it was simply Wright's time.

Lawrence completed 25 of his 41 passes for 319 yards as he and Meyer both earned their first NFL win many miles from home. The win also snapped the London curse on rookie quarterbacks, who had been 0-5 since the NFL began staging regular season contests in 2007.

Meyer, who came out of retirement to take his first NFL job, was fired just 13 matches into his first and only season after a number of personal conduct issues were raised. Prior to the London game, Meyer – who is married – was filmed inappropriately touching a woman just one day after the Jags had suffered an agonising road defeat to the Bengals and, in December, he was accused of physical abuse on kicker Josh Lambo. Lambo insisted Meyer repeatedly kicked his leg during warmups before the Jags' final preseason game. When he told his coach to stop, Meyer allegedly said: 'I'm the head ball coach. I'll kick you whenever the fuck I want.' He was fired on 16 December 2021, finishing with a 2-11 record. The Jaguars finished 3-14, securing the top pick in the draft for the second consecutive year.

For Miami, the loss to Jacksonville was a bitter blow. The Jags gatecrashed the return of Tagovailoa, who was making his first start in a month following his fractured rib injury. The second-year quarterback threw a pair of touchdowns to Waddle as he finished 33 of 47 for 329 yards, two touchdowns and one interception. 'I'm not 100 per cent, but I was 100 per cent ready to be out there,' Tagovailoa said. Dolphins coach Brian Flores bemoaned the consistency and his own coaching as his team – pegged to contend for a playoff berth before the season – left London with a frustrating 1-5 record. The Dolphins became the first team in NFL history to lose seven successive games followed by seven straight wins, securing a 9-8 record on the season. It wasn't enough as Miami missed the playoffs and coach Flores was surprisingly fired despite the winning record.

SECTION 3:

BRITISH PLAYERS IN THE NFL

Bobby Howfield

Denver Broncos 1968–1970
New York Jets 1971–1974

IT IS fitting that Bobby Howfield, the first British player to play in the NFL, was a kicker. It is perhaps even more appropriate that he transitioned to gridiron football in the United States after first making his name as a goalscoring striker in the football league with a fiery, volatile temperament – a perfect trait for success in the NFL.

Howfield began his association football career with Bushey FC, his local club just outside of Watford, the town where he was born. After signing amateur terms with Millwall in May 1957, Howfield became a professional footballer when he got his big move to Watford FC in September. He played two seasons at Vicarage Road, during which time he made 50 appearances for the 'Blues' and scored ten goals. While he had become a fan favourite due to his fierce right foot, the form of fellow striker Cliff Holton – as well as the arrival of new recruits such as Dennis Uphill – forced Howfield from his boyhood club to Crewe Alexandra where he spent the 1959/60 season, before moving on to Aldershot Town.

Howfield found himself in the headlines for the wrong reasons at Aldershot. His fiery temper saw him get suspended from the club following a dispute with club management, clouding his impressive form on the pitch. In the 1961/62 season, Howfield scored 23 league goals, which remained a club record for many years. Despite being something of a cult hero and the club's leading scorer, Howfield unceremoniously left Aldershot to return to Watford for a fee of £4,000 in July 1962, departing with a fine record of 44 goals in 76 league appearances.

Howfield was tasked with leading Watford's charge for promotion to the Second Division, and the match against Northampton Town on 27 October 1962 was the biggest match of the season given the Cobblers were leading the league and had signed former Watford striker Holton. With 19,000 in attendance, Howfield played an instrumental role and scored as the Hornets won 4-2 – but he was once again attracting the wrong kind of attention. A heated exchange led to Howfield punching Northampton player Alec Ashworth to thunderous applause from the crowd. Ashworth responded with a strike of his own, and both men were duly sent off. It was a rarity to be dismissed in this era, and Howfield is recorded as the only Watford player to receive a red card between August 1957 and November 1967.

Howfield continued his scoring form, with his 15 goals over 50 appearances for Watford proving to be enough to attract attention from Fulham in the First Division. The striker enjoyed a fairly successful spell at Craven Cottage as he scored nine goals in 26 appearances before moving stateside. Howfield joined the New York Americans of the International Soccer League for a brief stint in the summer of 1965, but subsequently returned to Aldershot in August 1965. In his second spell at the club, Howfield played in 34 matches across two seasons with ten goals to his name.

His association football career ended with a move to non-league Chelmsford City, where Howfield retired from soccer aged 31 – but his sporting career wasn't quite done yet. Howfield was sat in a pub with a friend when he read an advert in the paper for a 'kicking clinic', a trial for placekickers to try their might and sign with the Kansas City Chiefs from the American Football

League. His short time across the Atlantic in the Big Apple had clearly intrigued Howfield: 'I had enjoyed myself when I was in the United States [playing soccer]. I had made some friends in New York, I enjoyed the American way of life, so I decided to see if I could make it as a placekicker.' Armed with his ferocious right foot, Howfield attended the trial at Wembley Stadium and impressed the coaches so much with his first two attempts that they signed him right there and then, securing the former striker a pint after his friend allegedly bet him a drink that his venture into American football would be unsuccessful.

After jetting out to the States, it appeared Howfield would have to buy his friend a drink after all. The Chiefs discovered a new kicker, leaving Howfield at something of a crossroads before he signed with the Denver Broncos of the AFL in 1968. He kicked 30 of 30 extra points during his debut season – an impressive 100 per cent record – but struggled with field goals as he made an even 50 per cent with 9 of 18. He followed that up with 36 of 37 extra points and 13 of 29 field goals in 1969 before kicking 27 of 28 extra points with 18 of 32 field goals in 1970, Howfield's final season with the Broncos. His field goal percentage for the 1970 season was the highest of his career so far: 56.2 per cent was paired with a new career high of 81 points.

The Broncos finished 5-8-1 for the second successive year and Howfield decided to go to the city that stole his heart for a summer five years earlier: New York. He signed for the Jets in 1971 and the change of scenery did wonders for his game. Following a torrid first campaign in which the Jets – who had won the Super Bowl with iconic quarterback Joe Namath just three years prior – finished 6-8, Howfield came to life in 1972. He kicked 40 of 41 extra points and made a new career high in field goals at 73 per cent as he became a genuine star. He set a new record for points scored by a kicker (121 – a career-best) when, on 3 December 1972, Howfield converted six kicks at Shea Stadium and scored all of the Jets' points to lead his side to an 18-17 win over the New Orleans Saints. The winning 42-yard field goal was converted in the dying seconds but Howfield, who was developing a reputation as an apathetic Brit, showed little emotion to the New York media after securing the win: 'I'm still not really excited, and probably won't feel excited until I have my first beer!'

In 1973, Howfield continued to impress with a 100 per cent record on extra points and an admirable 70.8 per cent field goal rate, but his play declined drastically in 1974 which led to his decision to retire at the age of 37. Regardless, his 1972 season in which he led the AFC in scoring – and was second overall in the NFL – secured Howfield's reputation as a Jets legend.

Howfield was the first of a long line of British kickers in the NFL and a true trailblazer. He was the first British player to play in the league and did so for seven seasons, proving talent can indeed be found just across the pond.

Allan Watson

Pittsburgh Steelers 1970

JUST AS Bobby Howfield was performing for the Denver Broncos and making a splash as a kicker in 1968, Allan Watson had followed in his footsteps – but the Welshman was a little behind. Like Howfield, Watson was plying his trade as a kicker as he played for the Wheeling Ironmen in the Continental Football League, showcasing the immense talent trapped inside his right leg.

Watson was born in Blackwood, a small town in the Caerphilly area of Wales, and he attended the local high school before moving to Newport to attend the University of Wales. He starred as a footballer and wanted to find a career in sport, but failed to imitate the likes of Howfield in the English professional leagues.

Instead, Watson made the trip to the United States and found himself playing soccer for the Pittsburgh Phantoms at the age of 23. Unfortunately, his time in professional soccer would span just a single season as the league the Phantoms played in – the non-FIFA sanctioned National Professional Soccer League (NPSL) – merged with the United Soccer Association to form the North American Soccer League (NASL), a division which would be graced by the likes of Pelé, Franz Beckenbauer, Johan Cruyff and George Best. It was not a league that would be graced by Watson, as the Phantoms folded before the 1968 campaign due to poor attendances. They attracted an average home gate of just 3,122, the second lowest in the league.

Watson decided to try his hand – or foot – at American football and began kicking for the Ironmen, but his time with the West Virginia outfit again only lasted a single season as the team folded in 1969. Undeterred, Watson attended a try-out with nine other men vying for a spot on the Pittsburgh Steelers roster. Watson was beaten out for the role by Gene Mingo, who scored the first punt return for a touchdown in the American Football League back in 1960, but the Welshman still penned a deal to stay on the practice squad.

When Mingo struggled for form by kicking just 27.8 per cent of his field goals as the Steelers slipped to 4-6, Watson was called up to the main roster. He made his debut at Three Rivers Stadium in Pittsburgh's week 11 clash with the Cleveland Browns and nailed four extra points as Watson's Steelers won 28-9 to finish 3-3 in divisional matches.

The Steelers lost to the Green Bay Packers the following week as Watson kicked two field goals but missed the extra point after Terry Bradshaw, Pittsburgh's rookie quarterback selected first overall in the 1970 NFL Draft, hit Dave Smith on an 87-yard touchdown pass. Watson would miss an extra point as the Steelers fell to the Atlanta Falcons 27-16 in week 13 before a final-day defeat to the Philadelphia Eagles left the Pittsburgh with a 5-9 record.

Watson played in four games during the 1970 campaign, converting five of his ten field goal attempts in a tough season for the Steelers. His record wasn't particularly eye-catching given the league average that season was 59.4 per cent – an improvement of just under 7 per cent on the previous year – but the franchise opted to invite Watson to camp ahead of the 1971 campaign. They were reportedly enamoured with the Welshman's soccer-style technique as he used the instep of his foot to kick the ball.

Watson attended the 1971 camp and he was more experienced than the other kickers that attended the original try-out as he was entering his third season in football. He was perhaps surprised by the lack of care afforded to kickers and the wider roster during preseason: 'They expect you to take care of yourself, and report in shape. It's not their problem to worry about you.'

The soccer player-turned-Steeler impressed in camp, reportedly thumping pigskin after pigskin between the posts. Watson, living in East Liverpool, Ohio, was enjoying the scrupulous attention to detail of gridiron football. Kickers worked out once a day, charting the details of each kick including distance and the time period between snap of ball to the kick itself. 'A satisfactory time is between 1.2 and 1.4 seconds. You can't afford to take any longer than that or the chances are good that the kick will be blocked.' At least Watson understood the issue that would lead to his downfall.

Soccer-style kickers in the NFL and the general transition from association football to American football is traditionally thought of as being an easy switch, but that is not necessarily the case. 'When I first started kicking a football, I couldn't break the habit of booting the ball on a low trajectory, and quite often the kicks were blocked,' Watson admitted. Nine other kickers came to take his job but seven left after several rounds of camp, leaving Paul Rogers out of Nebraska and free agent Greg Fries as the threats to the Brit's job.

Watson understood that, even back then, the NFL really stood for 'not for long': 'This is one occupation that you never know how long you're going to be employed.' After originally surviving camp as the Steelers kicker, Watson was replaced by Roy Gerala after the Canadian had left the Houston Oilers. Gerala would go on to lead the AFC in scoring in 1973 and 1974, and was named to the Pro Bowl in 1972 and 1974 as the Steelers won three Super Bowl championships during his tenure.

Watson would eventually find a home in the short-lived World Football League (WFL), playing for the Chicago Fire in 1974 and the Chicago Wind the following season after the team rebranded. However, he struggled greatly in his final season, making one field goal from six attempts in a disappointing campaign that ended prematurely as the WFL folded.

While Watson would not leave his mark on the NFL in the same way Howfield did with the Broncos and Jets, he proved kickers could hail from Wales and still find a way into the dizzying heights of professional football. It was becoming a British pastime.

Mike Walker

New England Patriots 1972

MIKE WALKER, another soccer player who switched codes to play in the National Football League, took a famously unconventional route to become the third British player in league history. While Walker did not last long in the NFL, his journey from budding soccer player to the New England Patriots is a tale that has stood the test of time.

The story of how Walker landed in Foxborough begins with *Sports Huddle*, a sports talk radio show hosted by Eddie Andelman with his friends Jimmy McCarthy and Mark Witkin. The show aired on WBZ but soon moved to WEEI, the leading sports radio channel in New England. *Sports Huddle* debuted in 1971 and, as it established itself as a popular place for fans to tune in, the trio were looking for ways to genuinely help their local teams – including the Patriots who were suffering from particularly woeful kicking. Andelman was intrigued by the trend of soccer or rugby players becoming kickers in the NFL, focusing on their different style. He commented on how these kickers used the inside of their feet to strike the ball after a sideways run up. Most importantly, these players were proving to be accurate.

On 27 November 1966, the Washington Redskins and New York Giants took part in the highest-scoring match in NFL history, with the men in blue coming away 72-41 winners. The record was powered on the leg of the two teams' kickers: brothers Pete and Charlie Gogolak. Pete, from Cornell University, kicked for the Giants while Charlie, from Princeton, did so for Washington as they combined for an NFL record 14 extra points. Andelman questioned how these brothers from Budapest in Hungary were so skilled, attributing it to their soccer pedigree.

On their talk show, the trio lamented the Patriots' disappointing kicking that cost them a memorable 1970 win over the high-flying Baltimore Colts – who would go on to win Super Bowl V – as New England made only two of five field goal attempts in a desperate 14-6 defeat. In their last season in Boston before moving to Foxborough, two Pats kickers combined for just eight converted field goals from 22 attempts, the third-lowest conversion rate across the league.

Andelman was aware of the 'Kicking Karavans' which had travelled across Europe and the United Kingdom looking for kickers in the late 1960s and early 1970s so, using the special teams woes for content, the host and his sidekicks decided to find a European kicker for the Patriots. They dubbed the venture 'Search for Superfoot' and what started as a joke became an international hunt.

The trio called plenty of different outlets and prospective kickers before their big call came through. The *Daily Mirror*, a popular tabloid newspaper in Britain, decided to back the idea and create a kicking contest to find Andelman's soccer-style kicker for the Patriots. The *Mirror*'s advert calling for kickers to enter the contest reflected the lack of understanding and acceptance of the sport across the Atlantic, referring to American football as 'a rough and tumble game where the players turn out like spacemen in helmets and pounds of padding'.

The contest saw 16,000 Brits enter, with regional heats held across the country. The radio hosts even joined Patriots coaches in watching prospective kickers attempt to impress in places such as Goole, Maidstone and Welsh town Pontypridd.

With the *Mirror* and American partner Westinghouse Broadcasting picking up expenses for the contest, 12 soccer players remained as the finals were held in Oxfordshire on 15 May 1971. In the drizzling rain at a US Air Force base, Mike Walker – a 21-year-old from Cornforth, Lancashire who had been entered into the contest by his father – took a sip of tea on the sideline before running onto the field to nail a pair of 55-yard field goals. It was enough to impress the coaches and the hosts. Walker had won a cash prize and a two-week trial at the Patriots' training camp.

Dubbed Mike 'Superfoot' Walker, he was a complete rookie when it came to American football but his amateur soccer background with Carnforth Rangers helped him. The former bricklayer was overwhelmed by the media coverage afforded to him at the training camp and subsequently returned to England, but he impressed the coaches enough that they kept him on their practice squad.

Walker practised his kicking while away from the team and he returned to training camp in 1972, beating out several experienced kickers to win the starting job. His debut, a preseason clash against the iconic Raiders in rowdy Oakland, was the first game of American football he had ever experienced. The Brit was taken aback by the crowd's abuse. 'They would scream things at you, knowing full well that you were fresh off the plane, not knowing their game, to try to disrupt the way you kicked,' Walker said. 'But I was a good kicker, I didn't let that stuff bother me too much. You were obviously a local professional player, getting paid in my case many, many thousands of dollars more than I'd ever made when I was back in England.' Armed with his nickname even in match programmes, Walker appeared in eight games for the Patriots in 1972, and while he was perfect when it came to extra points, he made just two of eight field goals with a career-long of 36 yards.

Struggling with a thigh injury, Walker was cut by the Patriots during the offseason and never appeared for the Los Angeles

Rams, with whom he spent the 1973 season. He retired after that campaign and became a liquor salesman, as well as a permanent fixture in Pats folklore. There was historical irony in the fact that the New England Patriots turned to a Brit for help, and while Walker wasn't the superstar Andelman, McCarthy and Witkin hoped for, he paved the way for future soccer star kickers, including compatriot John Smith.

John Smith

New England Patriots 1974–1983

THE NEW England Patriots' interest in English kickers remained after Mike 'Superfoot' Walker. After they signed John Smith, the Oxfordshire-born star proved to be one of the more successful imports in league history.

Smith had dreamed of making it as a professional soccer player since he was born in Leafield, Oxfordshire in December 1949. Smith was reportedly an excellent sportsman and impressive player, excelling in soccer to the point where he was offered a professional contract at 16 years of age. However, his interests had evolved as Smith turned down the offer to focus on pursuing a career in education, training as a teacher at King Alfred's College at the University of Winchester between 1968 and 1971.

Upon graduating, Smith travelled to the United States in 1972 as he continued to chase his dream of teaching. Smith was teaching and coaching soccer at a summer camp when he was asked to try kicking a football, and he enjoyed the experience as he found he had a knack for it. The Brit's fling with American football became a prosperous marriage following a successful trial at the New England Patriots after he approached the franchise and asked for a chance. With the league in the midst of the 'soccer-style' kicking trend, the Patriots decided to give Smith a shot.

When the Patriots were scrimmaging with the Washington Redskins at training camp, Smith had a rude awakening. The

Brit was juggling a soccer ball on the sideline when New England coach Chuck Fairbanks cried for his name and ordered him to kick. Smith ran onto the field and kicked the field goal without his helmet, left behind on the other field alongside the soccer ball. He took to the field for the Patriots in the 1973 Hall of Fame Game against the San Francisco 49ers, who won the preseason contest 20-7. Smith, heavily jeered and abused by both opposition fans and players alike, was hoping to win a professional contract but struggled in the game and was subsequently cut from the team.

It was certainly not the end of Smith's American dream. The Patriots saw potential in the former soccer star and sent him to spend the 1973 season with the New England Colonials in the Atlantic Coast Football League. 'My wife and I both wanted to travel, so we thought, "What the heck, let's go over and see what it's all about,"' Smith said. 'My dad always used to say to me, "Have a go and give it all you got." I really thought it would end up just being a kind of vacation.' The vacation became a permanent residency as Smith impressed and re-signed with the Patriots in 1974, where he became the starter – and the Brit starred to arguably become the most consistent specialist in the NFL. After beginning his career in style with All-Rookie honours, Smith was named to the Patriots All-Decade Team for the 1970s, and he followed that up with the best season of his career to open the 1980s. Smith led the league in scoring across both 1979 and 1980, and he made each of his 51 extra points and 26 of 34 field goals during the latter season to earn a place at his first and only Pro Bowl.

The Brit is part of a tragic piece of history from that season, too. On 8 December 1980, the Patriots were facing their AFC East rival the Miami Dolphins in a nationally televised game on *Monday Night Football.* With a playoff spot on the line, the game was tied 13-13 in the final seconds of the match when Smith – such a huge fan of The Beatles that the Brit was forced to sing songs from the band during his rookie season – lined up to kick the winning field goal. The camera was pinned on Smith, who had made two field goals in the match already, when news suddenly broke that John Lennon had been murdered. Legendary broadcaster Howard Cosell announced the tragic news right before Smith's kick was blocked, and the Dolphins went on to win in overtime. Smith, frustrated with the offensive line after his kick was blocked, didn't hear of the news until reporters entered their locker room. 'The press was talking about two things: the fact that we'd lost the game and we had a lead in the fourth quarter, and then it changed to John Lennon,' Smith recalled. 'It put things in perspective.'

During his time in New England – particularly between 1976 and 1980 – the Patriots were considered one of the better teams in the NFL, going 50-26 over the four seasons but failing to win a playoff game as they fell to the Oakland Raiders in 1976 and Houston Oilers in 1978. In the 1982 campaign, the Patriots battled the Dolphins in the infamous 'Snowplow Game'. Played 12 December amid a snowstorm at Schaefer Stadium, Smith kicked the only points to cement himself in football folklore as the Patriots won 3-0.

Smith injured his right knee – his non-kicking leg – and underwent arthroscopic surgery that kept him out of much of the 1982 season. He returned before the end of the campaign but it ended in familiar fashion, with the Dolphins defeating the Patriots 28-13 in the Wildcard Round of the 1982 postseason. Smith retired after the 1983 campaign as the second-highest scoring player in Patriots history behind Gino Cappelletti. At the time of writing, Smith's total of 692 points places him fourth behind Stephen Gostkowski, Adam Vinatieri and Cappelletti.

Mick Luckhurst

Atlanta Falcons 1981–1987

MICK LUCKHURST embarked on a long career in both the NFL and television, and the Brit even established himself as a key member of the players' association despite growing up in St Albans, a small cathedral city in Hertfordshire. Following a playing career spent solely with the Atlanta Falcons, Luckhurst was named to the executive committee of the NFL Players Association where he acted as player spokesman – not bad for a kicker who figured he would rather play rugby than American football.

Born in Redbourn, Luckhurst attended St Columba's College in his home county but always dreamed of going to America and earning a sports scholarship. He arrived at St Cloud in Minnesota via an exchange programme, and quickly learned the athleticism necessary to prevail in American sports was vastly different to back in the United Kingdom. 'Within about a day I realised I wasn't tall enough, couldn't jump high enough and wasn't good enough to play basketball,' said Luckhurst. 'I wanted to stay, so I had to find an alternative.' Luckhurst played rugby in the States and secured a sports scholarship at the University of California Berkeley, where he would play both rugby and American football for the Golden Bears.

Luckhurst was instrumental in leading the Golden Bears to their first national collegiate rugby title in 1980 and showed off his trusty left boot by making 14 of 17 penalty kicks and 18 of 19 conversions. He impressed on the football field as well, holding the record for the longest field goal in team history for some time with a 54-yard effort against Oregon State in 1979. Despite his success in the gridiron arena, Luckhurst never considered a career in the NFL a possibility. 'Even after my senior year at Cal, I wasn't seriously thinking that I would play in the NFL,' he recalled. 'I thought it'd be lovely to give it a shot but I really thought I'd probably go to Australia or New Zealand to play rugby, and just have a laugh doing that.' He went undrafted in 1981, but Luckhurst wouldn't wait long to find a home in the NFL.

The Englishman wasn't drafted as teams were conscious he had kicked for just two seasons, but Luckhurst was offered free agent deals by 18 teams. Luckhurst shared an agent with Atlanta quarterback Steve Bartkowski, who also played for the Cal Golden Bears in college. Despite the Falcons having a kicker in Tim Mazzetti, it was clear the franchise were looking for a new kicker and Luckhurst went to the try-out. He performed well, beating out eight other kickers to claim the starting position for himself. 'Walking out onto the field with my helmet in hand, knowing I was the only one left and I was actually the kicker, was one of the greatest days ever.' He was offered a 'whopping' $3,000 signing bonus with a first-year salary of $30,000, but Luckhurst truly realised he had made it when a fan handed him his rookie card in a supermarket: 'That alone was a dream come true.'

Luckhurst played for the Falcons for seven seasons and kicked 115 field goals from 164 attempts along with 213 extra point conversions from 216 attempts. The Brit retired as the franchise's all-time leading scorer with 558 points and was surpassed by Morten Anderson in 2000. With the only rushing attempt of his career, Luckhurst scored a rushing touchdown for the Falcons in their 1982 playoff game against the Minnesota Vikings. A fake field goal led to the 17-yard scoring rush, capping off a performance in which Luckhurst also kicked a field goal and an extra point to become the only player in playoff history to do all three. 'I've been accused of looking like I'm carrying a loaf of bread, but it's amazing how fast you can run when you've got NFL players chasing you down,' Luckhurst said before revealing his biggest regret after scoring. 'I handed the ball to the referee [as his celebration] because Herschel Walker always did it and said, "I'm coming back soon." I should have slammed it and celebrated because I never got close to coming back again! I don't regret it though, because it wa a fun, brilliant day – unfortunately, we lost the game.' The 30-20 defeat at Minnesota was the only playoff appearance of Luckhurst's career.

Luckhurst's rushing touchdown was the longest Falcons scoring run until Jamal Anderson's 34-yard touchdown against the San Francisco 49ers in 1999. 'It was quite funny because suddenly the guy on television said "and that breaks Mick Luckhurst's record", and that must have been the most embarrassing record that any team ever had – their field goal kicker had the longest run for a touchdown! I think everyone at the franchise took a massive sigh of relief when Jamal scored.'

With rugby and soccer playing such a prominent role in the British sporting mainstream, kicking has always been a confusing position for British fans to wrap their head around. Luckhurst understood the position is unique – and doesn't necessarily disagree with the English perspective. 'I really do see how hard it is to play as a lineman – defensive or offensive – or a linebacker and the abuse that comes to their bodies; often tackling is more painful than being tackled! For the English fans, you're just a kicker – until there's three seconds left, you're down by one, and you've got a 48-yard field goal,' Luckhurst warned. 'Suddenly, there's not one player on that team that wants to be you and not one of them thinks they can do your job. You never know which points are going to be crucial, and the vast majority of all games are decided by the kicking points – and so as a kicker, there's pressure on you every minute of every game.' Luckhurst also revealed he earned respect from his team-mates by making tackles on special teams when needed: 'Today, I don't walk very well and I look a bit older than I am because I did go down and make a tackle.'

While mentally arduous, Luckhurst commented on the strange feeling of exhaustion he would suffer after an American football game. 'I'd be more physically tired [than rugby] yet I would be on for maybe minutes, possibly seconds. You just can't switch off,' he said. 'While you're off the field, you have to be ready to go at any moment. Anything can happen.' Luckhurst admitted he wasn't afraid of taking the game-deciding kicks as he was prepared for it. The mental aspect of the position meant the Brit looked for positive aspects of the high-pressure moments. 'The nerves were positive because it got me fired up and focused – but didn't interfere with my ability to perform.'

Luckhurst knew he had to perform and is aware of the raised standards of kickers in the modern game. 'I always compare kicking to Roger Bannister and the four-minute mile: once kickers realised they could kick 70 per cent or 80 per cent, they did – and now I think the norm will become 90 per cent,' Luckhurst said. 'When I kicked, if you made 70 per cent of your attempts you were considered a top kicker, but now you'd be cut from the NFL.' Luckhurst retired having made 70.1 per cent of his field goal attempts.

After retiring, Luckhurst transitioned to television where he worked alongside friend and legendary quarterback Dan Marino. They worked together covering the NFL as well as the World League of American Football. 'Wherever we went, people wanted Dan to throw them the ball so they could say they caught a ball that Dan Marino threw,' Luckhurst recalled.

Luckhurst – who was part of the ceremonial coin toss at Wembley Stadium when the Atlanta Falcons faced the Detroit Lions as part of the 2014 slate of International Series matches – became a popular figure among British audiences in the 1980s as Channel 4 boosted American football's popularity. With the game becoming increasingly accessible to Brits to both play and watch, Luckhurst hopes more compatriots will enter the league to inspire the next generation. 'There was me and John Smith – no one other than that, and we were kickers,' he said. 'Now, there are players in the NFL that are British and not just kicking: they're playing offensive line, defensive line, and other positions. They get to come [to America] to go to college, and then one player makes it and a 10-year-old watches them and suddenly goes, "Gosh, I would love to do that" – and it becomes a part of the dream.'

For Luckhurst, his dream took him away from Hertfordshire and rugby all the way to the bright lights of the NFL and the record books of Atlanta.

Vince Abbott

San Diego Chargers 1987–1988

'IF YOU step back and think about what has happened to me, it's unbelievable,' Vince Abbott told the *Los Angeles Times* in his polite British accent back in 1987. He certainly was not wrong.

Abbott was born in London in 1958, but he didn't stay in the capital long. He traversed the globe, living in Ireland, Australia, New Zealand and the Bahamas as he attended 16 schools by the time he was 15 years of age. His love for sport was perhaps the only constant in his life, and Abbott – given his British background and time spent in other countries fond of the sport – was a keen rugby player. He joined the University of Washington with the intention to play rugby but saw two women at practice and was apprehensive about getting physical with members of the opposite sex in a competitive environment.

After leaving rugby behind, Abbott attended try-outs for the football team, using his soccer-based kicking style to make 30 out of 30 attempts in the pouring rain. His coaches ensured he had a place on the team and the Englishman was subsequently redshirted, meaning he was forced to sit out his freshman year to learn the ropes of the programme and the sport. While the United States and United Kingdom are very similar, something was clearly lost in translation as Abbott thought this meant he could play somewhere else. He quit Washington and had already enrolled at Cal State Fullerton by the time he figured out he was wrong – and he had to sit out a year on the West Coast, too.

Following his graduation, Abbott went undrafted in 1981 and received no professional contract. Between 1982 and 1986, he attended NFL training camps in San Francisco, Miami, Chicago, Tampa and Los Angeles where the 49ers, Dolphins, Bears, Buccaneers and Raiders each rejected him. In fact, failing to earn a roster spot became such a theme for Abbott that NFL records claim he was cut from the Rams, despite the kicker never attending their training camp. He played in the USFL for the Los Angeles Express in 1983 and made 21 of 30 field goals only to get cut before the start of the following season. Abbott didn't mind too much, though. He used the time to get his head down and work as he chased the NFL dream that had so far proved elusive. Abbott would practise at his alma mater and his wife Sarah would support him as best she could; the two would go to the field each night with 12 footballs and she would hold the ball while he kicked until well after dark.

Abbott got his long-deserved break in 1987. He attended a training camp and preseason with the San Diego Chargers where he went seven of eight on-field goals – four of which were over 40 yards in length. The Brit was so impressive that the Chargers traded iconic kicker Rolf Benirschke, who had been with the team since 1977, to the Dallas Cowboys. 'You should have heard the boos,' Abbott recalled. 'I had replaced their hero, and now look what I was doing.' He made an immediate impact as a rookie, making two of three field goals from 32 and 33 yards respectively – with the latter tying the match with just over three minutes to play – against the Kansas City Chiefs on his debut.

In week seven against the Cleveland Browns, Abbott successfully made a 20-yard kick to tie the game with 1:46 remaining before his 33-yard winning field goal in overtime secured a 27-24 victory for the Chargers, who moved to 6-1 – their best start since their first season in 1961. Abbott's crucial influence continued the following two weeks as he made three field goals against the Indianapolis Colts – including a game-winner from 38 yards – and kicked three field goals to help the Chargers to a 16-14 win and an 8-1 record. After kicking 13 of 22 attempts during his rookie campaign, with seven misses coming from over 40 yards, Abbott retained his place on the Chargers roster for the 1988 season.

Asked what his secret for success was, Abbott said: 'I just kick it. Where it goes is where it goes. I can just do my best and hope it gets through the uprights.' The Brit held his own during his sophomore campaign, making 8 of 12 field goals in 12 appearances as the Chargers struggled to a 6-10 record. The 1988 season would prove to be his last, ending his career a perfect 13 of 13 on game-winning field goals.

His journey from London to Los Angeles, from rugby to the NFL, had sculpted Abbott into the clutch kicker he became – and he understood the reason he could handle the pressure of game-winning kicks stemmed from the effort he put in to overcome all the hardships he endured over the years. 'Making kicks in training camps where, if you miss it, you are cut immediately,' Abbott concluded to the *Los Angeles Times*. 'When you have been on the spot as much as I have, you get used to it.'

Lawrence Tynes

Kansas City Chiefs 2001-2002
Scottish Claymores 2002
Ottawa Renegades 2002-2003
Kansas City Chiefs 2004-2006
New York Giants 2007-2012
Tampa Bay Buccaneers 2013

LAWRENCE TYNES, along with Osi Umenyiora on the same New York Giants team, became the first British player to win a Super Bowl championship while on an active roster. The Scottish-born superstar kicker's journey from playing soccer in Campbeltown to lifting the Vince Lombardi Trophy on two occasions is one that saw Tynes's career come full circle while going beyond any of his wildest dreams.

Lawrence James Henry Tynes was born in Greenock, Scotland in May 1978 to an American father – a member of the US Navy – and a Scottish mother. Tynes grew up in Campbeltown, a small town with a population of under 5,000, where he attended St Kieran's primary school with his two brothers, dribbling a football around the loch when they walked to school. He developed an eye for sports early and, while he enjoyed playing shinty, he was infatuated with soccer. 'We had two or three recesses per day, so I always couldn't wait for those to go play soccer,' Tynes recalled. 'I used to always put on my Celtic strip, just to feel like Paul McStay.'

Tynes played for the Campbeltown Boys, and he continued to play soccer when he arrived in America aged 11 – but his eyes were truly opened by American football.

Tynes arrived in Florida after his father was stationed back in the States and he was at a disadvantage when it came to football as he had never played the sport, unlike his colleagues. He would travel with his Milton High School soccer team around south-eastern America but he soon realised the sheer popularity of American football. 'On Friday nights, there was literally 10,000 people at a high school game – and our town was only around 10,000 people! Every person in town was at the games, they were a big deal,' Tynes added, before explaining how he transitioned from soccer to football. 'Our PE teacher asked me if I could kick because he knew I played soccer, so during class in my junior year, I went out to the practice field to kick and never stopped. If he never asked me to kick, I don't think I would be talking right now.' Similar to the likes of Bobby Howfield and Allan Walker before him, Tynes utilised his soccer ability to become an accurate kicker – but he was keen to emphasise the mental fortitude required at the position. 'There's a lot of people that can kick a football, but not a lot of people can do it on Sunday when the pressure is on. Kicking the ball, per se, is not necessarily difficult if you have a soccer background - but doing it under the gun and to win games is hard.'

After graduating high school, Tynes walked-on at Troy University in Alabama but he soon earned himself the scholarship he craved. He started all four years as a Trojan and earned All-American honours, yet Tynes – who played alongside Umenyiora at Troy, too – still never thought a career in pro football was an option. 'I just didn't think it was possible. There are 32 people in the world that get to kick a football, why would they want me?' While Tynes went undrafted in 2001, he signed with the Kansas City Chiefs as a free agent but endured a difficult spell with the team. He was cut before the 2001 season but re-signed ahead of the 2002 campaign, where Tynes was allocated to the developmental league close to home. 'At the time, NFL Europe was around so I kind of knew I was going to go there because it was a minor league,' Tynes said. After a month of training camps in Tampa, Florida where he had to beat out a number of kickers for a spot in NFL Europe, Tynes was allocated to the Scottish Claymores, ensuring he would return to play football in Scotland.

Tynes figured Scotland was where he was going to land, particularly as the kicker had worked with Claymores special teams coach Thomas McGauhey in Kansas City. 'It was mad, very full circle. I never in a million years thought I'd be in Scotland playing American football.' His time with the Claymores helped him develop his game, although Tynes acknowledged the frustration of getting less reps as he split snaps with English bare-footed kicker Rob Hart. 'What was interesting about NFL Europe was European kickers would kick everything short. Some games I wouldn't take a field goal because there were no attempts outside of 35 yards.' Tynes understood why this was the case: international players like Hart – who Tynes labelled a 'really good kicker' – helped bring awareness to the game. The 2002 season was beneficial to Tynes as he would go visit his grandma in Greenock after practice, allowing him to stay in touch with his roots. The Claymores ended the 2002 season with a 5-5 record.

Upon returning to North America, Tynes signed with the Ottawa Renegades in the Canadian Football League, and he will always treasure his time north of the border. 'The CFL is really where I felt I belonged and understood I could play,' he said. 'It's not a small league, it's just not as popular as the NFL.' Tynes harboured dreams of making it in the NFL, and he re-signed with the Chiefs ahead of the 2004 season. Tynes subsequently beat out legendary kicker Morten Anderson to claim the job and held it for three seasons, compiling a field goal conversion rate of 78.2 per cent before he was traded to the New York Giants ahead of the 2007 season. The Giants sent a 2008 seventh-round conditional pick for the Scottish-born placekicker, and the innocuous trade soon became historic.

The Giants had lost Pro Bowl kicker Jay Feely to Miami in free agency, and Tynes soon beat out unproven kickers in Josh Huston and Marc Hickok to become the franchise starter. Halfway through his first season, the Giants flew to London to face the Miami Dolphins in the first International Series match at Wembley Stadium. Of course, Tynes was destined to score the first points. 'It just makes sense that I was the one who scored the points, because I'm from the UK,' he said, smiling. 'It's an awesome piece of history to claim.' The Giants left London with a 13-10 win and went on to clinch a playoff berth with their 10-6 record. After a pair of road wins against the Tampa Bay Buccaneers and the Dallas Cowboys, New York arrived in Green Bay to face the Packers at Lambeau Field.

On that freezing cold day in Wisconsin, Tynes made the first of his two career-defining kicks. It was -18 degrees Celsius with a wind chill of -31 when Tynes stepped up to the plate in overtime. He had missed his previous two attempts, but the Scot saw his opportunity to thwart Brett Favre and the Packers. Before his attempt, no kicker had made a field goal of over 40 yards while game time temperature was below freezing. His 47-yard effort with 12:29 remaining in overtime appeared to be sailing wide right, but it hooked back inside and over the crossbar to send the Giants to the Super Bowl as 23-20 winners over Green Bay, becoming the NFC champions. The conference-winning kick still stands as the longest postseason field goal made at Lambeau Field. Tynes recalled a 'funny' story about the match, commenting on how the conditions affected players' bodies. 'I had a kick-off in the middle of the match and I felt something pop – but it was so cold, I was not going to pull off the layers to go see it. After I made the kick and ran off the field, I pulled off my sock and right by my ankle, my foot had just swelled up to like a baseball because my socks were keeping the pressure of that fluid in there,' recollected Tynes. 'When I pulled everything off, I almost passed out looking at it because I had busted all the blood vessels in my foot.' The injury was so severe that Tynes didn't kick until the Thursday before Super Bowl XLII, and while he was advised not to kick in the championship game, there was no way he was going to sit it out.

On 3 February 2008, the New York Giants took on the New England Patriots in the Super Bowl. The Patriots were vying to become the first undefeated team since the Miami Dolphins in 1972, and the first team to ever do so with the longer schedule. While the odds were stacked against the Giants, Tynes claimed the team believed they could at least compete with the Patriots after losing their regular season contest to Tom Brady and co. by just three points. 'We knew we had the advantage; we were the underdogs,' Tynes insisted. 'We knew what kind of pressure they were under to become the first-ever 19-0 team in NFL history, so we had a lot of confidence going into that game. Of course, it takes some luck, right? We have the crazy helmet catch as well as some other unbelievable plays in that game and we ended up winning it.' The Giants, largely thanks to Eli Manning's heroics and David Tyree's unbelievable catch, emerged 17-14 winners to secure Tynes a championship ring. 'It was a good year getting traded from the Chiefs, to win a Super Bowl in my first year in New York.'

He wasn't done there, though. Tynes became the first player in NFL history to have two overtime game-winning field goals in the playoffs when he did it in the NFC Championship Game once again. On 22 January 2012, Tynes nailed a 31-yard chip shot to defeat the 49ers in rainy San Francisco before converting two field goals and an extra point as the Giants defeated the Patriots in Super Bowl XLVI to claim his second championship title.

While the elements were different, the question remained: which NFC Championship-clinching kick did Tynes prefer? 'The Green Bay game is the one I'm most known for,' he said after pausing for a moment. 'It was the third-coldest game in NFL history. It was terrible; you could throw water up and by the time it came to the ground, it would be an icicle – yet I hit a 47-yard field goal. I have no idea how I did that.' He was more confident when he stepped up to take the kick at Candlestick Park. 'It was short, but muddy and wet conditions meant anything could go wrong. I definitely relied on my past experiences and knew I had been in that position before and done it.'

Tynes lived an incredible career that took him from Scotland to New York, embarking on careers in NFL Europe, the CFL and NFL. He retired as a two-time Super Bowl champion, the 2012 NFL scoring leader and a Giants legend after scoring 586 points for Big Blue – the second-most in franchise history. 'When you're in the moment, you don't think about it but being away from football now and thinking back on what I accomplished, it's cool – I'm really proud,' Tynes said while declaring he never forgot his roots on the field. 'I felt like I was carrying the flag for Scotland when I was playing.'

Osi Umenyiora

New York Giants 2003-2012
Atlanta Falcons 2013-2014

OSI UMENYIORA certainly has a claim to being the greatest British player in NFL history. Born in Golders Green in the London borough of Barnet to Nigerian parents, Umenyiora is a proud advocate of his ties to both the African nation and the United Kingdom. He is of Igbo descent, a native from the town of Ogbunike. His full first name – Ositadimma – pays homage to his heritage as it means 'from today on, things will be good'. With total dedication and passionate play, Umenyiora ensured that his career was, at the very least, most definitely good.

Umenyiora remembers little when it comes to his time spent in London, although he recalls earning plenty of gold stars at school. 'I'm not trying to be funny, but my gold stars would be almost off the chart!' he declared. It's not just the gold stars that Umenyiora remembers when it comes to London, as he also recalls McDonald's, *Rocky IV* and the cold, wet weather. Fortunately, Umenyiora wouldn't have to worry about the bleak climate for too long as his family moved from London to Nigeria when he was seven years old.

At 14 years of age, Umenyiora moved to Auburn, Alabama to pursue a better education. He lived with his sister and attended Auburn High School, where he began to play American football for the first time – and it was certainly a new experience. 'I had never even heard of American football before. When I arrived, my friends told me to go to a high school game and I was just completely lost,' Umenyiora recalled. 'It was the strangest thing to see, especially if I didn't know what it was. I only knew football and basketball.' He started playing American football in his junior year after his older brother's friends recommended the sport to him due to his size and athleticism. 'I realised the game was popular in America – it was so much bigger than everything else. I didn't have a lot of friends in high school at the time, so I just did it as a way to fit in.' Umenyiora befriended team-mate and future NFL legend DeMarcus Ware in high school, and the two men embarked on their careers in college alongside one another, too.

In fact, the story of how Umenyiora got to college is remarkable. He received no scholarship offers and wasn't even considered by schools as he was a relatively unknown entity. His senior season had ended, but Umenyiora had failed to attend a mandatory class – driver's education – and was summoned to the principal's office where he received an in-school suspension due to his repeated absences. His suspension was overseen by the school's running backs coach, who asked Umenyiora what he wanted to do with himself now high school was set to finish, and the budding star simply replied he wanted to go to college. The coach called his former college team-mate Tracy Rocker, the defensive line coach at Troy State, who happened to be in Auburn at the time. Rocker stopped by the school to test Umenyiora's measurables and athletic capabilities: 'He told me, "You're really not that good of a player, but you're an athlete," so he called his head coach Larry Blakeney, who stated if Rocker thought I was good enough to receive a scholarship, he should offer one,' Umenyiora said. 'They gave me a scholarship and I went to Troy. Crazy story.'

Umenyiora played for the Troy State Trojans where he started out on the interior of the defensive line playing nose tackle. In his junior year, Umenyiora's coach moved him to defensive end as he wanted the Brit to earn more money once he reached the NFL. 'That's when my career took off and flourished because I was able to really utilise my athleticism.' In 2002, Umenyiora set records at Troy in tackles for loss in a single season (20.5) and sacks in a single game with four against Florida A&M en route to a 15-sack season, the second-most in NCAA Division I. Umenyiora's legacy as a Trojan was secured in 2014, when he was inducted into the Troy University Sports Hall of Fame. 'That was crazy – especially when you consider how I got to college, right?' Umenyiora said, struggling to get the words out while laughing. 'I got into a college hall of fame. I mean, it was incredible. I couldn't make the ceremony because I was actually playing when it happened, but just knowing they made a video and celebrated my experiences – incredible.'

Despite starring at Troy, Umenyiora did not receive an invite to the NFL Scouting Combine – which meant he had to work hard to get noticed by scouts. 'I had a little stopwatch and timed myself running the 40, doing drills – just ridiculous stuff. There weren't a lot of teams that attended my first pro day, but around 26 showed up to the second one,' Umenyiora recalled. 'Teams don't share information, so I had to travel to all the interested teams for almost three weeks to give them my information.' When the 2003 NFL Draft came, Umenyiora expected to be selected in the fifth or sixth round, so he was sitting at home in his pyjamas just watching the event unfold. He received a call from his agent, who suggested the New York Giants – who were incredibly impressed by his ability – were set to draft him in the second round, 56th overall. 'I looked up at the TV and saw the guy come on stage and struggle to read the name, and then I realised it was real,' Umenyiora said, smiling. He was thrilled to get the move to New York, although the Brit wouldn't have minded where he landed. 'Even if I got drafted by the Bengals, I would have been ecstatic! Just making it to the NFL was like a dream,' Umenyiora added. 'Whenever you think about American football, there are three or four teams that comes to mind and it's the Giants, the Cowboys, Green Bay, etc. They're the teams that you think of, so I was very excited.'

After his rookie campaign, Umenyiora began to find success in 2004 as he started the last seven games of the season and tallied seven sacks. In 2005, the Brit began to truly establish himself as one of the league's premier defensive ends in football, achieving 14.5 sacks and 70 tackles, second only to the 16 sacks of Oakland star Derrick Burgess, as Umenyiora earned All-Pro recognition and his first trip to the Pro Bowl. 'The coaches called the whole team together and they said they were going to announce who made the Pro Bowl before announcing my name and then [Michael] Strahan's. There was nothing like it, knowing where I come from: from being born in England and moving to Nigeria, the whole story – and suddenly being told I'm one of the best players in the world at this position. It was mind boggling,' Umenyiora remembered. 'Outside of that first Super Bowl, it was probably the best feeling I've ever had in football. I remember it vividly.'

Umenyiora starred in 2007 as well, which would prove to be a huge year for both the defensive end and the Giants. He recorded six sacks in a single game as New York defeated the Philadelphia Eagles 16-3 to move to 2-2, and he followed it up in week seven when Umenyiora hit San Francisco 49ers quarterback Trent Dilfer with a sack and forced a fumble which he returned 75 yards to score the first touchdown of his career. Umenyiora finished with 13 sacks on the year as the Giants booked their place in Super Bowl XLII, pitting Big Blue against the unbeaten New England Patriots.

The Giants, who had finished the season 10-6, defeated the Tampa Bay Buccaneers, Dallas Cowboys and Green Bay Packers to reach the championship game in Arizona. While New York were set to face the vaunted Pats, Umenyiora was more concerned with the Cowboys in the Divisional Round. 'Dallas that year were probably the best team I had ever played against – they had 13 Pro Bowlers on their roster,' he declared. 'They had beaten us twice handily, but we beat them when it mattered.'

Umenyiora, who would never eat before games due to crippling nerves, recalled how he was forced to motivate and encourage Hall of Fame defensive lineman Michael Strahan and his team-mates ahead of the clash with New England. 'I was never a big speech guy – it was usually Strahan who did most of the talking – but I remember the day of the game just sitting there at breakfast, reading the paper when it hit me,' Umenyiora recollected. 'If we, as a defensive line, don't play well, we're going to lose this game. This game was literally on our shoulders. I pulled Strahan to the side and told him, and he was like, "Yeah, yeah, whatever" and carried on eating. I grabbed him again and said, "Listen to me, bro. If we don't play our games, then this isn't going to happen," and I think at that point the gravity of the situation had sunk in. Strahan always considered me the joking guy, but I was dead serious.' Umenyiora realised Tom Brady and the Patriots offence needed to get hit early and consistently to throw them off their game, and he believed the Giants were capable of the upset – but it was down to their defensive line.

During the first quarter, Umenyiora began to believe the offensive line could not deal with the Giants defensive line. 'We were hurrying, hitting, and getting to Brady – I could see he was getting frustrated,' the former Giants defensive end said. 'We really started to believe after the first and second quarter; that's when we knew we were going to win.' The Giants defence began to ooze confidence and they held the all-conquering Pats offence to just 14 points – their lowest total of the season. With Eli Manning's late touchdown pass to Plaxico Burress sealing a 17-14 win for the Giants, Umenyiora had won the Super Bowl for the first time – and he referred to it as the pinnacle of his career. 'Not only did we do something that nobody gave us a chance to do, but my defensive line and I were the main reason we won that game. I was a big part of probably the biggest upset in Super Bowl history – it's something that will never be forgotten,' the Brit said, grinning as he remembered the celebration parade down the Canyon of Heroes.

He experienced the parade again four years later. The Giants defeated Brady and the Patriots once more, winning Super Bowl XLVI 21-17. Umenyiora and his team were more assured going into the second championship match as they had done it before. 'It was weird how confident we were. Honestly, I wouldn't say we were a better team than the Patriots, because we weren't. We were just a bad matchup for New England,' said Umenyiora, who took great pleasure in assuming the role of David to the Patriots' Goliath. 'Everybody who played for New England and Bill Belichick all carried themselves with a certain swagger, and they beat everybody else but they couldn't beat us. Maybe I'm imagining things, but you could feel them come down a peg when they were around the Giants – and I definitely take pride in that.'

After injury issues began to rear their ugly head, Umenyiora signed a two-year deal with the Atlanta Falcons. The move worked out for him off the field as that was where he lived while playing for the Giants, but the Falcons were struggling after going 13-3 the season before Umenyiora's arrival. 'They were such a good team for the years prior to me getting there, but then I arrived and we sucked,' Umenyiora sombrely admitted. 'I root for Atlanta to this day. I want them to win so bad because of the people who are there; they are a top-class organisation, so overall I had a really good time.'

When looking back over his championship-winning and success-laden career, Umenyiora expressed a single regret: he didn't flaunt and celebrate his international status in the NFL enough. 'When I was playing, I wish I had known how big the game was going to become out here, because I would have been waving that Union Jack and planted it in the middle of the field. Boom! It would have been an image forever,' the Brit, who is a leading advocate for the development of the international game in both the United Kingdom and Africa, said with a grin etched across his face.

Umenyiora's career résumé compares among the best in the league, and certainly among international players. He is a two-time Super Bowl champion, two-time Pro Bowler, both a First-Team All-Pro and Second-Team All-Pro, and he led the NFL in forced fumbles in 2010. When it comes down to assessing the greatest international players in NFL history, one thing is for sure: Ositadimma Umenyiora's football career was most certainly good.

Rhys Lloyd

Baltimore Ravens 2005
Green Bay Packers 2006
Frankfurt Galaxy 2006–2007
Carolina Panthers 2007–2009
Minnesota Vikings 2010

FROM THE white cliffs of Dover to the NFL via Frankfurt, it's safe to say Rhys Lloyd took every opportunity available to him during his career as a kicker. A self-confessed lover of sports, Lloyd – a passionate Chelsea FC fan – harboured dreams of becoming a professional footballer. In more ways than one, he achieved those dreams.

Lloyd first discovered the United States when he represented England in a soccer tournament in Daytona, Florida where he was exposed to the branding and marketing of the bigger teams like the Dallas Cowboys, San Francisco 49ers and Miami Dolphins. His family moved to Minnesota, an area he would remain tied to throughout his career, and Lloyd became increasingly involved in football – but he never became infatuated with the sport like he adored soccer. 'Even when I was playing, I never really fell in love with it. Growing up in England was like a completely different world and I'm a massive soccer fan,' he said, before commenting on his frustration with the word 'soccer' rather than 'football'. 'I was at Chelsea as a youth kid and that was the dream, but I always played rugby and cricket and pretty much any sport you can get your hands on as a kid. When you're 15 and moving to the States, people are interested in you because of your funny accent, but sports is an easy way to meet and become friends with people. Nothing was planned, it sort of fell in my lap.'

Minnesota, like most Midwestern states, worships football. The culture surrounding the gridiron sport is immense, which perhaps makes the Vikings' postseason near misses that extra bit more painful. For Lloyd, the culture was infectious; he increasingly got into the sport after moving there as a teenager. While attending Eastview High School in Apple Valley, Lloyd played soccer and had taken up track and field during the offseason to stay fit. During a spring break trip to Florida, his PE teacher asked the Brit if he wanted to take up kicking for the school team, which Lloyd accepted so long as it didn't interfere with his soccer schedule. When it came to his first game, Lloyd certainly acted like a rookie. 'They dressed me and I didn't have a freaking clue what was going on,' he remembered. 'I didn't know how to put the pads on, I felt like a toddler – they were literally pulling my pants up and putting the right pads in the shorts and whatnot. I was clueless.' Thanks to his sporting endeavours, Lloyd lettered in both soccer and football before graduating.

Lloyd then attended Rochester Community and Technical College, a two-year bridge between high school and university. He impressed while studying graphic design and was a two-time All-American kicker before transferring to Minnesota to play as a placekicker, punter and kick-off specialist for the Golden Gophers in 2003 and 2004. 'I treat the University of Minnesota like Chelsea and England – it's in my blood. Even when I go back onto campus, it just has a different feel to it,' Lloyd said with a smile. 'There's something about college football; I don't watch a lot of NFL – not because I'm not interested, but I don't make a point to watch it like I do with Chelsea. College football, though, I make a point to watch every single week because they're kids who play because they love the sport. I don't want to say that I'm part of the family because it's just corny, but I'm always going to be part of that culture.'

Perhaps the highlight of his college career came when Lloyd kicked the game-winning field goal in the 2003 Sun Bowl to lead Minnesota to a win over Oregon, but the Brit savoured every moment as a Gopher. 'Everyone always gets so excited by the fact that I played in the NFL, but it doesn't even scratch the surface of what it's like to play in college. In college, you're playing in stadiums that fit 110,000 and they're all students. It's basically a bunch of kids getting drunk and going apeshit. It's a mixed bag in the NFL: some of them are fair-weather fans, but in college, win, lose or draw, the fans are there until the fourth quarter because it's a party. It's different.'

Lloyd was an undrafted free agent and signed with the Baltimore Ravens, but he was released prior to the start of the regular season before a short stint with the Green Bay Packers the following spring. His agent asked about NFL Europe, and Lloyd was intrigued. 'I was happy to go if it kept the dream alive, and I got paid to go over to Europe for six months – happy days!' With allocation rules in place, there were only a handful of places available but Lloyd was confident he would land in Frankfurt. Aaron Hosack, a receiver who played alongside Lloyd in college before joining the Minnesota Vikings, was returning for his second season at the Galaxy and had utilised backroom politics to secure a spot on the team for the Brit – so long as he was drafted by the coaches. Lloyd was picked by Frankfurt, although the NFL Europe draft was certainly less glamorous than its far more popular American equivalent. 'It was less a draft and more like picking players at school and not wanting to be last,' Lloyd recalled. 'I'm so glad I went to NFL Europe. I didn't want to do it at first but it was an incredible experience living in Frankfurt for six months.' Lloyd played at a number of iconic stadiums, including the Olympiastadion in Berlin and the

Amsterdam Arena, the home of AFC Ajax. A keen soccer fan, Lloyd immediately bonded with Frankfurt fans due to their soccer style of support and the enormous following for the team. 'I loved it because they were doing soccer songs but with different words. I was looking around like, "Shit, this is unreal." I was playing a foreign sport in a foreign country, but it was amazing. It was a lot of fun.'

Lloyd signed with the Ravens upon his return to the NFL and managed to survive final roster cuts after he nailed a 55-yard field goal in the preseason finale defeat to Atlanta. He endured a difficult season in Baltimore and hovered between the gameday roster and the practice squad before he was claimed off waivers by the Carolina Panthers on 26 December 2007.

Lloyd enjoyed the best spell of his career at the Panthers, where he led the league with 30 touchbacks in 2008. 'Carolina just felt like home. I hung around some of the greatest players ever [in Baltimore]: Ray Lewis, Deion Sanders, Ed Reed. They were good guys, but there was definitely a divide in that locker room – and it was all about money,' said Lloyd, whose family returned to the area soon after his retirement due to their fondness for Carolina. 'The locker room was incredible; you don't get starstruck on the pitch when you're playing because everyone is on the same level, if not financially. I never felt I could just sit down at a table with Ray Lewis in Baltimore. In Carolina, I hung out with Steve Smith all the time. It was such a cool environment and I love the Panthers.'

During his playing days, Lloyd was a great advocate of developing the sport on a global scale. He helped host 'Super Bash', an annual Super Bowl party in London, and always wanted to play at Wembley Stadium in an International Series clash but he unfortunately never got the chance. 'At the end of the day, it was never about playing football. I just thought I could play at Wembley,' Lloyd revealed. 'It was the wrong sport and that would hurt, but to step out onto that pitch and play would have meant everything.' Lloyd does not believe international franchises – like the long-rumoured team to be based in London – would work in the NFL given the logistics and scheduling issues, but he insists the sport must continue to grow on a global scale to be taken seriously in the long run. 'Your typical American will claim it's the biggest sport in the world but it is only really played in America. How can you call yourself world champions when it's state-to-state play? It's obviously the biggest sport in America, but it's so minute compared to other global sports.'

Lloyd believes Germany would be the best new market for the NFL to explore, citing his experience in Frankfurt as proof that the country is invested in American football already. 'Germany would be a great place to go and hold a game; they are football nuts. They are invested in their local teams like the London Warriors, teams that are literally just playing down the park,' he said. 'They aren't getting paid for it, they just have a good following.' As Lloyd spoke glowingly of Germany's potential, the NFL soon confirmed regular season games were coming to the country. In February 2022, the league announced a four-year deal to broaden the International Series to continental Europe with games split between Bayern Munich's Allianz Arena and Deutsche Bank Park in Frankfurt.

For a man with ties to both Frankfurt and London, Lloyd certainly approves of the NFL's path to international recognition.

Tim Shaw

Carolina Panthers 2007
Jacksonville Jaguars 2008
Chicago Bears 2009–2010
Tennessee Titans 2010–2012

TIM SHAW was born in Exeter, a small city in south-west England with a population of just over 120,000. It is an area close to my own heart as I spent my university years in the rugby city, with Exeter Chiefs proving to be particularly successful recently. Rugby never interested Shaw, though. He had his sights on another sport across the Atlantic.

Shaw attended Livonia Clarenceville High School where he starred as a running back. In 2000, he broke the Michigan High School Athletic Association (MHSAA) record for most touchdowns in a single season with 48 in just 13 games. A year later, he broke the record again with 51 scores in 14 appearances. He became the first player to eclipse 100 career rushing touchdowns in MHSAA history, scoring 306 points as a senior – ranked third all-time – and 288 as a junior, placing him fourth all-time in the association. As a junior, Shaw inspired the team to their first semi-final appearance before leading them to the state final as a senior.

Across his glittering high school career, Shaw rushed for over 2,500 yards and was classified as a three-star recruit before attending Penn State, opting to join the Lions over offers from Big Ten rival schools such as Michigan and Michigan State. Shaw received minutes on special teams and was named the unit's captain, where he impressed enough to earn snaps and playing time on defence. Shaw's remarkable athletic ability meant he became a starter at linebacker alongside the likes of Paul Posluszny and Dan Connor, two winners of the Bednarik Award, bestowed upon the best defensive player in college football.

The trio formed what many consider to be the best linebacking corps in Penn State history, with Shaw named an Academic All-American in 2006. He was selected in the fifth round of the 2007 NFL Draft by the Carolina Panthers, where he slotted back into a special teams role. However, his time in Carolina was short-lived as he was cut before being signed by the Jacksonville Jaguars in November 2008.

Shaw appeared in three games for the Jaguars during the 2008 season as the team went 5-11, a sharp drop following their 11-5 record in 2007. He played for the franchise during preseason for the 2009 campaign but was suddenly released as part of the final roster cuts. The Chicago Bears picked him up just nine days later, after opening-week injuries to linebacker duo Pisa Tinoisamoa and the legendary Brian Urlacher forced the team to sign cover.

He impressed in the Windy City and set a club record for special teams tackles with 30 on the season, including an eight-tackle performance in which he forced and recovered a fumble against the Detroit Lions. His performances caught the eye, and Shaw was named to *USA Today*'s All-Joe Team for 2010; a line-up dedicated to honouring the NFL's unsung and underrated players.

After Shaw left the Bears ahead of the 2010 season, the Tennessee Titans claimed him off waivers and the linebacker found a home in Tennessee. He played in 48 matches across his three seasons with the team, leading the Titans in special teams tackles in 2010 with 20 and was subsequently named the unit's captain for both 2011 and 2012. During his time in Tennessee,

Shaw was an advocate for American football in the UK, promoting the 'Super Bash' in 2011 alongside Osi Umenyiora and Rhys Lloyd. 'This is a great opportunity for me to connect two things that I love – football and my heritage,' Shaw said. 'It's important to me to represent my home country in a positive way and try to relay what the game of football has done for me.'

While charging from sideline to sideline leading the Titans' special teams corps, Shaw began experiencing twitching and weakness in his right arm late in the 2012 season, in which he played each of Tennessee's 16 regular season games as they compiled a 6-10 record. Team doctors assumed Shaw had pinched a nerve and ordered MRI exams for his shoulder, with tests highlighting nothing was wrong. Shaw continued to struggle with the nagging issue and cited pain lifting weights during training camp the following year. 'I remember a specific drill in preseason with the Titans,' Shaw recalled. 'We were doing this punt coverage drill and all we're doing is running and crossing behind someone to fill each other's lanes or just play off each other as far as going to make a tackle. And I fell, on my own. No one was on me, no one was near me. I just tripped and fell, and it was embarrassing.' Shaw was released during Tennessee's final cuts on 31 August 2013.

On 19 August 2014 – 349 days after he officially left the NFL – Shaw revealed he had been diagnosed with amyotrophic lateral sclerosis (ALS) when he took part in the viral Ice Bucket Challenge. He retired from the NFL having made 128 total tackles across his six-year career, forcing three fumbles and making two fumble recoveries.

Since retiring, Shaw has worked as motivational speaker and author while giving back to football and spreading awareness of ALS. 'To be able to play the game as long as I did was a gift,' he said.

Graham Gano

Washington Redskins 2009–2011
Carolina Panthers 2012–2019
New York Giants 2020–present

IN LAWRENCE Tynes and Graham Gano, it appears the New York Giants have a knack for attracting and signing Scottish kickers. They both have military fathers, which is perhaps why the duo have showcased their mental fortitude by making tough kicks in crucial moments. Gano is no stranger to adversity in a career that took him from Angus to New York City via Florida, Las Vegas and Super Bowl 50. He is a firm believer that setbacks are all part of the overarching plan, with each incident and obstacle helping to forge Gano into the kicker and man he is today.

Gano was born in Arbroath, a town in Scotland's eastern region of Angus, in April 1987, while his father, Mark, was stationed at Canadian Forces Base in Newfoundland as a US Navy master chief petty officer. Mark – a Vietnam veteran – was the latest in a family with a rich military history; Gano's great-grandfather Richard and grandfather Raymond also served. Gano spent his formative years living on a farm in Fettercairn where he remembers his golden retriever, the countryside and his thick accent. 'Nowadays, I joke with people and say they wouldn't understand me back then because my accent was so strong,' Gano said in a voice more America than Aberdeen. 'I feel I'm a little disconnected because it's been so long [since he returned], but I'm still from Scotland.' Gano was so proud to hail from Scotland that he grew up dreaming of playing for the Scottish national football team. Soccer was his favourite sport as a child, playing with his brothers around their farmland, which showed that kicking a ball was always part of Gano's destiny – and it became clearer once he touched down in the United States.

There were a couple of reasons why Gano did not want to play American football as a child. One was his dream of playing for Scotland. The other key reason was because he didn't want to wear the tight pants that are part of the uniform, so Gano opted to play 'the real football' with loose shorts on and shunned gridiron in favour of soccer even after moving to the United States – until fate intervened. 'The first time I gave American football a shot was my freshman year of high school, and it was only because their team didn't have a kicker. I showed up for soccer, but they didn't have a programme for the boys. My mum couldn't pick me up, so I thought I'd give kicking a go.' Gano attended JM High School in Cantonment where he became an immediate kicking star. Gano became the starter for the Aggies and was an All-American First-Team selection by *USA Today* as he turned heads with his achievements. He played in the CaliFlorida All-Star game and made a 50-yard field goal in the match to boost a developing reputation as a clutch long-range kicker.

During his senior season in high school, Gano made three field goals over 55 yards (57, 64 and 65) and even had a monster 71-yard field goal negated by a penalty. 'I think we were playing Washington High School and they jumped offside, so coach took the first down – but the referees didn't even think we were kicking the field goal! They thought we were punting,' Gano recalled. 'I remember the referee sprinting back to try and figure out if I made the kick or not. It was so far and dimly lit I could barely see, but the guys on the sideline were like, "Dude, you made that kick!", which was pretty cool.'

Gano credits soccer and his faith for his ability to kick a ball a very long way. His brother was a professional soccer player in Germany and would teach Gano how to strike the ball properly, which helped offensively despite playing as a goalkeeper. 'At the end of my soccer career, I could consistently send a goal kick to the other penalty box. For as long as I can remember, I've been able to kick a ball a long way so I tried to make the most out of it.' As a senior in high school, 36 of his 38 kick-offs were touchbacks and Gano averaged over 42 yards per punt as he showcased his ability and thumped the ball to the other end of the field at will.

Ranked as the third-best kicker in the nation, Gano attended Florida State University where he played as a kicker and punter for the Florida State Seminoles from 2005 to 2008. He spent most of his college career as a punter, but he finally got his chance once the starting kicker graduated ahead of Gano's senior season. During the 2008 campaign, Gano finished first in his conference for field goals made, percentage of field goals converted and 50-yard field goals made as he collected the Lou Groza Award, given to the best kicker in college football. 'We weren't as successful as I would have hoped but still being able to play for Bobby Bowden, one of if not the greatest college football coach of all time, was a dream come true,' Gano said. He led the ACC in field goals per game and had the highest field goal percentage in the conference, becoming the first kicker in FSU history to convert over 90 per cent of his field goals in a season with a conversion rate of 92.3 per cent. He left a lasting impression as a Seminole because, despite only kicking for a single season, Gano finished second in school history in 50-yard field goals behind two-time Lou Groza Award winner Sebastian Janikowski, who was selected in the first round of the 2000 NFL Draft by the Oakland Raiders.

The final game of Gano's collegiate career was the 2008 Champs Sports Bowl, where the Seminoles triumphed 42-13 over the Wisconsin Badgers. Thanks to a performance which included three successive punts that were either downed or bounced out of bounds at the opposition one-yard line, Gano is one of only two punters to ever be named the MVP of a bowl game. 'I was celebrating because we had won and then people told me I was the MVP – and I just started laughing. It was a memorable way to end my college career.'

The 2009 NFL Draft came and went and Gano was left to find work as an undrafted free agent. The Scot was disappointed following his successful senior season, but it developed a chip on his shoulder that stayed with him across his professional career. He was signed by the Baltimore Ravens, but his brief stint with the franchise was over when Gano – who admitted he wasn't prepared to kick in the NFL at that stage – was waived prior to the start of the season. Eager to get to work, Gano signed with the Las Vegas Locomotives of the United Football League, although he was reluctant to take the opportunity as he had never even heard of the league. 'We practised at Casa Grande, Arizona in the middle of the desert – we literally had sandstorms, scorpions and roadrunners on the field. It was chaos, but my agent thought it was a good opportunity to get film and it was a blessing in disguise.' Gano made 13 of 16 field goals as he led the league in scoring and field goals made, leading the Locomotives to the championship in overtime. He caught the eye of NFL teams while in Nevada, including the Washington Redskins.

On 8 December 2009, Gano signed with Washington. He impressed in what was left of the 2009 season before establishing himself as a clutch kicker in 2010; Gano struck three overtime game-winning field goals against the Green Bay Packers, Tennessee Titans and Jacksonville Jaguars. 'It was always a dream of mine to be able to hit game-winning field goals,' Gano said. 'You prepare yourself mentally in practice to be ready for those situations so that when the time comes, you won't be as nervous.' He remained the starter in Washington for the 2011 campaign where he made 31 of 41 field goals – and five of the ten misses were blocked. Despite a banged-up offensive line contributing immensely to his drop in form, Gano was surprisingly cut by Washington ahead of the 2012 season. He felt he had finally found his rhythm as a kicker in the NFL, but Gano knew the hindrance was simply all part of the plan and he would soon be back in the NFL.

Gano recalls being out of football for around ten weeks when he and his wife sat down at their dining room table. 'We're a spiritual, Christian family so we sat and prayed. We asked God if football was supposed to be in my life – and if not, I was ready to figure it out,' Gano added. 'The very next day, I was in Carolina.' On 20 November 2012, Gano signed with the Carolina Panthers, replacing Justin Medlock as the starting kicker. His time in Carolina became the most successful and stable spell of his career. 'Coach [Ron] Rivera was great. He gave me an opportunity to come in and he believed in me for a long time. When I'm done playing, I'll still pull for Carolina and that's always going to be home,' Gano said. He contributed to a number of NFL initiatives and charity work during his years in Carolina, and while Gano left a lasting impression off the field, he and the Panthers certainly made a mark on it.

During the 2015 season in which the Panthers went 15-1, Gano kicked 146 points to break Jim Kasay's 1996 team record for most in a season. He also used his powerful leg to great effect, recording NFL-best statistics with 69 touchbacks and an average kick-off distance of 72.0 yards. The Panthers surged through the playoffs, defeating the Seattle Seahawks and Arizona Cardinals to reach Super Bowl 50 at Levi's Stadium in Santa Clara, California. Despite outgaining their opponents by 121 yards and earning ten more first downs, the Panthers lost 24-10 to the Denver Broncos. League MVP Cam Newton struggled against the vaunted defence, and Gano – so reliable throughout the 2015 campaign – missed a field goal that cannoned off the right side of the goal post. 'We won a lot of games and really changed the perception of the franchise: we beat the Patriots, won three consecutive division titles and went to a Super Bowl after one of the best seasons ever. We came up short, but that season was incredible – nobody expected it.'

Following their Super Bowl heartbreak, Gano continued to perform for the Panthers. Against the New Orleans Saints in the 2017/18 playoffs, he recovered from an early miss to make four field goals, including a 58-yard attempt that tied Pete Stoyanovich for the longest field goal made in postseason history. It showed the kind of form he was in: Gano was named to his first Pro Bowl in 2017. He duly took advantage and penned a four-year deal worth $17m with the Panthers in March 2018 and showed his worth later in the year when he made a 63-yard game-winning field goal as time expired to defeat the Giants. His performance earned him NFC Special Teams Player of the Week honours, and tied the non-altitude-assisted field goal record set by Tom Dempsey in 1970 and matched by David Akers in 2012.

However, injuries began to pile up and frustrate Gano before he was released by the Panthers on 30 July 2020. Once again, the Scot understood it was merely all part of the plan and he didn't have to wait long to find out where the next stage would lead him. Gano joined the Giants in August 2020 and immediately made an impression when he set a franchise record with three field goals of at least 50 yards against the Cowboys. 'I wasn't sure what to expect at first, but I remember talking to Lawrence [Tynes] and I was able to pick his brain about the organisation. It's top class, the ownership is great,' Gano said. 'They really take care of the players and there's a reason why they've won four Super Bowls. They know what they're doing.' On 15 November 2020, Gano signed a three-year, $14m contract extension to keep him in New York through 2023. The Giants have endured difficult seasons during his short time in the Big Apple – 6-10 in 2020 and 4-13 in 2021 – but Gano is confident the franchise will turn it around soon. 'I want to help the team win again and get to the playoffs or even the Super Bowl,' he said. 'I still feel I can play for a long time, so we'll have to see if my family want me to keep playing!'

The 34-year-old has gone through a lot to get to where he is in the NFL today. He believes his experiences, such as playing goalkeeper in soccer and the pressured environment of Florida State, have shaped him into a top kicker. Gano is more than that, though; he is a well-spoken man with a genuine heart. He understands his job is a privilege, referring to the NFL as 'a kid's game' he is lucky enough to play for a living, so Gano is constantly seeking ways to be a positive influence within society. 'I'd like people to remember me for being consistent, hardworking and selfless while making an impact in the community that will last longer than my time here.'

Gano still has family over in Scotland, although he admits rather guiltily that he hasn't been able to return since he was young. He'll surely get a chance to make amends soon, but even after travelling from Europe to America, taking his chance at Florida State, dropping down to the UFL to keep his dream alive, bouncing back in the NFL and playing in a Super Bowl, Gano has never forgotten his roots: 'I'm still proud to be Scottish.'

Jack Crawford

Oakland Raiders 2012–2013
Dallas Cowboys 2014–2016
Atlanta Falcons 2017–2019
Tennessee Titans 2020
Arizona Cardinals 2021

A LONDON boy through and through, Jack Crawford had dreams of making it as a basketball star when he arrived in the United States. His journey has taken the Brit from school with Harry Potter to American football in Dallas – and an emotional London return in the 2014 International Series.

Crawford grew up in Kilburn, an area in north-west London, where he attended the City of London School alongside *Harry Potter* star Daniel Radcliffe. Aged seven, Crawford was diagnosed with alopecia universalis, a rare autoimmune condition which causes the total loss of all hair on the body. While he was interested in American football through movies like *Any Given Sunday* and *Remember the Titans*, Crawford's first love when it came to sports was basketball. 'I followed in my brothers' footsteps really, they played basketball. I was introduced to the East London Royals, based out of Whitechapel through our school basketball coach,' recalled Crawford, described by fellow British NFL star Menelik Watson as a 'monster' on the court. 'A guy scouted me, and he had ties to an American camp. He said they were looking for international talent and he gave me the details, so I went over when I was 15. They then wanted me to stay but my dad insisted I finished my GCSEs, so I took them and then transferred over.'

Crawford moved to Longport, New Jersey in 2005 where he attended St Augustine Preparatory School. The Brit intended to pursue a career in basketball but he couldn't play for the school team as a sophomore due to international eligibility rules surrounding transfers. While living with a friend who played both basketball and American football, Crawford opted to join the football team despite having no prior experience. 'I was a lot bigger than a lot of the kids, even in America,' said Crawford. 'I thought about playing both ways, and then I considered not playing at all so I could focus on basketball – but then a lot of guys came to me, including [former New York Jets general manager] Terry Bradway. He encouraged me to play to see if I enjoyed it.'

At first, Crawford played on both sides of the ball. He was deployed on offence as both a receiver and tight end while the Brit also wreaked havoc as a defensive end. Despite his early success in high school, Crawford was playing football rather reluctantly: 'I didn't like that it was outside, cold and muddy. I wanted to be inside playing basketball.' He made 12 touchdown receptions and received All-Area and All-Parochial honours en route to being ranked the 15th-best defensive end in the nation by Scout.com. He received just one scholarship offer to play basketball in college, but football was a different matter. 'I had the whole country almost: Tennessee, Miami, Florida, California. I started to realise this was where my best path may lie. I didn't even play basketball in my senior year because I just wanted to focus on football.' Crawford accepted a scholarship offer from Pennsylvania State University, nearby to where he was living with his host family.

The Brit played in all the Penn State Nittany Lions games as a true freshman, appearing at defensive tackle and tight end while others in his class were redshirted. Instead, the coaching staff wanted Crawford to get to work immediately due to his striking physique. However, there was still a learning curve to be respected given Crawford was so unfamiliar with the sport and he suffered a particularly haunting early experience. 'In practice, the quarterback is wearing a red jersey so you don't touch him – you don't even get close to him,' said Crawford. 'It became a habit; I broke through the offensive line against Coastal Carolina – my first game – and the quarterback tried to pump fake me, but I got to him for the sack. I just touched his chest and turned around as if the play was over, but he still had the ball in his hand and scrambled for a first down. My heart was beating and I was hyperventilating because there were like 80,000 fans at that game alone.' The best remedy for such a harrowing experience is patience and practice, and Crawford's potential was soon realised.

As a sophomore, Crawford replaced Aaron Maybin at defensive end and started all 13 games, ranking ninth in the Big Ten Conference in tackles for loss with 15 and tenth in sacks with 5.5. He impressed during his junior year despite ligament damage in his right foot before starring as a senior with 6.5 sacks. After four years at Penn State, Crawford declared himself available for selection in the upcoming 2012 NFL Draft.

'The draft is a little bit overrated – people put too much emphasis on it, especially college kids,' Crawford said. Draft day is a stressful time for all players, and Crawford simply wanted to get through the emotional roller coaster by chilling and playing video games during the draft to take his mind off it. Unfortunately for him, his host family and friends all gathered together to support him and watch. 'I suspected I was going to get drafted in the fourth, fifth or sixth round – but there was always the hope in the back of your head that you could get selected earlier,' Crawford added. 'Then you get worried if you're going to get drafted at all. My friend called me during the day to wish me good luck. I was like, "Bro, don't call me man. You know it's the draft – I thought you were a team!" I was annoyed and hung up. It was an intense day.' Perhaps more so than most players, Crawford was also concerned about where he was going to end up, as he didn't want to go to certain places. While California was appealing, the idea of having to move away from his friends and family on the East Coast was daunting. 'The TV changed and said the pick was in, and then I got a call saying it was from the Oakland area,' remembered Crawford. 'Once I got drafted, it was a big weight off my shoulders. It felt like forever seeing other guys picked before you, but we were all celebrating.' Crawford was selected by the Oakland Raiders in the fifth round of the 2012 NFL Draft, 158th overall.

Crawford was a backup for the Raiders in his rookie season, appearing in just four games and making five tackles. He struggled to adjust to the speed of the professional game compared to college, and the Brit admits he needed time that Oakland ultimately didn't afford him. Crawford also struggled with locker-room politics as he transitioned to the professional arena. 'The Raiders weren't as organised as the other teams I played for or as they are now,' he revealed. 'We had a younger head coach and a lot of vets; it felt like we were isolated in our own little groups. We just weren't a proper team. We didn't have any cohesiveness.' Crawford played on special teams and established himself on the defensive line in his sophomore season, but he was released by the Raiders during final cuts in August 2014. 'It was a blow. I remember getting back to my house, crying and thinking I had nothing to do tomorrow,' Crawford said. 'It was a feeling that stuck with me because I never wanted to feel that again.' With a chip on his shoulder, Crawford was handed an immediate reprieve by the Dallas Cowboys – and there was no time to waste.

'I went out with a friend to drown my sorrows with alcohol, and the next morning I woke up to a call from my agent who told me I was joining the Cowboys and they wanted me there tomorrow,' Crawford recalls while smiling to himself. 'I'm hungover and I had to pick up everything and move from Oakland to Dallas in 24 hours.' The Brit dragged himself onto the three-and-a half-hour flight to Texas to sign a deal with the Cowboys just days after he was cut. The cultural difference between the Raiders and America's Team was immediately clear: 'Dallas felt like a real team, from the offence to defence. Oakland was very segregated.' Due to his relentlessness and dedication in training, Crawford began to turn heads within the Cowboys organisation. He had a better rapport with the Dallas coaching staff, and he began to improve his game. 'In football, you can't be scared of making mistakes. If you are, you'll lose every single time. Rod Marinelli changed the game for me because he said this position is about going, not thinking,' Crawford said. 'As soon as that pressure of being perfect every time was gone, I started to make plays and all my hard work and effort started to translate.' He saw clear improvements in his game early into his tenure in Dallas, and Crawford had his greatest moment against the Jacksonville Jaguars.

After missing three games with injury, Crawford returned for the International Series clash at Wembley and he registered the first sack of his career. 'Technically, my first real sack was on a Saints punter who tried a fake punt, but I don't count it!' Crawford said, laughing. 'When you go all the way back to London – born and raised – and play in front of your friends and family at Wembley Stadium, it felt like fate. It was my time; it was meant to be.' He added a forced fumble and two more tackles to his sack as the Cowboys emerged 31-17 winners in London.

Crawford spent three years with the Cowboys before departing in free agency. 'I made some close friends: [Tony] Romo, Dez Bryant, DeMarcus Lawrence, Tyrone Crawford. We were like a family on that team – it was completely different from Oakland. Playing for the Cowboys, meeting Rod Marinelli and implementing that mindset definitely helped to extend my career.' The Brit hit free agency in 2017 and was unconvinced he would receive any offers; he was injured for much of 2016 and simply hoped to receive the chance to impress on a training camp roster.

Suddenly, Crawford was heading to Atlanta on a three-year deal. 'I refused to get my hopes up – maybe it's the English in me. My agent called and said I was joining the Falcons on a $10 million deal; I never thought I would get that much money,' Crawford said, revealing he cried after putting down the phone. Crawford was thrilled to join the Super Bowl runners-up, particularly due to Dan Quinn and his reputation. He said former team-mates had talked glowingly of the defensive guru, and Crawford soon learned his new coach's methods differed to Marinelli and the Cowboys. 'Dallas had to be the hardest programme to play for; they ran us into the ground. Marinelli was a Vietnam vet with an old-school mentality, so we were hitting full pads every day in training camp. In Atlanta, they took the pads off halfway through as a break on our body – everybody in Dallas thought I was so lucky!'

Crawford spent three years in Atlanta as the team endured some turbulent times, although the Falcons made the playoffs in 2017 only to lose to the Philadelphia Eagles in the Divisional Round. The Brit signed with the Tennessee Titans in 2020 where he registered two sacks before joining the Arizona Cardinals for the 2021 campaign.

While the sport may not have totally captured the imagination of Crawford, he has developed a different appreciation for the game than when he played *NFL Blitz* with his brothers back in London – and he hopes more international players get involved to play sport in the coming years. 'The curiosity is there,' the Brit said. 'After playing for ten years, it's the ultimate team game; there's no other sport where everybody relies on everyone else so much. You could have [Tom] Brady and a great team, but special teams could lose you the Super Bowl.'

Menelik Watson

Oakland Raiders 2013-2016
Denver Broncos 2017

THE ODDS were never in Menelik Watson's favour. In the United States alone, just over six per cent of high school football players will play in college, and around one per cent will play in the NFL. When you factor in the obstacles along Watson's journey from Manchester to Oakland, California, the chances of him making it in the NFL were highly improbable.

Watson was born in December 1988 to single mother Novlyn McFarquhar, who raised him and his three brothers on Anson Estate in Longsight, a Manchester neighbourhood notorious for gun crime and gang wars. As a child, Watson was close with his brother Iler – people even thought they were twins as they wore similar hand-me-down clothes. His mother did her best to make a living, but Watson would often go hungry, forced to eat ketchup out of free sachets at restaurants. Watson's brothers spent time in prison as the influence of the area began to leave its mark, but something changed when he was nine years old: Iler taught him about basketball.

Watson had always been interested in sport, with his mother keen to get him involved in soccer or rugby to take advantage of his developing physical gifts. His hopes of excelling in soccer were shattered when Watson snapped his ankle in a '100 against

100' game of football, with the bone piercing through his skin. Despite medical warnings to not play sport, Watson was determined to excel. He didn't have the money to play regularly, but after attending Burnage High School for Boys, Watson's outlook changed. His school was once attended by British former professional basketball player Nick George, who starred for VCU in the United States. Suddenly, there was a path for Watson to follow.

Watson began to play basketball and joined the Manchester Magic where he met British American John Amaechi, a former British Basketball League MVP who played for the Cleveland Cavaliers, Orlando Magic and Utah Jazz. 'If it wasn't for John Amaechi, I wouldn't be here,' Watson uttered. Basketball was £2 a session and Watson couldn't afford the bus home, but he was determined to succeed. Amaechi and club director Joe Forber organised work for Watson, allowing him to play for free in exchange for his helping hand in sweeping around the centre, mopping the court, checking the balls and refereeing. Watson was earning his keep.

It was while playing for Manchester Magic that Watson landed on his dream: he wanted to go to America, play in college, and make it in the NBA as the first British born-and-raised star. At a Christmas basketball tournament in Manchester back in 2006, just days after Watson's 18th birthday, he was spotted by American–Peruvian coach Rob Orellana. 'Probably the most instrumental person in my growth,' Watson labelled him. Orellana was impressed by Watson's size and unique lateral speed, and offered the Brit a place at his basketball academy in Gran Canaria. Alongside future Great Britain small forward Ashley Hamilton, Watson would train three times a day in pursuit of scholarship offers from colleges. The resurfacing of a foot injury threatened to derail Watson's dreams as he was forced to sit out a lot of action, but the birth of his daughter – named Orellana as a touching tribute to the impact of Rob – intensified his situation.

Watson pushed himself upon his return, and he earned his ticket to the 'land of opportunity'.

After receiving a number of offers, Watson chose Marist College, enticed by their NCAA Division I basketball programme. He was forced to redshirt his first year due to eligibility rules, but Watson had another problem with the Poughkeepsie school – he realised the coach was more of a salesperson than a basketball coach. 'The coach was a fucking arse. He was not a great human – and that's me being kind,' Watson said. Condemned to a year on the sidelines, Watson began a downward spiral fuelled by alcohol and drugs. It was a far cry from his time in Gran Canaria. 'I wasn't really in the basketball gym, I was running around campus chasing girls,' Watson recalled. 'When I got to college, I did all the things I wasn't able to do in Spain. I let go of the rope; I got lost. I hit a really deep depression.' His dreams of being the first British-bred NBA star was fading rapidly – and then, in his second year at Marist, Watson had an epiphany.

Watson was done. He was done with smoking, drinking, and any other distraction from his ultimate goal of providing for his daughter. He understood Marist was not the place for him and informed his coach he would not return for a third season. Watson's initial plan was to return to England, find a trade and 'sell a load of drugs on the side'. While a successful sports career was what he longed for, he truly wanted money in his pocket to ensure a stable life for Orellana. 'The biggest thing was being OK with coming home, and if someone saw me stacking shelves in Asda, my ego wouldn't be hurt – I'd be OK. When I came to that conclusion, my friends asked me about American football.' It was not the first time Watson had heard someone suggest football.

When playing for the Magic as a teenager, his American team-mates would warn Watson that once he got to the States, he would be enticed into football – but he thought nothing of it. 'I used to say, "I'm never going to play American football" and "Rugby is way better"! It's funny how things turn out.' With two years remaining on his visa, Watson figured he would take the opportunity to try his hand at football and, if it didn't work out, he would return to his homeland. His thoughts were always with his daughter, who was soon turning five years of age, and Watson was adamant football was set to be his final opportunity. 'If I wasn't in the NFL in two years, I was going home,' he said. 'It was a lot of time to miss with nothing to show for it.' He informed father-figure Orellana of his decision to leave Marist in pursuit of a football career, and Orellana was thrilled to hear the news. Watson's former coach organised a flight for him to head to San Diego – and opportunities soon came flying his way.

When Watson first arrived in America, he came with one bag and the tracksuit he was wearing. The bag contained a pair of basketball shoes, two pairs of shorts and three T-shirts. During his time at Marist, Watson became bogged down with self-considered luxuries: watches, jackets, even a fake chain. He lost himself at Marist, and realised such items were no good for him as he embarked on a life in football. 'I needed to get back to that kid from Longsight who used to open the fridge and see nothing. The kid that used to eat butter and ketchup to keep going.' Watson, ready for a new beginning, flew to San Diego where he lived with legendary state basketball coach Ray Johnson, a friend of Orellana's. He spent the summer moving heavy furniture, coaching basketball and picking the brain of Johnson and his friends. Watson didn't cut his hair or beard as he wanted to be natural – and more importantly, he didn't want to change his appearance for anyone else. His time spent with Johnson helped mature his mindset: Watson was done chasing girls, he was back chasing dreams.

With football season just around the corner, Watson went to San Diego's Exos Gym – an elite facility where plenty of prospects go for pre-draft workouts – but Watson was there to test his athletic ability to simply understand if he could make it as a football player. He took a trainer out onto the grass and, in regular sneakers from a two-point stance, Watson ran a 4.68s 40-yard dash. 'When the guy clocked it, he laughed as he told me the time – I didn't know if it was good or not!' After running it again, Watson clocked a 4.72s dash. Standing 6ft 5in and weighing more than 300lb, Watson passed the eyeball test – and his freakish athleticism was starting to turn heads.

He visited a number of junior colleges in California. The Brit's sheer size and athleticism made him an attractive prospect, but he found the perfect home at Saddleback College. He visited the beautiful campus in Mission Viejo and everything felt right, from the people to the natural scenery. As Watson arrived to meet with coach Don Butcher, he bumped into future Chicago Bear Kyle Long – son of Hall of Fame defensive end Howie Long – in the hallway. The two immediately hit it off, but Watson wanted to impress Butcher, a respected and experienced assistant coach. Butcher quickly summoned head coach Mark McElroy as well as the offensive and defensive coordinators in an attempt to woo the Brit, who felt comfortable in the building. His search was over. 'It felt like home, like these were people I could call and depend on if I ever needed anything.' As Johnson sorted the paperwork, training camp was just weeks away and Watson was raring to go – but his mentor flew over to speak with him about an urgent potential opportunity.

Orellana didn't waste any time in getting to the point once he arrived in San Diego. 'He said, "Menelik, I think you can be heavyweight champion of the world in boxing." Rob really believed in me, so I thought fuck it, I grew up fighting anyway. Let's give boxing a go.' With the 2012 London Olympics right around the corner, the timing was near-perfect, but Watson would have to act fast. The duo drove up to Los Angeles where they met and worked out for Oscar De La Hoya's Olympic training coach, Osmar Alaniz. It was a once-in-a-lifetime opportunity, and Alaniz – who helped the 'Golden Boy' win gold at the 1992 Barcelona Games – worked on Watson's movement and striking, with the Brit impressing during his unofficial trial. After assessing his physique and potential, Alaniz declared he could get Watson ready for the London Olympics and even echoed Orellana's belief that the Manchester-born star could be world heavyweight champion – but he needed to start tomorrow. No football, no Saddleback, just boxing. 'It made me understand how athletic I was. To go from being in that depressive state of self-sabotage in college to being told by Oscar De La Hoya's coach that I could be heavyweight champion of the world in five months. It was surreal. Rob was so excited for me – he kept saying he was going to be like Don King – but I specifically remember feeling like I was going to disappoint him.' Watson insists his recovery from depression, paired with his daughter and family being back across the Atlantic, was the only reason he didn't get into boxing. He didn't want to feel isolated or alone. Watson needed a team around him; a group of like-minded individuals uniting towards one common goal. The Brit reluctantly told Orellana that he wasn't going to pursue boxing, but Watson vowed he would make it in the NFL. It was a promise he would keep.

At this point, Watson was still yet to even pick up a ball, let alone put on the equipment. He attended his first practice session at Saddleback still rocking the rugged look he had sported since moving to California, with an untamed beard and long hair adding to the mystique of the team's latest recruit. 'Everyone was looking at me like, "Who the fuck is this guy?" I probably looked like I just came out of jail.' Watson's team-mates showed the Brit how to appropriately put on his gear, and he became a new man: 'I felt like I could run through a wall and be OK.' He took to the field as a defensive end, but his coaches advised against the position due to the scheme run by Saddleback, which relied on smaller, quick edge rushers to spread the line. Long – who Watson had immediately befriended upon arriving at the junior college – inspired the move to offensive line, as he had started on the defensive equivalent himself and insisted the position was 'way easier'. Watson approached McElroy, an offensive mind, about joining his unit – and the coach was thrilled with the idea.

The Saddleback Bobcats already had a good offensive line, but there was a gap at centre. Watson was told he had a shot of making it under the tutelage of offensive line guru Damien Watters Sr. Coach Watters believed he was destined to be a tackle, and Watson committed himself to being a student of the sport and his coaches. 'I knew nothing so I just wanted to soak it all in,' he said. Watters, who spent extra hours with Watson after practice on the field and in the film room, was impressed by Watson's appetite to learn and improve – which he did at a rapid rate. Pass protection was the aspect of the position that came easily to the Brit, who confidently insisted it was the first skill he mastered. 'Kyle [Long] said to me, "Menelik, just envision the quarterback is the basket. Don't let him get to the basket."' By presenting football in basketball terms, it clicked. Watson confessed that run blocking was still confusing; Saddleback once called a pass play and he barrelled downfield to run block. It was a moment neither his coaches nor team-mates would let him live down for the remainder of his time on the team, but the Brit was picking up the sport quickly – and that was no joke.

Watson got thrown into his first taste of live action in the third game of the season against Pasadena, with Saddleback leading comfortably. After watching Long channel his anger to dominate the position, Watson utilised his own aggressiveness and almost immediately came to blows with a defensive end. 'He was talking shit, telling me he was a crip and I said to him, "I don't give a fuck about your gang. They're not on the field right now – they can't save you." I couldn't wait to get into my first fight, because in my head I thought I could legally beat up other players.' The two men were separated by their team-mates and Coach McElroy furiously pulled Watson out. McElroy bellowed at Watson that such behaviour was unacceptable, and he would kick the Brit off his team if similar scenes were repeated. They weren't – the incident stuck with Watson. 'I realised the best way to get guys was between the whistles: I was going to punch opponents in their chest so hard it almost felt personal – and any chance I got to bury them in the run game, I did.' Watson therefore assumed the role of peacemaker while Long was the fiery member of the offensive line, implementing their very own 'good cop, bad cop' routine in Southern California.

Watson was given his first start soon after, and he never looked back. He was disciplined and dedicated: Watson attended each of his classes and would immediately complete homework so he could spend his free time watching film and observing NFL offensive linemen to mimic their moves. Watson played in just eight matches for Saddleback, but his rapid development paired with tremendous size began to capture national attention. Scouts and coaches from major college football programmes visited Saddleback to see Long but left with Watson in mind, too. The University of California were the first to offer the Brit a scholarship, but others soon followed suit.

Watson recalled when legendary Oklahoma coach Bob Stoops came to Saddleback to personally offer a scholarship to the Brit, only for him to not recognise the enormity of the gesture. 'My coach burst out laughing and he was like, "That's Bob freaking Stoops man! You really are English." I didn't truly understand the process or know my worth.' In his heart, Watson truly wanted to go to the University of Southern California – his 'dream' school – to play for the USC Trojans and he met with head coach Lane Kiffin. It didn't go particularly well, as Watson felt uncomfortable with the coach's demeanour and veiled intentions. He was offered the scholarship he craved after meeting with USC assistant coach Ed Orgeron, but Watson turned down the opportunity to fully explore all the options available to him. His team-mates were surprised and confused as to why their new British offensive lineman, who had barely played the sport in his life, was getting so many offers from major schools – but Watson knew why. 'After the games, while y'all are looking for the next party and where the girls are at, I go back to my apartment and watch film,' Watson would tell them. 'Then I go to sleep early so I can work out and illegally stream NFL games, just watching offensive linemen all day.' His room-mate would bring girls back to their room, but he never disturbed Watson, who had one goal in mind: to reach the NFL. His dedication paid off come visiting time.

Watson admits his visits were strange, particularly at the University of Washington. 'I didn't know how serious the players took it. They took me to a strip club – why was I in a strip club?' The tour to find Watson's next chapter continued as he checked out Rutgers and Auburn, and he liked the prospect of the Tigers – but admitted he felt the coach was, like his Marist basketball coach, more of a salesperson. 'He gave me the whole Cam Newton spiel, telling me I needed to be a brand. I wanted to come to a programme and learn football – he lost me there. I could have had a nice place, money in my pocket, trained at nice facilities and played SEC football – but I felt I was going to be too comfortable at Auburn, and I didn't want to feel comfortable.'

Watson found what he wanted when visiting Florida State. It was his 'worst' visit, but the team possessed talent and the path from the school to the NFL was well trodden. Watson then met with offensive line coach Rick Trickett, a former US Marine and Vietnam veteran, and the pair hit it off – despite Trickett originally visiting to see Long. 'He said, "I think you can go to the NFL. I'm going to coach you hard, but promise me one thing: if I hit you, don't fucking hit me back!" We laughed and shared that moment, and I knew this guy had my best interests at heart.' The Brit had some concerns, but it was decided: Watson was a Seminole.

Watson believes joining the Florida State Seminoles was the best decision he ever made. As part of a recruiting class alongside the likes of Ronald Darby, PJ Williams, Mario Edwards and future first overall pick Jameis Winston, Watson became an instant hit on the offensive line – and even became the de facto mouthpiece for Trickett: 'The younger guys were super disciplined when coach was there but as soon as he walked off, everyone started messing around. I let it slide for like a week, and then one day – tired and pissed off – I called everyone cowards and told them to grow up. From then on, we took it seriously and found success.' With two years of eligibility left, Watson was originally meant to redshirt and play in his senior year, but he improved so quickly he soon found himself starting for the Seminoles. Watson started at right tackle in every contest in 2012 except for the 6 October match at North Carolina State when he was dehydrated with a 105°F fever. He allowed one sack all season as Florida State stormed to the ACC title.

Watson declared for the 2013 NFL Draft, forgoing his senior year as he neared ever closer to the NFL. Florida State, led by Winston, went on to win the National Championship the following season – but Watson didn't mind. As Watson attended the draft at Radio City Music Hall in New York as one of the top prospects in the United States, he was set to accomplish his ultimate goal.

After he interviewed with 26 of the league's 32 teams, Watson was convinced by his agent to attend the draft rather than staying in Atlanta to watch the event unfold with both his English and American families, only to not get drafted on the first day. 'I didn't care where I got drafted, but I remember the look on my mum's face that first night. She was so upset for me. When the Ravens picked Matt Elam 32nd – after they had told me they would select me if I was available – I just stood up and walked out. I got back to the hotel where all the drafted guys were celebrating, and I changed and took off running. I must have run over 20 blocks until I reached the Empire State Building, where I sat on the curb. I was angry.' Watson eventually calmed down and returned to the hotel to spend time with his family, and he didn't have to wait long to realise his dream. With the 42nd overall pick, Watson was selected by the Oakland Raiders.

Amazingly, Watson was upset when he got drafted by Oakland. He assessed their roster and realised they had plenty of tackles already, so he was concerned he wasn't particularly needed. Regardless, the Brit put his head down and worked through rookie minicamp and organised team activities. Watson insists he put on 30lb – approximately 13.5kg – of muscle that offseason, but it wasn't balanced; his body didn't have time to adjust or adapt. Finally, the growth took its toll. As Watson was leaving the training facility before preseason training began, he jumped into an impromptu workout with his trainer. 'On the last rep of the last exercise we did, I popped my calf – that was the beginning of the end of my physical gifts. From that moment, I was playing catch-up for the rest of my NFL career.' With an inch-and-a-half hole in his calf, Watson belatedly told the Raiders three days after the injury occurred as he was concerned about two things: how the team would take the news, and their suboptimal facilities.

'You got to understand man, when I arrived in 2012, the Raiders organisation was in the dark ages. I got off the bus and there was a grey cloud over the building, and when I walked in I was like, "Woah, this is an NFL franchise?" There was no kitchen, and the gym was run-down. They had a medicine ball that had "Wisniewski" written on it. I went up to centre Stefen Wisniewski and asked if he put his name on the ball, and he told me it belonged to his uncle – who played in the 1970s and 1980s.' The equipment wasn't the only archaic aspects of the franchise. Rehabilitation was a new experience for Watson as he had never suffered a muscle injury to this extent, so he followed the franchise's instructions. The Raiders had a protocol in place whereby injured players would prove their fitness prior to returning to the field; players would go out with trainers to do sprints and cone drills. The Brit had reservations over the system:

why was he being treated like a wide receiver or running back? He felt he needed to do power training, not work on agility and speed.

Despite not fully recovering from his injury, Watson – craving the respect of his team-mates and coaches, particularly after head coach Dennis Allen repeatedly told him he 'hadn't done shit' as a rookie – rushed himself back onto the field. Sure enough, his calf popped again during the first physical drill. Watson was furious and an explosive argument broke out amid training. 'I'm from England, I had never played this game before and I of all people thought it doesn't seem like the ideal protocol. The next day was the first day they said, "Alright, linebackers over here. Receivers over here. Linemen over here." We started doing stuff that was more conducive to what we were doing on the field. I had to have a screaming match with an experienced trainer, and he was stubborn about it – but not too stubborn to realise I was right.'

Watson returned from injury but was part of the poor Raiders side that lost 28-20 in New Orleans and allowed the Saints to compile seven sacks in the preseason defeat. The Brit then approached his coaching staff with an idea when he returned to training. 'It was probably the most brazen thing I did in the NFL. I went up to coach [Tony] Sparano and I asked him if I could play left tackle. He gave me this look like, "You're not serious." I started against Seattle at left tackle – the first time I had ever played the position – in the last week of preseason. I played my ass off, and I got named the starting left tackle for the Oakland fucking Raiders after playing the sport for two years. After my experience at the draft, it was a big "fuck you" to the league.' Unfortunately, the frustrating narrative of Watson's career reared its ugly head: the first practice after he was named the starter, the Brit tore his meniscus. He believes his injuries made him stronger – particularly mentally. Watson would need to be strong in August 2015, as he tore his Achilles in the third preseason game against the Arizona Cardinals. He was ruled out of the entire 2015 season, meaning Watson would have to find form once he was fit in the all-important contract year of 2016.

Watson returned in the Raiders' third game of the 2016 season – and one moment stands out for him in that win over the Titans. Tennessee defensive stalwart Jurrell Casey ran a contained rush on Watson as the Raiders went for a power run play, and Watson tossed the 136kg defensive lineman to the floor as Oakland took off on a 30-yard run. 'I thought nobody could stop me when my body felt like that.' As Watson went to run downfield, his calf popped again. 'It was the first time I questioned God. Why me? I repeated that question over and over and over.' Watson returned in two weeks, but Austin Howard had been awarded the starting role and the Raiders were on a three-game win streak. Coach Jack del Rio didn't want to mess with the formula, leaving Watson frustrated and upset – but he understood the team was winning. 'Even though I was in a contract year, how dare I act so selfishly? There was no time to mope around the place, I wanted to make sure I made the most of every opportunity. Every time I came on the field, I was fucking somebody up.'

Despite a week 15 win over the San Diego Chargers to move to 11-3, Howard was replaced by Watson for the home game against the Indianapolis Colts. The Raiders were set to make the playoffs and Watson wanted to show what he could do – but this would be remembered as the tragic match where Derek Carr, the Raiders quarterback receiving MVP considerations, broke his ankle. 'I remember Derek's face and seeing his ankle joint dislodged. I couldn't believe it: Derek was the MVP, we were the best line in the NFL and it all went out the window.' While the Raiders won the game 33-25, it was the last time they tasted victory. Rookie quarterback Connor Cook came in for his NFL debut after backup Matt McGloin picked up an injury against the Denver Broncos in the Raiders' 24-6 loss to close the season, before their campaign was ended in the playoffs by the Houston Texans.

The loss in Houston was Watson's final game with the Raiders and he signed a three-year deal with the Denver Broncos, but calf and pectoral injuries derailed his time at Mile High. 'I played my NFL career using half my athleticism because any time I would push myself, I would tear something. I couldn't push myself to the limit because I was scared to pull anything – but I enjoyed every second.' This is the sentiment the Brit from Longsight, some 5,187 miles and a whole world away from Oakland and the NFL, still carries with him today.

He has questioned how different his experience would have been if he was drafted by a different team with different training methods, but Watson puts his 'amazing' journey to the National Football League down to one thing: discipline. 'As an 18-year-old kid walking into a college football programme, I wouldn't have come out the same player – Florida State have the most beautiful women on any campus in America, and I know that because I saw them in person! But I maintained my discipline. I had evolved from my time at Marist. It's not rocket science: if you want to be successful, you need to do your research and be disciplined in your approach. It's that simple. Growing up in Longsight, my brother got shot at 15. My older brother was in jail at that age. I know people murdered at 13. I used to think, "This is my destiny? With a father who had a bunch of kids and didn't give a fuck?" Nobody was going to come save us or show us how to live, and I always knew the streets were there – worst-case scenario, I could sell drugs. Sport saved me. Everything was stacked against me, and I just wanted to see how far I could get.'

Forget the one per cent; Watson's story from Longsight to the NFL is truly exceptional. The boy who left Manchester and became a man in the United States had a simple message: 'I'm not special or chosen. I'm not superhuman. I'm a regular guy that dedicated himself to something – and got it done.'

Jay Ajayi

Miami Dolphins 2015–2017
Philadelphia Eagles 2017–2019

JAY AJAYI was always going to be a threat once he reached the NFL. The London-born Arsenal fan was born to Nigerian parents and moved to Maryland when he was just seven years old. Ajayi's earliest American football memory was Super Bowl XXXVII, where the Oakland Raiders met the Tampa Bay Buccaneers to decide the champions of the 2002 NFL season.

Ajayi was just nine as he watched Jon Gruden's Buccaneers dominate to win 48-21. 'It was the first Super Bowl I remember watching,' he said. 'I really didn't know what it was. I don't think I truly understood the size of the Super Bowl until high school when I started playing and realising I liked American football.' Ajayi eventually moved to Texas where he attended Frisco Liberty High School, impressing as a senior as he rushed for 2,240 yards and 35 touchdowns. It was a testament to Ajayi's incredible natural athleticism that he earned a varsity letter as a member of the 4x400m, 4x200m and 4x100m district championship teams. His power, speed and evasive ability caught the eye of colleges, and Ajayi committed to Boise State University.

The Brit redshirted as a freshman at Boise State for the 2011 season but struggled with off-field issues and was arrested for shoplifting from a local Walmart. In 2012, Ajayi returned to action and immediately impressed over 11 games. He rushed for 548 yards and four touchdowns on the year, including a sensational 118-yard performance and a score against New Mexico in just his second career game. In his sophomore season, Ajayi started 12 of the Broncos' 13 matches with over 100 yards rushing in six of them. His best outing came against Nevada, scoring three touchdowns and torching the Wolf Pack for 222 yards en route to a sensational breakout campaign in which Ajayi tallied 1,425 yards and 18 touchdowns.

As a junior at Boise State in 2014, Ajayi became the first player in school history to rush for over 100 yards in ten different games across a single season. Ajayi wreaked havoc as he set a Boise State record with 1,823 rushing yards. His 28 rushing touchdowns were second nationally only to Wisconsin's Melvin Gordon. The Broncos defeated the Arizona Wildcats 38-30 in the 2014 Fiesta Bowl with Ajayi scoring three touchdowns and registering 134 yards on the ground, and the Brit capped off his tremendous season by declaring his eligibility for the 2015 NFL Draft. He finished his collegiate career with 678 rushes (third all-time at Boise State) for a tremendous 3,796 yards (third) and 50 touchdowns (tied second). Ajayi became the first and only player in school history with three games of over 200 yards rushing, a feat he would also accomplish in the NFL in just a single season.

Ajayi was selected by the Miami Dolphins with the 21st pick in the fifth round of the 2015 NFL Draft, becoming the 14th running back taken that year. A quiet rookie campaign disrupted by an injury sustained in preseason meant Ajayi tallied just 187 yards and a single touchdown, but he showed what he was capable of in his sophomore campaign. After the Dolphins lost Lamar Miller to the Houston Texans in free agency, Ajayi was named the backup to veteran back Arian Foster, although Foster suffered a groin injury – which would lead to his eventual in-season retirement – in a week two defeat to the New England Patriots, leaving the Brit to lead Miami's backfield.

Ajayi soon made his mark: he crushed the Pittsburgh Steelers with a 204-yard and two-touchdown outing before going for 214 yards and a score against the Buffalo Bills. In doing so, Ajayi became the fourth player in NFL history – along with OJ Simpson (twice), Earl Campbell and former Dolphins star Ricky Williams – to rush for over 200 yards in successive games, picking up back-to-back AFC Offensive Player of the Week awards. In week 16, Ajayi spectacularly rushed for 206 yards and a touchdown to become just the fourth player in NFL history to record over 200 yards rushing in three separate games in a single season – and the only player to do it so early into their career. He led the Dolphins to the postseason where they suffered a wildcard defeat to the Steelers and was named as an AFC selection to the 2017 Pro Bowl. To cap off a terrific year, Ajayi was ranked 69th on the NFL Top 100 Players of 2017 as voted by his peers.

If 2016 was a year of individual glory, 2017 was when Ajayi's team achieved success. While he got off to a fine start with 122 yards in a 19-17 win over the Los Angeles Chargers, Ajayi failed to find the end zone through the first eight weeks of the season. The Brit was the only NFL rusher with over 100 carries yet to score, and Miami decided to cash in. On 31 October 2017, Ajayi was traded to the Philadelphia Eagles for a fourth-round pick in the upcoming 2018 draft.

Ajayi wouldn't rush over 100 yards in a single game for the Eagles during their incredible 2017 run, but the Brit was a valuable component in an offence that stormed to the number one seed in the NFC playoffs, even without injured starting quarterback Carson Wentz. They defeated the Atlanta Falcons in the Divisional Round before topping the Minnesota Vikings in the NFC Championship Game, with Ajayi tallying 99 yards from scrimmage in the 38-7 win to advance to the Super Bowl, where the Eagles were set to face Tom Brady and the New England Patriots.

Did the Brit – in just his third season in the NFL – worry about facing the all-conquering Patriots and the league's serial winner on the biggest stage of the sport? 'I didn't really care that it was Tom Brady, I was just worried about my own team,' Ajayi said. 'At the end of the day, there was a lot of excitement but it's just another game. I'm an extremely confident person, so I didn't think the moment was too big for me.' Ajayi rushed for 57 yards as the Eagles won 41–33 – their first Super Bowl win in history – and the London-born star was ready to celebrate the moment in Minnesota, some 4,015 miles from the Big Smoke: 'It's what I worked for throughout my whole career,' said Ajayi. 'Some people play for so long and don't win, so it was amazing to get that under my belt.'

Unfortunately, Ajayi's career unravelled almost as quickly as it had peaked. He began the 2018 season with a pair of touchdowns in an 18-12 win over the Falcons but his season ended prematurely after Ajayi suffered a torn ACL during a loss to the Vikings in week five. He re-signed with the Eagles in November 2019 after running back Darren Sproles was placed on injured reserve, but Ajayi made just three appearances before his release just over a month later. He officially retired on 8 January 2022, appearing as an honorary captain for the Philadelphia Eagles in their regular season finale against the Dallas Cowboys.

Efe Obada

Carolina Panthers 2017–2020
Buffalo Bills 2021
Washington Commanders 2022

THE RISE of Efe Obada is astonishing, unique and improbable, all wrapped in one. It's the type of tale that belongs in theatres, Hollywood or urban legend. Better yet, it's a story that is still far from finished.

Obada is a special human being first and an elite sportsperson second. His extraordinary story begins in Nigeria, where Obada was born before he moved to the Netherlands with his mother and sibling when he was eight years old. After spending two years in the country, his mother decided to send her children to the United Kingdom to try to improve their lives. The exact details of how he arrived in London are unclear; it has been reported that Obada was trafficked into England, but he has never disclosed the details. He arrived in London an abandoned homeless child, allegedly spending nights sleeping rough before a security guard offered them shelter in the tower block he was working shifts in. Obada then found temporary accommodation with a friend of his mother before he was swiftly placed into foster care, growing up in over ten different foster homes across Stockwell and Lambeth. His traumatic experiences began to shape an incredible unrelenting mentality. 'Growing up in foster care made me realise that I had to make something shake for myself. No one was coming to save me so I had to do it myself,' Obada said. 'It made me determined but also immensely grateful for the life I have, and I never take anything for granted.'

At the age of 22, when most American football players are either in high-level college programmes or in the NFL, Obada was working in Grace Foods, a warehouse in Hertfordshire's Welwyn Garden City. He had never considered playing sports before, let alone the obscure and unfamiliar game of American football. The Brit had played soccer back in school but he never once thought he could go professional – instead, a chance meeting with a friend saw Obada's path to the NFL begin. Standing 6ft 6in tall, Obada was urged to take up American football with the London Warriors: 'I remember seeing the Super Bowl on TV way back in the day, but I never took any notice of it. I knew about the sport and the different clubs in London but was never seriously involved due to all the issues in my life at the time.' The South London-based outfit were reigning back-to-back national champions, and Obada – armed with the physical stature and the necessary attitude – began to impress.

It was at the Warriors where he was spotted by Aden Durde, the defensive coordinator at the time, and he formed a strong bond with Obada. 'From day one, he's the first person that believed in me and took time out of his life to coach me up. He invested in me when nobody else did.' When Durde had the opportunity to work as an intern coach with the Dallas Cowboys in 2014, he recommended the iconic franchise take a look at Obada. The Brit worked out with the team before their International Series clash with the Jacksonville Jaguars at Wembley Stadium and the Cowboys saw his potential. After just five games with the Warriors where he was deployed at both tight end and defensive end, Obada was on his way to Texas – and he will always be thankful to Durde. 'He facilitated the opportunity with Dallas, and that changed the whole trajectory of my life,' Obada said.

'He's family and always will be. I owe him a lot. He's always trying to coach me – we can't have a regular conversation now without him offering up advice! He's definitely a big influence on my career.'

In April 2015, the Cowboys signed the inexperienced Obada as a free agent. The Brit, settled at defensive end, spent the next year bouncing between the practice squad and free agency, desperately hoping for stability and a chance to prove himself. Obada also joined the Kansas City Chiefs and Atlanta Falcons in 2016 but the result was always the same: the Brit was released without making it to the field. Instead of letting the adversity affect him, Obada simply remembered what Durde had told him: 'He would say, "Don't feel sorry for yourself. Why do you feel sorry for yourself?" – and that's something that really stuck with me. We all go through life and can feel down, but it really impacted me. When things get hard, I don't feel sorry for myself and just keep pushing.' His patience and perseverance paid off in 2017.

The International Player Pathway programme was launched in 2017 to give international athletes the chance to make it in the NFL and Obada was part of the first intake after being spotted by Will Bryce, Head of Football Development at NFL International. Through the programme, Obada was guaranteed a position on an NFC South team after the division was randomly selected to be awarded a special 11th practice squad spot specifically designed for an international player. On 25 May 2017, Obada was signed by the Carolina Panthers. As part of the conditions of the programme, he was ineligible to make the 53-man roster during the regular season, but the Brit signed a reserve/future contract with the franchise in January 2018.

A strong preseason ensured Obada became the first NFL International Player Pathway graduate to make the 53-man roster. It was the culmination of years of hard work and dedication: 'I was determined. There was a lot of pressure to make it on to the active roster but I kept my head down and kept grinding.' Obada also praised the influence of coach Ron Rivera on his career: 'It was a blessing for me that I landed at the best team. Until you've played around the NFL, you won't realise how great coach Rivera is. He gave me my start in the league when most coaches probably wouldn't have and really helped me develop as a man and a football player.' If arriving in Carolina was luck, his debut against the Cincinnati Bengals in week three gave Obada the opportunity to showcase his talent.

The defensive end got his NFL career off to a dream start. Obada secured a sack and an interception as the Panthers went on to win 31-21. The Brit was awarded the game ball for his exceptional performance and named NFC Defensive Player of the Week. He signed a one-year contract extension with Carolina in January 2019 and went on to play for the Panthers in the International Series clash against the Tampa Bay Buccaneers. Under the lights of the new Tottenham Hotspur Stadium in London, Obada was made an honorary captain for his special homecoming: a 37-26 win over the Buccaneers with the Panthers defence recording seven sacks on quarterback Jameis Winston. It was an emotional moment: 'Going back to London to play was a dream. In the family section after the game, I sobbed my heart out. It was so overwhelming and surreal to play at home, especially seeing how dramatically my life had changed.'

Obada spent the 2020 season with the Panthers and had the most productive campaign of his career to date with 5.5 sacks – taking down the likes of future Hall of Fame quarterbacks Aaron Rodgers and Tom Brady – a forced fumble and two fumble recoveries. Obada entered free agency with optimism after proving he could contribute effectively in the NFL, but admitted he will always adore Carolina: 'I loved the team, the fans, the city; Carolina will always hold a special place in my heart,' the Brit said. 'The fanbase is amazing – they still cheer for me now – and I feel the staff really helped me develop as a player.' It was announced in April 2021 that Obada had switched conferences to join the Buffalo Bills under defensive guru Sean McDermott. Obada signed with the new-branded Washington Commanders to reunited with Rivera ahead of the 2022 NFL season.

The Buffalo Bills excelled in 2021, winning the AFC East with an 11-6 record while Obada contributed 3.5 sacks. He found confidence within the familiar defensive scheme set by coordinator Leslie Frazier and defensive line coach Eric Washington, who worked with Obada throughout his time in Carolina. He was on a team pursuing a shot at Super Bowl glory – a far cry from Welwyn Garden City – but his biggest gripe with being a British player in the NFL? Things can often be lost in translation. 'Sometimes I have to slow down and enunciate a little bit just so that they can understand me, but then sometimes I have to fake an old English accent because some of the fellas can be really childish!' Unfortunately, Obada's Bills came up short in one of the NFL's greatest matches: a 42-36 defeat to the Chiefs in Kansas City.

It's been a long road or Obada – from Nigeria to Washington via the Netherlands, London, Dallas, Kansas, Atlanta, Carolina and Buffalo– and he puts his success down to an insatiable work ethic. 'I don't consider myself to be a great athlete, or particularly smart or talented – I just work hard,' he declared. 'There's so much more I want to achieve before I can call myself a success. I want to keep improving and winning and providing for my family.'

A selfless and approachable NFL star, Obada continues to build on a legacy that other international players can use as motivation and inspiration. 'If people remember me at all, I want them to remember my immense gratitude for the opportunity and the fans – I never took a single day in the NFL for granted.'

Jermaine Eluemunor

Baltimore Ravens 2017–2018
New England Patriots 2019–2020
Las Vegas Raiders 2021–present

WHEN THE International Series was launched in 2007, its desired product were players like Jermaine Eluemunor. His story, from a sports-loving kid desperate to make it as a pro, is exactly what the NFL and American football needs as it seeks to expand around the globe.

As a 12-year-old boy, Eluemunor watched the inaugural International Series match with his eyes glued to the television as the Miami Dolphins and New York Giants battled in his home city of London. 'That was the first game I ever watched – literally my first time ever seeing or hearing about the game. It changed the whole trajectory of my life. I was in the middle of figuring out what I wanted to do and seeing that opened my eyes and I was like, "Damn, this is what I'm supposed to do with my life."' It was a nice twist of fate, as the young Brit stumbled across the gridiron showdown while flicking through the channels trying to find the Arsenal match.

As a young man growing up in Chalk Farm, Eluemunor bounced around a number of sports searching for the perfect fit. He knew he wanted a career in sport, whether it be as a player or as a staff member. He attended St Patrick's Catholic Primary

School before going to Haverstock, where he played a number of different sports – football, basketball, rugby, and a lot of cricket. 'Every sport you can play in England, I tried, because I was so big on sports,' he said. He recalled how Talacre Community Sports Centre – a brand-new sports complex – was around five minutes from his home: 'I went to a bunch of little camps and sporting events over there so that's where I got my start in sports.' After laying eyes on American football when the NFL came to Wembley in 2007, Eluemunor became interested in the sport too and, incidentally, his dad moved stateside in February 2008, just after his 14th birthday.

The move was unexpected, but Eluemunor enjoyed life in Danville, New Jersey where he enrolled at Morris Knolls High School, although his football career stuttered as a difficult home life began to take its toll. 'Football wasn't going too well because I was going back and forth between London and America, and we were really struggling over in the States to make ends meet. It was my sophomore year, and we returned to England.' However, the future NFL star begged his father to come back and let him play football, a sacrifice Eluemunor will never forget. 'He had a great job offer in England which he turned down because I wanted to be over here to play football. I knew it was what I was meant to do and it took a lot of begging, but he agreed to come back and struggle a little bit longer just so I could achieve my dreams,' Eluemunor emotionally recalled. 'I owe my success to him because he took that leap of faith and gave me the chance to make something of myself. They call America 'the land of opportunity' but moving over from England, it was really hard to make ends meet. He was sleeping on the floor in this little condo and I was sleeping on a futon for a good couple of months before it got too much and he wanted to move back home, so it was a struggle.'

Eluemunor now stands at 6ft 4in and weighs 156kg, and his impressive size was what helped him realise he was meant to play offensive lineman. While playing defensive tackle in his senior year of high school, his coach suggested he switched to the offensive side of the ball: 'I didn't know any of the technique. Kick step, sliding – I didn't know any of it. I probably pass blocked like four times in my entire high school career, and there was no technique. It was literally just jumping the guy, getting my hands on him and standing there!' Eluemunor was accepted at Lackawanna College in Scranton, Pennsylvania where his coach moved him to offensive line due to his size and physical nature. Eluemunor has no regrets: 'It came out of nowhere to be honest, but it turned out to be the best move ever.' It certainly would be as the Brit was named to the all-conference second team in 2013, highlighting his potential to a number of leading football programmes around the country.

Eluemunor's next move proved to be a far more difficult choice. His success at Lackawanna led to 35 colleges actively recruiting him, and he struggled to make – or rather, finalise – a decision. The Brit originally committed to UCLA, then flipped to Arkansas. 'I had commitment issues! When you go from not being recruited and people saying you suck, to schools you have only seen on TV or YouTube offering football scholarships, I wanted to accept them all. I wanted to go to every single school, and I didn't know what a commitment was. I didn't realise fans would jump on social media to talk about it! I didn't think anything of it.' Luckily for Eluemunor, Texas A&M head coach Kevin Sumlin knew about his lack of understanding with the system and asked the budding offensive lineman to visit the college last because he knew he would ultimately play for the last one.

As an Aggie, Eluemunor redshirted in 2014 and only made one appearance in 2015 as the backup right guard, playing in the Music City Bowl. However, 2016 proved to be the big break the Brit craved. Eluemunor started 12 of the 13 games in his senior season, and he attributes his development in football to his offensive line coach Jim Turner: 'Coach Turner whipped me into shape – I owe lots of success at A&M to him and coach Sumlin for believing in me and seeing what I was capable of, because I had a really bad coach my junior year. I'm not afraid to say it: he was terrible. He didn't pay attention to me and sent me down the wrong path in terms of coaching, but my senior year restored the confidence that would set me up for the rest of my career.'

Ahead of the draft, Eluemunor confessed he had no idea what the process was, only that he had to work his way up draft boards. Eluemunor impressed at the NFLPA Collegiate Bowl – a postseason college football all-star game for draft-eligible players – and it was there he met Hall of Fame tackle Jackie Slater, who was working as an offensive line coach for the game: 'He told me I could be a great tackle in the NFL, even when I was being used as a guard. Hearing that from Jackie Slater, one of the best tackles to ever do it, definitely helped my confidence.' The Brit had to earn an invite to the NFL Scouting Combine and did so thanks to his performance at the NFLPA game. Eluemunor attended the 'freaking dope' combine in Indianapolis, and it dawned on him just how far he had come: 'All I could think was: who thought back in 2008 that I would make it here? It was ridiculous.'

Eluemunor was carrying a hamstring injury at the combine, which lowered his value. Draft analyst Mike Mayock – who, as chance would have it, would later become Eluemunor's general manager at the Raiders – had the Brit in his revered top 100 list of prospects. Eluemunor experienced a roller coaster of emotions before he was selected by Baltimore in the fifth round: 'I was confident I would get picked in the fourth round, and then the fourth round passed and I was like, "Oh shit, will I even get fucking picked now?!" I had been watching the draft since 2008 and had always wanted to hear my name called. It didn't matter what round it was – it was a surreal moment.' After waiting over two days, the Ravens spent their 159th overall selection on a Brit from Chalk Farm. Eluemunor had made it to the big time.

His time in Baltimore had 'ups and downs'. Eluemunor admits he had the chance to become a starter under John Harbaugh, but he couldn't seize the opportunity as he was still learning the ropes at the professional level: 'I had to adjust to the speed of the game, but I feel like I had a good rookie year.' Eluemunor did have a successful debut campaign – he was named to the 2017 PFWA All-Rookie Team.

He was traded to the New England Patriots in 2019, which Eluemunor admits was a culture shock given the franchise's ability – and mentality – to consistently strive for championships under the stewardship of Bill Belichick and Tom Brady, the most successful duo in league history. 'Expectations are high and the standards are even higher; you have to meet the requirements they ask of you every single day – and that's to be a professional. Bill Belichick expected a lot because he traded a fourth-round pick for me.'

His time in Foxborough was short as an ankle injury derailed his progress in the 2020 season, but the time spent around Belichick and Brady left a lasting impression on Eluemunor: 'It was just crazy to be around two of the best to ever do it. It made me want to join them and try to cement my name in history. Just being around those two motivates you to be great.'

To be honest, Eluemunor needs little motivation. The physical giant from Chalk Farm has cultivated a successful start to his career, playing for renowned franchises alongside legendary names, and he's ready to achieve more. 'I believe I'm going to be a Pro Bowler and All-Pro. God wouldn't have put me in the NFL and blessed me with the opportunities, the skills and the talent for no reason. If I wasn't meant to become one of the best, then why would I have gone through everything I have to get here? I didn't come here to be average or mediocre.' His defiant attitude and willingness to prove himself among the best in a traditionally alien sport back in his homeland means Eluemunor's arrival in Las Vegas to join the iconic Raiders franchise feels right. The

Raiders are all about grit, strength and determination, traits the Brit possesses in abundance: 'I've always thought I am a typical Raiders lineman – a big, physical guy who just likes to hit people. I was meant for this franchise; the fact that I get to put on the silver and black and represent the Raiders is an honour. I have high expectations on myself after the coaches placed their trust and confidence in me, and hopefully I can stay here for the rest of my career, if everything goes to plan.' Everything is going to plan thus far, albeit with notable and unforgettable help along the way from his father and coaches at Texas A&M.

From the Big Smoke to Sin City, Eluemunor feels at home amongst the brightest lights. With the attitude and mentality the Brit possesses, it's only a matter of time before he shines too.

Jamie Gillan

Cleveland Browns 2019–2021

THE LATEST in a long line of Scottish kickers in the NFL, Jamie Gillan decided to excel in punting rather than the placekicking favoured by Lawrence Tynes and Graham Gano. He certainly ensured his inherent passion for rugby did not go to waste.

Born in the Scottish Highlands near Inverness, Gillan – like many athletic Scots before him – began his life playing rugby. He spent four years at Duncan Forbes Primary School and Culloden Academy, playing for Highland RFC. His team was incredibly successful, and Gillan firmly believes coach Donnie Flockhart was the best coach he ever had as the team never lost a game during his time there. Gillan then attended Merchiston Castle School for three years after receiving a scholarship to play rugby. At this stage, Gillan was set on playing the sport and living among the Highlands – American football was nothing but a bore to him.

Gillan attended Merchiston in Edinburgh from ages 13 to 16, and he even claimed the U16 Scottish Schools Cup. His father – a military man who worked in anti-submarine warfare for the Royal Armed Forces – was relocated to Maryland, and the budding rugby star made a choice. Gillan opted to follow his family to America, ensuring he would spend the final two years of his high school life in the States. 'I miss Scotland a lot, my friends and family are all over in Scotland but there are major opportunities out here.' His opportunity certainly came after Gillan enrolled at Leonardtown High School and attended football games.

As Gillan neared graduation, it became clear the Leonardtown Raiders needed a kicker. After attending several games as a fan, Gillan decided to try his luck. He went to practice soon after and impressed special teams coach Brian Woodburn so much he made the Scot the kicker right there and then. Gillan played in five regular season games and Woodburn was enamoured with his awe-inducing kicking style. He labelled Gillan the 'Scottish Hammer' thanks to his powerful kicks and the name stuck, much to the displeasure of the Scot. His thunderous kicks drew attention from college football programmes, namely Kentucky, Delaware State, Old Dominion and Towson. They all approached him with walk-on or grayshirt opportunities, neither of which would have allowed him to play football while receiving a scholarship, but Gillan had a plan. He was intent on returning to Scotland to play rugby unless he received a full scholarship. Bowie State, a Division II school, stepped up to the plate – but they were soon topped by a Facebook post from the University of Arkansas Pine Bluff.

Gillan's friend saw a post on Facebook claiming that UAPB needed a kicker, so the Scot put his highlights tape into the post and he received a call later that day offering him a full scholarship to join the Division I school. Gillan celebrated that night and woke up the following morning with a hazy recollection of the scholarship, and he didn't know where Arkansas was: 'I'm not going to lie to you, I had never heard of the state of Arkansas in my life!' Gillan didn't mind where the school was located; as long as it was a scholarship, where he would receive free food, gym and football, he was in. He got on the plane to head to UAPB and quickly did his research – Gillan didn't even know it was a historically black school until he arrived. In fact, the Scot assumed 'HBCU' was a sponsorship rather than the acronym for historically black colleges and universities established before the Civil Rights Act of 1964 to primarily serve the African–American community.

It was a different culture and Gillan was certainly in the minority as a white Scottish man, but it didn't affect him due to a childhood spent moving around different locations and customs. 'I wasn't treated any differently being white, because I didn't act any different, because I'm me. What you see is what you get with me.' Unfazed by his new setting, Gillan made an immediate impression thanks to his work ethic and athleticism – and his stats showcased his fine performances.

Across his four-year career as a UAPB Lion, Gillan tallied 9,024 yards across 214 attempts, averaging a sensational 42.2 yards per punt. In 2018 alone, Gillan thumped 71 punts for 3,015 yards – with his longest punt recorded at a mega 80 yards. The Scot also nailed 19 punts for over 50 yards while 27 were pinned inside the opposition 20 as the 'Scottish Hammer' quickly became a weapon of mass destruction. Gillan displayed his versatility at UAPB too as he made 20 of 29 field goals in his senior year with a career-long conversion of 47 yards.

Gillan's career appeared at a crossroads after graduating from UAPB. He wasn't invited to the NFL Scouting Combine and Pine Bluff didn't have a pro day. He was even running out of footballs to train with, after punting them so hard they began to deflate. Gillan had his heart set on making it in football, so he drove for three hours to Jonesboro, a city in the north-eastern corner of Arkansas, to take part in the Arkansas State pro day. When he arrived, nobody knew who Gillan was but, throughout his workout, the Scot went from unsung prospect to the name on everybody's lips. Despite being a punter, Gillan showed off his athleticism as a 6ft 2in potential gadget on special teams, the type of player special teams coaches dream of. He recorded a 4.6s 40-yard dash as well as impressive performances in the long and broad jumps, but while he caught the eye and garnered some traction, only two punters were selected in the 2019 NFL Draft. It didn't take the Cleveland Browns long to sign Gillan as an undrafted free agent just weeks after bringing him in for a pre-draft workout.

After he nailed a 74-yard punt in preseason against the Indianapolis Colts, Gillan was named the starting punter for the Browns, beating out veteran Britton Colquitt for the role. The Scot and his hammer of a leg had arrived in the NFL and he wasted no time in making some noise. He earned AFC Special Teams Player of the Month in September following a terrific period which included 11 punts inside the 20 and only 19 return yards allowed. He finished his rookie campaign with 28 of his 63 punts downed inside the 20 to earn a spot on the Football Writers Association's All-Rookie Team.

Unfortunately, Gillan appeared to lose his mojo soon after. He struggled for form in 2020 and 2021 and was ultimately waived by the Browns on 22 December 2021. The Buffalo Bills signed him to their practice squad, but he left the franchise just days after their defeat to the Kansas City Chiefs in the AFC Divisional Round of the playoffs.

Afterword

THE NATIONAL Football League has the lowest percentage of foreign-born players among the major sports leagues in North America. As of 2017, approximately 3 per cent of active players are international, although the rise of the International Player Pathway (IPP) Programme – which helped Efe Obada break through – is sure to affect that number going forward.

The IPP has grown each year since it was launched in 2017 and, as of 2020, 19 of the 32 NFL franchises have signed international players as a direct result of the system. There are three British representatives in the 2021 intake: Berlin Thunder defensive end Adedayo Odeleye, Winnipeg Blue Bombers linebacker Ayo Oyelola and University of Utah offensive lineman Bamidele Olaseni. They will be hoping to earn a chance in the NFL like Obada did so effectively, while the draft sees more and more international and British talent with every passing year. Through names like Michigan linebacker David Ojabo – the Nigerian-born budding star who grew up in Scottish city Aberdeen before moving to the United States at 17 – and USC's Sam Oram-Jones, the future of British American football, particularly in the NFL, is bright.

In terms of the future of American football in the United Kingdom, one of the most exciting areas to develop and grow is the women's game. The Women's Contact league began in 2012 and has experienced steady growth annually. When it started a decade ago, the league was played in 5v5 format, known as the Sapphire Series. The league became a two-tier system in 2016, with Division One and Division Two each housing a North and South conference. After a banner year in 2017/18, all divisions moved to 7v7 – the current format – and there are plans to extend to 9v9 in the upcoming 2022 season, in which 19 teams from across the country are registered to take part. In 2020, the league was rebranded in favour of a more conventional and perhaps appropriate name, the National Women's Football League (NWFL).

The league, which takes place in the summer, also provides developing players with the opportunity to compete in the NWFL Super 11s, an 11-a-side format that allows women to play the familiar NFL version of the sport. In its current state, the Super 11s consists of three full-day training sessions before concluding with a North versus South game. The series has previously acted as trials for the GB national team, too.

The GB national team is perhaps the best representation of the women's game in the United Kingdom. At the 2019 International Federation of American Football Women's European Championship, Britain – led by captain Phoebe Schecter – came agonisingly close to securing glory on home soil as they defeated eventual champions Finland 18-14 only to miss out on the title on head-to-head results. They secured a silver medal following sensational performances from star running back Ruth Matta, who plies her trade with the Boston Renegades in the United States. Matta is a six-time UK National Champion with the Birmingham Lions, and a two-time Offensive Player of the Year. 'The British American Football Association has to do a better job of promoting our female teams because they really are the beacon for the sport. They've been the most winning team from juniors, men's, flag, whatever – so really pushing them forward would be good,' Schecter said. 'In order for it to be the norm, you do have to push people and promote the game. It's about finding ways to celebrate the females within this pretty awesome sport.'

This is where the potential of the women's game is so exciting. Figures like Matta and Schecter can drive the sport forward, particularly with the national team captain working for 11 months as a coaching intern with the Buffalo Bills, where she became the first-ever female NFL coach to hail from Britain. Schecter, a dual citizen, only got into the sport as a way of keeping in touch with her roots after she arrived in the UK. She is always looking to promote the sport and hosted a successful U19 girls football development day in November 2021 as part of the general focus of the NWFL to increase football participation among young women. 'Hopefully one day the NFL Academy, which is based in London, will bring on a female athlete – that would be a pretty cool next step,' said Schecter,

Her story can truly inspire the next generation to take advantage of Britain's impressive standing among European nations when it comes to football. Why limit themselves to excelling on the continent? 'American football doesn't have to just be for Americans or Canadians; we can be great at this sport. Ten years from now, I don't see why the British women's side couldn't win a world championship, especially with this great young talent and coaches.' Schecter believes the potential inclusion of flag football at the 2028 Los Angeles Olympics will further legitimise the game in the United Kingdom, and, moving forwards, she is hoping to run camps to further encourage participation in American football among young women.

As well as Schecter's initiatives, NFL UK debuted a weekly show on Twitter and Instagram called *Her Huddle*, which features key and leading women voices in football. The future for American football – across all codes and genders – has never been brighter on British soil. Long may it continue.

Acknowledgements

I MUST acknowledge the exceptional help of David Tossell, who orchestrated a number of the interviews and provided invaluable advice on how to pitch the idea to publishers. David's expertise in the area made the whole process far smoother than it otherwise would have been, and I appreciated his help immensely.

Anthony Wootton offered his knowledge of the Tea and Coffee Bowls, with his remarkable insight helping to shed light on an incredible story. It simply would not have been possible to tell the tale in such detail without Anthony's research and kindness in sharing his work.

Thanks to my friend Rory Macnair as well, for his knowledge of the ever-growing women's game in the United Kingdom.

I'm incredibly grateful for my friends who helped read and edit the book, sharing the burden as I stressed out – Sasha, Dylan, Oscar, Sarah, Kieran, Barney, Robbie, Ox and Ferg. Your time and energy spent assisting *The Special Relationship* is incredibly appreciated.

Finally, a special thanks to Dad for giving me this idea, supporting my career and instilling the belief that this was ever possible. I will never be able to effectively articulate how much it means to me.

Notes

AUTHOR INTERVIEWS

Jay Ajayi, Will Blackmon, Jack Crawford, Jermaine Eluemunor, Gary Imlach, Graham Gano, Roger Goodgroves, Rhys Lloyd, Mick Luckhurst, Efe Obada, Matt Ryan, Phoebe Schecter, Lawrence Tynes, Osi Umenyiora, Menelik Watson, Anthony Wootton.

SECTION 1

CHAPTER 1: The Silver Cup and a Golden Reception

Prater, Ernest, 'American Football at the Crystal Palace: Charging a Passage for the Man With the Ball', *The Graphic*, December 1910

Cuneo, Cyrus, 'Football in its Most Dangerous Form: An American Footballer Armoured for the Game', *Illustrated London News*, November 1910

CHAPTER 2: A Spot of Tea and Coffee

Nickleson, Allan, 'Canucks Take Yanks', *Canadian Press News*, February 1944

Knight, Eric, *Instructions for American Serviceman in Britain* (War Department, Washington, 1942)

'8,000 Irish Fans Puzzled by US Football Game', *Stars and Stripes*, 16 November 1942

Wootton, Anthony, The Tea Bowl: The game that stopped the war (BBC *Sportshour*, October 2019)

Peter Young quote, 'He demonstrated leadership …'

Gail Thompson quote, 'My dad said …'

Steve Daniel quote, 'Paul was revered …'; 'Fine display put …'

Wootton, Anthony, *NFL: When American football came to London in World War Two* (BBC, November 2019)

George Hees quote, 'I came face-to-face …'

Graff, Gene, 'Blues Blank Canadians, 18-0', *Stars and Stripes*, March 1944

CHAPTER 3: The GI Bowl and the End of WWII

Lee, Ray, 'Shuttle-Raders Sink Navy Lions, 20-0', *Stars and Stripes*, November 1944

Official Program: Army vs Navy (November 1944)

Wentworth, John, 'Warriors Overcome Shuttle-Raders, 13-0', *Stars and Stripes*, January 1945

CHAPTER 4: The US Air Force Europe Sports League

Dunn, Dennis, '"It's Moider," London Cries at AF Football Game', *Stars and Stripes*, December 1952

Crawford, Russ, *Le Football: A History of American Football in France* (Lincoln: University of Nebraska Press, 2016)

British Pathé, *US Air Force Football Final Aka American 'Grid' Football* (1952)

Slappey, Sterling, '"Jolly Good" Say British of Yank Football', *Stars and Stripes*, December 1952

Fan quote, 'the battle's …'

Crawford, Russ, *The Long History of American Football in the UK* (Sport in American History, October 2016)

Graphic story, 'At some secret …'

'Grid Deaths Show Sharp Drop in 1st Half of Season', *Stars and Stripes*, November 1955

Coffey, John, *United States Air Forces In Europe 1952 Football Championship Final Official Programme* (December 1952)

CHAPTER 5: The 1980s: Greed, Gridiron and Channel 4

'It was both entertaining and bewildering for the Britons …', *Sunday Express*, August 1983

John Marshall quote, 'We never expected …'

Eskenazi, Gerald, 'Tex Schramm Is Dead at 83; Builder of "America's Team"', *New York Times*, July 2003

Tomasson, Chris, 'Vikings recall NFL's first game in London: "When we kicked anything, it was a pretty big deal."', *St Paul Pioneer Press*, October 2017

Rickey Young quote, 'Because we were …'

Darrin Nelson quote, 'They didn't really …'

'Bess paces Vikings as football invades Great Britain', *Greenville News*, August 1983

Guy Horchover quote, 'It's rather good …'

London Ravens History (BritballNow.co.uk)

Crawford, Russ, *The Long History of American Football in the UK* (Sport in American History, October 2016)

Tony Wells quote, 'American football is …'

Sunday Express excerpt, 'All those endless …'

Rozelle, Pete, *American Bowl 1986: Chicago Bears vs Dallas Cowboys Official Match Programme* (NFL, August 1986)

When the Super Bowl Bears shuffled off to London to meet the Cowboys (ESPN, October 2019)

Mike Ditka quote, 'The fans were …'; 'Let's be honest …'

Bill Smith quote, 'One of the …'

CHAPTER 6: The World League of American Football: The Rise and Fall of the Monarchy

Tench, Matt, 'American Football: End of the World League', *Independent*, September 1992

Dufresne, Chris, 'Europe Takes to WLAF, but Will It Catch On Here?', *Los Angeles Times*, May 1991

Mike Lynn quote, 'It's an absolute …'

Mark Mandell quote, 'The ratings are …'

Larry Kennan quote, 'It's a fun …'

Eichel, Larry, 'In Europe, WLAF's Game Was More Than Football', *Philadelphia Inquirer*, June 1991

Cassidy, Alex, *American Football's Forgotten Kings: The Rise and Fall of the London Monarchs* (Pitch Publishing, September 2015)

Orlando Sentinel quote, 'a rather arduous …'

'The Spectacle's the Thing As Monarchs Capture Title', *New York Times*, June 1991

Stan Gelbaugh quote, 'This is tremendous …'

Maguire, Ken, *Thanks, WLAF! Player parlayed London life to Super Bowls* (Federal News Network, February 2021)

Dedrick Dodge quote, 'No amount of …'

'Fate of WLAF will be decided by NFL owners', *Deseret News*, October 1991

Bruce Dworshak quote, 'Our future hangs …'

CHAPTER 7: NFL Europe

Elliott, Keith, 'American Football: Plan for smaller World League: The London Monarchs may be transplanted to Millwall in 1994', *Independent*, March 1993

Nick Priestnall quote, 'I have heard …'

Cress, Doug, 'The New World League: Retooled, and Ready to Start Saturday', *New York Times*, April 1995

Jerry Vainisi quote, 'Some of our …'

O'Hagan, Simon, 'Monarchs seek to rule the world', *Independent*, March 1995

Gareth Moores quote, 'The UK has the …'

Cassidy, Alex, *American Football's Forgotten Kings: The Rise and Fall of the London Monarchs* (Pitch Publishing, September 2015)

Brad Johnson quote, 'We did have a quarterback …'

Reid, Pete, *Sweet Dreams: The Scottish Claymores Conquer the World* (Dear Scotland, August 2009)

Fox Sports announcer quote, 'For a millennia …'

Halling, Nick, 'American football: Monarchs look to wider market as World League adopts new identity', *Independent*, April 1998

Oliver Luck quote, 'It makes sense …'

Kröner, Andreas, 'Kirmes, Hot Dogs und Eiertanz', *Der Spiegel*, April 2004

Jörn Maier quote, 'Certainly a lot …'

Patrick Venzke quote, 'A college …'

Gregory, Sean, 'America Is Exporting a Rotten Product to Great Britain', *TIME*, October 2013

John Williams quote, 'One of the …'

NFL folds Europe league, to focus on regular-season games abroad (ESPN, June 2007)

Uwe Bergheim quote, 'Despite the …'

Fantin, Alessandro, *A look at NFL Globalization strategies - Exporting football to Europe* (American Football International, September 2019)

Mark Waller quote, 'NFL Europa has …'

SECTION 2

2007

Giants vs Dolphins

NFL Considers Adding 17th Game To Season (*News on 6*, May 2007)

Mark Waller quote, 'It is preliminary but …'

Wembley to host Dolphins & Giants (BBC, February 2007)

Roger Goodell quote, 'The international popularity …'

John Mara quote, 'It will signal …'

Gough, Martin, *Giants beat Miami at wet Wembley* (BBC, October 2007)

Cam Cameron quote, 'I can't imagine …'

2008

Chargers vs Saints

NFL to return to the United Kingdom in 2008 (NFL.com, January 2008)

Roger Goodell quote, 'The game in London …'

Bandini, Nicky, 'NFL confirm 2008 Wembley fixture', *Guardian*, February 2008

Roger Goodell quote, 'Playing a limited number …'; 'Maybe it's because the …'

Dean Spanos quote, 'This is another positive …'

Shawne Merriman quote, 'He just told me …'

Clayton, John, *Brees agrees to six-year deal with Saints* (ESPN, March 2006)

Drew Brees quote, 'I just felt that …'

Kahn, Michael, *Saints top Chargers in London NFL battle* (Reuters, October 2008)

Sean Payton quote, 'It was a bit …'

2009

Patriots vs Buccaneers

Pats to face Bucs in London (Sky Sports, December 2008)

Joel Glazer quote, 'The Tampa Bay …'

Patriots rout Bucs in front of sellout Wembley crowd in London (NFL, October 2009)

Brandon Meriweather quote, 'I just happened to …'

Raheem Morris quote, 'Tom, he's the guy …'

Bill Belichick quote, 'It's been a …'

Tom Brady, 'We had plenty of …'; 'All the flashbulbs …'

Smith, Scott, *All in! Tom Brady, Bucs team up to pursue championships* (Buccaneers.com, March 2020)

Bruce Arians quote, 'Tom is the most …'

2010

Broncos vs 49ers

Williamson, Bill, *London trip could be a disaster* (ESPN, January 2010)

Pat Bowlen quote, 'Our organisation has …'

Josh McDaniels quote, 'The previous games …'

London Calling: 49ers vs. Broncos on Oct 31 (49ers.com, January 2010)

Joe Staley quote, 'I've never been to …'

Vernon Davis quote, 'I've been waiting …'

Love, Tim, *San Francisco 49ers rally past Denver Broncos in London* (BBC, October 2010)

Shawntae Spencer quote, 'We got to get …'

Mike Singletary quote, 'The people here …'

Josh McDaniels quote, 'It was a very …'

2011

Bears vs Buccaneers

'Wilson, Stephen, Bears put on show in London', *Toronto Star*, October 2011

Roy Williams quote, 'We had a squirrel …'

'Forte runs for 145 yards, Bears beat Bucs 24-18', *Sports Illustrated*, October 2011

Matt Forte quote, 'When you get the opportunity …'

DJ Moore quote, 'I was pretty much …'

Raheem Morris quote, 'The problem with us is …'

Sherry, Matthew, *Any Given Sunday: The NFL's epic 100-year history in 20 games* (Weidenfeld & Nicolson, September 2020)

George Halas quote, 'football players are …'

2012

Patriots vs Rams

Ingle, Sean, 'Razzle meets dazzle as NFL comes out of the shadows in the UK', *Guardian*, October 2012

Sam Bradford quote, 'It was surprising …'

Andy Richmond quote, 'There was no …'

Pats score on 1st 5 possessions, rout Rams in London (ESPN, October 2012)

Sam Bradford quote, 'You can't ask …'

Rob Gronkowski quote, 'That was a …'

Tom Brady quote, 'I don't know …'

Bill Belichick quote, 'The stadium was …'

2013

Steelers vs Vikings

Big London crowd revels in Vikings' win over Steelers (NFL.com, September 2013)

Adrian Peterson quote, 'They were just …'

Adrian Peterson, 'It was electric …'

Greg Jennings, Adrian Peterson lead Vikings past Steelers (ESPN, September 2013)

Matt Cassel quote, 'You throw a ...'

Greg Jennings quote, 'It would have ...'

Ben Roethlisberger quote, 'We are in ...'

NFL: Minnesota Vikings beat Pittsburgh Steelers at Wembley (BBC, September 2013)

Leslie Frazier quote, 'I think I'll ...'

49ers vs Jaguars

Gregory, Sean, 'America Is Exporting a Rotten Product to Great Britain', *TIME*, October 2013

Shahid Khan quote, 'Everybody needs to ...'

Colin Kaepernick, 49ers demolish Jaguars in London (ESPN, October 2013)

Paul Posluszny quote, 'Kaepernick is a stud ...'

Gus Bradley quote, 'We can take ...'

Jim Harbaugh quote, 'The beginning of ...'

Haislop, Tadd, *Colin Kaepernick kneeling timeline: How protests during the national anthem started a movement in the NFL* (Sporting News, September 2020)

Colin Kaepernick quote, 'I am not going to ...'

Wagner, Kyle, *Colin Kaepernick Is Not Supposed To Be Unemployed* (*FiveThirtyEight*, August 2017)

Benjamin, Cody, *Roger Goodell says NFL was 'wrong for not listening' earlier, encourages all to peacefully protest* (CBS Sports, June 2020)

Roger Goodell quote, 'We, the National ...'

Corran, Davidde, 'San Francisco 49ers ravage Jacksonville Jaguars at packed Wembley', *Guardian*, October 2013

Maurice Jones-Drew quote, 'This year hasn't ...'

Jim Harbaugh quote, 'He looked like ...'

Paul Posluszny quote, 'It was one ...'

2014

Dolphins vs Raiders

Wilson, Ryan, *Philbin accepts responsibility for causing distraction with QB situation* (CBS Sports, September 2014)

Joe Philbin quote, 'One of the functions …'

Tafur, Vic, 'A jolly old break before game prep', *San Francisco Chronicle*, September 2014

Andre Holmes quote, 'I was surprised the …'

Kevin Boothe quote, 'These kids are …'

Eisen, Rich, *The Rich Eisen Show* (April 2019)

David Shaw quote, 'As hard as it …'

'Steve Sabol's "Autumn Wind" poem a lasting tribute to Oakland Raiders', *East Bay Times*, August 2016

Smith, Cory, *Dolphins vs. Raiders: Score and Twitter Reaction from Wembley Stadium* (Bleacher Report, September 2014)

Mike Wallace quote, 'I don't know …'

Ryan Tannehill throws 2 TDs as Dolphins drub Raiders in London (ESPN, September 2014)

Dennis Allen quote, 'Obviously, we did …'

Lions vs Falcons

Lions rally from 3-TD deficit as Falcons suffer historic collapse (ESPN, October 2014)

Desmond Trufant quote, 'It felt good …'

Jeremy Ross quote, 'We don't give …'

Cassius Vaughn quote, 'I knew Prater …'

Matt Ryan quote, 'This is as …'

Katzenstein, Josh, 'Matthew Stafford likely to break Bobby Layne's record', *Detroit News*, October 2014

Matthew Stafford quote, 'It'll probably mean …'

NFL: Detroit Lions beat Atlanta Falcons 22-21 at Wembley (BBC, October 2014)

Alistair Kirkwood quote, 'There are logistic …'

Cowboys vs Jaguars

Tony Romo throws 3 TD in return as Cowboys beat Jags in London (ESPN, November 2014)

Tony Romo quote, 'Anybody who's had …'

Blake Bortles quote, 'We kind of …'

Jason Garrett quote, 'That was the …'; 'Didn't seem like …'

Slater, Matt, *NFL Wembley: Seven years until London Jaguars? Rams? Raiders?* (BBC Sport, September 2014)

Mark Waller quote, 'To permanently …'

Boren, Cindy, 'Referee Gene Steratore explains overturned Dez Bryant catch', *Washington Post*, January 2015

Gene Steratore quote, 'Although the receiver …'

2015

Jets vs Dolphins

Ingle, Sean, 'Caution key to London NFL franchise as Jets face Dolphins at Wembley', *Guardian,* October 2015

Alistair Kirkwood quote, 'The early kick-offs make …'

Bandini, Nick, 'New York Jets win in London to heap more misery on Miami Dolphins', *Guardian*, October 2015

Todd Bowles quote, 'He came up …'

Bills vs Jaguars

Ingle, Sean, 'Jacksonville Jaguars seal Wembley win over Buffalo Bills in thrilling finale', *Guardian,* October 2015

Gus Bradley quote, 'We have been in this situation …'

Telvin Smith quote, 'You can't even see Gus's eyes …'

Jaguars rally to beat Bills 34–31 after blowing big second-half lead (ESPN, October 2015)

Gus Bradley quote, 'What we're seeing …'

Rex Ryan quote, 'I've never known …'

Lions vs Chiefs

Ingle, Sean, 'Alex Smith conducts Kansas City Chiefs' Wembley rout of Detroit Lions', *Guardian,* November 2015

Alex Smith quote, 'It was a lot of fun but …'

Gamble, Andrew, 'Alex Smith's unthinkable comeback: Washington Football Team quarterback finally returns after traumatic injury', *Independent,* October 2020

Jared Goff quote, 'I will be able to …'

2016

Colts vs Jaguars

Wells, Mike, *Luck retires, calls decision 'hardest of my life'*, (ESPN, August 2019)

Andrew Luck quote, 'I've been stuck in this process …'

Redskins vs Bengals

Bengals travel to London for home game against the Redskins (Yahoo, October 2016)

Marvin Lewis quote, 'We're not going …'

2017

Ravens vs Jaguars

Lewis scores 3 TDs as Jaguars rout Ravens in London (ESPN, September 2017)

Allen Hurns quote, 'It's been three straight …'

Saints vs Dolphins

Ingle, Sean, 'New Orleans Saints beat Miami Dolphins in Wembley stinker', *Guardian*, October 2017

Sean Payton quote, 'It doesn't have to be …'

Jay Ajayi quote, 'We didn't put …'

Cardinals vs Rams

Urban, Darren, *Cardinals To Play Rams In London In 2017,* (azcardinals.com, December 2016)

Michael Bidwill quote, 'In 2014, I attended the …'

Somers, Kent, 'Arizona Cardinals take on Los Angeles Rams, hope the sequel to London game is much better', *Arizona Republic*, November 2017

Harold Goodwin quote, 'That was like one of …'

Vikings vs Browns

Hangst, Andrea, *Browns and Vikings take different approaches in traveling to London,* (Dawgs by Nature, October 2017)

Mike Zimmer quote, 'We've had sleep people ...'

2018

Seahawks vs Raiders

Bishara, Motez, *NFL London: Seattle Seahawks right ship on overseas trip* (CNN, October 2018)

Jon Gruden quote, 'It was a great flight ...'

Tahir Whitehead quote, 'It's a good feeling to ...'

Titans vs Chargers

Bacharach, Erik, 'How the Titans ended up in London to face the Chargers in their first international game', *The Tennessean*, October 2018

Marcus Mariota quote, 'The thing about where I'm ...'

Searles, Graham, 'Philip Rivers steers LA Chargers to nailbiting win over Tennessee Titans', *Guardian*, October 2018

Philip Rivers quote, 'I remember ...'

Chargers withstand Titans' late rally, hold on for 20-19 win (ESPN, October 2018)

Philip Rivers quote, 'He ran a ...'

Jordan, Gary, 'NFL London 2018: Tennessee Titans at Los Angeles Chargers', *The American*, October 2018

Mike Vrabel quote, 'When that drive started ...'

Eagles vs Jaguars

Simpson, James, *Philadelphia Eagles vs Jacksonville Jaguars: Super Bowl champions are rookies in London* (Sky Sports, October 2018)

Michael Bennett quote, 'I like going to Harrods ...'

'Jacksonville Jaguars players arrested in London over unpaid £50,000 drinks bill', *Guardian*, October 2018

Barry Church quote, 'There was definitely a ...'

NFL at Wembley: Eagles beat Jaguars in front of record crowd (BBC, October 2018)

Chris Long quote, 'It did feel like ...'

2019

Bears vs Raiders

Sherry, Matthew, *Any Given Sunday: The NFL's epic 100-year history in 20 games* (Weidenfeld & Nicolson, September 2020)

Christopher Halpin quotes, 'We want our teams to …'; 'This is one of …'

Richie Incognito quote, 'It's first class …'

Josh Jacobs rallies Raiders past Bears 24-21 (ESPN, October 2019)

Richie Incognito quote, 'They were talking …'

Josh Jacobs quote, 'We were up for the challenge …'

MacInnes, Paul, 'Oakland's early arrival pays off against Bears and Jacobs profits', *Guardian*, October 2019

Jon Gruden quote, 'I'm so proud of …'

Panthers vs Buccaneers

McCaffrey scores 2 TDs to lead Panthers past Bucs 37-26 (ESPN, October 2019)

Bruce Irvin quote, 'When one guys makes …'

Joey Slye quote, 'I played the ball from …'

Christian McCaffrey quote, 'I felt like every …'

London Falling: Bucs Sacked by Panthers in International Series Home Game (Buccaneers.com, October 2019)

Bruce Arians quote, 'The punt drops were …'; 'Throw the damn ball …'

Bengals vs Rams

Cincinnati Bengals vs Los Angeles Rams: Sean McVay faces former assistant Zac Taylor in London (Sky Sports, October 2019)

Zac Taylor quote, 'It's frustrating for everybody …'

Klein, Gary, 'Rams' Todd Gurley looking forward to this London trip for a change', *Los Angeles Times*, October 2019

Todd Gurley quotes, 'I like London, but …'; 'Those fans are a …'

Kupp has 220 yards receiving as Rams roll 24-10 in London (ESPN, October 2019)

Jared Goff quote, 'I joke about it …'

Texans vs Jaguars

No looking back: Watson on point as Texans top Jags 26-3 (ESPN, November 2019)

DeAndre Hopkins quote, 'It's great to play …'

2021

Jets vs Falcons

Costello, Brian, 'Jets can't overcome slow start in loss to Falcons in London', *New York Post*, October 2021

CJ Mosley quote, 'Falling back in a …'

Robert Saleh quote, 'Study the tape …'

Rathborn, Jack, 'Kyle Pitts revitalises Atlanta Falcons as NFL London rejoices at breakout display', *Independent*, October 2021

Arthur Smith quote, 'Kyle stepped up today …'

Dolphins vs Jaguars

Jags end 20-game skid with 53-yard FG to beat Dolphins 23-20 (CBS Sports, October 2021)

Urban Meyer quote, 'I don't think anyone …'

Matthew Wright quote, 'Just not a huge talker …'

Tua Tagovailoa quote, 'I'm not 100 …'

Stroud, Rick, 'Former Jaguars kicker Josh Lambo says he was kicked by Urban Meyer during warmups', *Tampa Bay Times*, December 2021

Urban Meyer quote, 'I'll kick you …'

SECTION 3

Bobby Howfield

Payne, Colin, 'Watford FC forward who became a Denver Broncos and New York Jets star', *Watford Observer*, February 2021

Bobby Howfield quote, 'I had enjoyed …'; 'I'm still not …'

Allan Watson

Burcham, Dave, Allan Gets His Kicks (*Evening Review* [Ohio], August 1971)

Allan Watson quote, 'They expect you …'; 'A satisfactory …'; 'When I first started …'; 'This is one …'

Mike Walker

Jones, Richard, 'The forgotten story of Lancashire's American Football ace', *Guardian*, January 2012

Daily Mirror advert, 'a rough and …'

Mike Walker quote, 'They would scream …'

Gonsalves, Rick, *Placekicking in the NFL: A History and Analysis* (McFarland, December 2013)

John Smith

Woods, Mark, *Smith is Patriots' UK connection* (ESPN, October 2009)

John Smith quote, 'My wife and …'

Ausiello, Jeff, *Ex-Pats kicker forever linked to Lennon* (ESPN, December 2010)

John Smith quote, 'The press was …'

Vince Abbott

Plaschke, Bill, 'Hey, Abbott! When at Last He Got the Call, It Was to Follow a Placekicking Legend in San Diego', *Los Angeles Times*, December 1987

Vince Abbott quote, 'If you step …'; 'You should have …'; 'I just kick …'

Tim Shaw

Titans LB Shaw Helping Promote Super Bowl in London (tennesseetitans.com, February 2011)

Tim Shaw quote, 'This is a …'

Birkett, Dave, 'Ex-NFLer Tim Shaw fights ALS: "What I see is a lot of hope"', *Detroit Free Press*, June 2015

Tim Shaw quote, 'I remember a …'

Mandell, Nina, 'ALS is slowly robbing ex-linebacker Tim Shaw of his muscles. But he won't let that stop him from living', *USA Today*, February 2017

Tim Shaw quote, 'To be able …'

Menelik Watson

Dillon, Dennis, 'Rapidly developing Watson bringing British Invasion to NFL', *Sports Illustrated*, April 2013

Shoesmith, Ian, *NFL Draft 2013: Menelik Watson swaps inner-city life for the big time* (BBC, April 2013)

Jamie Gillan

Forbes, Greg, *Path to the Draft: An Interview with the 'Scottish Hammer' Jamie Gillan* (ninetynineyards.com, February 2019)

Jamie Gillan quote, 'I miss Scotland …'

Withers, Tom, *Great Scot: Browns Rookie Punter has Scottish heritage* (Yahoo! May 2019)

Jamie Gillan quote, 'I'm not going …'

Stubbs, Roman, 'The Scottish Hammer: How Jamie Gillan went from Scotland to an HBCU to Browns rookie standout', *Washington Post*, September 2019

Jamie Gillan quote, 'I wasn't treated …'